A PIONEER CHURCHMAN

J.W.C. DIETRICHSON
IN WISCONSIN
1844–1850

EDITED AND WITH AN INTRODUCTION BY
E. CLIFFORD NELSON

MALCOLM ROSHOLT
and
HARRIS E. KAASA
Translators

PUBLISHED FOR THE
NORWEGIAN-AMERICAN HISTORICAL ASSOCIATION
BY TWAYNE PUBLISHERS, INC.
NEW YORK

Copyright © 1973, by
The Norwegian-American Historical Association

87732:53

Library of Congress catalogue card number: 73-8068

ISBN 0-8057-5443-1

MANUFACTURED IN THE UNITED STATES OF AMERICA

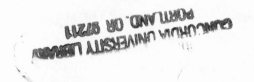

Foreword

With this volume, the Norwegian-American Historical Association begins an important relationship with Twayne Publishers, Inc., of New York. Twayne will issue all books approved and given basic editorial preparation by the Association, will supply copy-editing service, and will promote the sale of the volumes in our several series. The Association, in turn, will purchase copies of each book for distribution to its members, individual and institutional. We anticipate a happy and fruitful partnership with Twayne as well as an increased circulation of our publications.

The first book produced under this arrangement, *A Pioneer Churchman*, dealing with Pastor J. W. C. Dietrichson's work and travel in America, is a documentary that at first glance may seem to be of interest only to a limited number of theologians and church historians. A thoughtful reading, however, quickly reveals that its contents have much broader significance as a record of American frontier conditions and experience. If its main focus is on the beginnings of "ordered" religious life among the Norwegian immigrants—the transition from state to free church—its observations on this and a variety of other subjects will prove to be of concern to a much larger audience.

It is significant that Dietrichson was conscious of writing for the future—of supplying grist for the historian's mill—and he deliberately included in his accounts details that he thought would one day illuminate pioneer experience. Though conservative and rigid in his concepts of what constituted a properly structured church and imperious in his dealings with friend and foe alike, he was strikingly flexible and considerably in advance of his time in his attitudes, for example, to the blacks and Indians in American society. If he exaggerated the peril of the "sects" in Illinois and Wisconsin—especially the Mormons—he nevertheless offered a tightly reasoned interpretation of the direction taken by his vigorous missionary activity.

It must be pointed out, however, that Dietrichson did not fully understand the thoughts and emotions of his parishioners, immigrants largely of peasant origin who found much to their liking in the freewheeling—often crude—style and yeasty spirit of the American frontier. Nor did he, partly because of his social background and partly because of his missionary zeal in what he regarded as a hostile environment, present a picture that does justice to New-World institutions and life. There is irony in the fact that the Grundtvigian influence, so apparent in his theology, produced in him nothing like the feeling for the common folk so characteristic of the great Danish bishop.

But whatever the final judgment of Dietrichson—and of other clergymen of the Norwegian Synod—his *Travel Narrative* and *Parish Journal* together constitute an important document in Norwegian-American history. Until now, the absence of an English version of his story has marked a notable omission in Association publications.

Mr. Rosholt and Professor Kaasa have demonstrated great skill in turning Dietrichson's long, German-influenced sentences into a readable English that is true to his original Dano-Norwegian. Professor Nelson, able editor of the volume, has also contributed an invaluable Introduction that clarifies Dietrichson's religious views while it presents the churchman sympathetically as a person shaped by his origins and the early influences of his life.

The Association is happy to distribute to its members copies of this volume, the fifty-third in its forty-eight years of activity.

KENNETH O. BJORK

St. Olaf College
Northfield, Minnesota

Preface

This volume is an outgrowth of research in connection with the writing of *The Lutheran Church Among Norwegian-Americans: A History of the Evangelical Lutheran Church*, 2 vols. (Minneapolis, 1960). In seeking materials on one of the primary Norwegian immigrant communities in the American Midwest, my attention was called in 1947 to the carefully written Koshkonong (Wisconsin) Parish Journal covering the years 1844–1850. Einar Haugen, then professor at the University of Wisconsin, had discovered the document and had made it the subject of an article in the *Wisconsin Magazine of History* (March, 1946). Later I was given permission to examine and to microfilm the two-volume manuscript record. Strictly speaking, to call this record a "journal" may be inappropriate. But because the record is a chronicle reminiscent of a diary, it has been deemed permissible to refer to it as such. The two manuscript volumes of the journal are divided as follows: Volume I carries the account through the church year 1847–1848, that is, through Chapter V. Volume II includes the remainder of the record through Dietrichson's departure for Norway in 1850. The microfilm of the original journal has been placed in the library of Luther Theological Seminary, St. Paul.

Recognizing that the document had value and interest beyond providing source material for a small part of a rather -extensive history of the Evangelical Lutheran Church (the Norwegian Lutheran Church of America, which in 1946 changed its name to the Evangelical Lutheran Church, in 1960 merged with synods of Danish and German background to form The American Lutheran Church), I suggested to the Norwegian Conference of the Evangelical Lutheran body that the manuscript ought to be turned into English. The executive committee of the Conference then requested that I supervise the project, which, after several interruptions, has now been brought to completion.

In the work of translating the Parish Journal, I received the assistance of several individuals. The task was partially done by the late Reverend Olaf Lysnes, St. Paul, and myself, but the brunt of the labor was borne by Harris E. Kaasa, professor of religion and chairman of the department of religion at Luther College, Decorah, Iowa. I am especially indebted to Dr. Kaasa, who served as my research assistant during a portion of his senior year in Luther Theological Seminary. In addition to bringing the translation into publishable form, he provided no little help in tracing out elusive details and supplying information on obscure but significant historical items. Some of these have been incorporated into the editor's introduction and footnotes. It should be called to the reader's attention that there are no footnotes in the original journal.

The work in connection with the Koshkonong parish register soon led me to the reading of Dietrichson's *Reise blandt de norske emgiranter i "De forenede nordamerikanske Fristater"* (Stavanger, 1846) in which he reflects on the experiences of his first year in America. The chronicle seemed to be a natural companion piece to the Parish Journal. Then, one day in early 1971, I learned of an English translation of the *Reise*, prepared by Malcolm Rosholt, Rosholt, Wisconsin. Professor Kenneth O. Bjork, editor of the prestigious Norwegian-American Historical Association, Northfield, Minnesota, recognized that the now translated *Reise* and the Parish Journal belonged together, and, as such, would provide significant material for a portrait of early Norwegian-American economic, social, and cultural life, as well as being a primary source for immigrant church history in mid-nineteenth century. Consequently, knowing that I was to spend the summer of 1971 in Norway doing further research on Dietrichson, Bjork asked me to bring these two documents together, the one supplementing (and sometimes overlapping) the other, and to ready them for publication. This I was happy to do, for the task had been facilitated by Mr. Rosholt who had added helpful footnotes to those already present in Dietrichson's text of the *Reise*. It should be noted that Mr. Rosholt's translation was based on the American edition put out by Rasmus B. Anderson, Madison, Wisconsin, in 1896. Although pagination differs from the original (1846) book, the content is essentially the same. At least one interesting alteration occurs in the 1896 edition. Dietrichson refers in the 1846 edition to the church in which he was ordained as the "Opsloe Kirke." This spelling corresponds to his usage in the Parish Journal and to the designations found on maps of Christiania (Oslo) in the eighteenth and early nineteenth centuries. The American edition of Rasmus B. Anderson changed the spelling to "Oslo." In the present edition it was found advisable to place *The Travel Narrative* ahead of *The Parish Journal*, since the former in a way sets the stage for the latter.

The editorial task required, among other things, research in the library of the University of Oslo, in the Norwegian State Archives, and in the holdings of the Norwegian State Antiquary.

Numerous individuals lightened the editor's work both in Norway and America. I am especially grateful to Johan Hambro, the competent and genial secretary-general of Nordmanns-Forbundet (the League of Norsemen), Oslo, for taking a personal interest in the project and securing overseas passage for me in the summer of 1971. This assistance, together with a Ford Foundation faculty humanities grant from St. Olaf College, made it financially possible to carry the work to completion. I am also deeply grateful to Dr. Einar Molland, professor of church history in the University of Oslo, who shared with me his extensive knowledge of nineteenth-century Norway and directed me to significant sources hitherto unknown to me. Moreover, a word of appreciation should be extended to library staff members Gunnar C. Wasberg, Per Hveem, John Dahl, and Rolf Dahlø at Universitetsbiblioteket, Oslo; all lent their professional skills to my every bibliographical need. My gratitude must also be expressed to the staff of Norges Geografiske Oppmåling for providing me with photocopies of late eighteenth and early nineteenth-century maps of Oslo (Christiania), and permission to reprint them. Thanks are due to Mrs. Duane Kringen and Mrs. Philip Winter who painstakingly did the typescript, to Miss Charlotte Jacobson who prepared the index, and to Dr. Marie Malmin Meyer, emerita professor of English at St. Olaf College, who together with Professor Bjork, made some stylistic changes in the translation, and to Reidar Dittmann, Jr., Northfield, who drew several maps.

Although the Introduction includes a short biography of Dietrichson, it has been deemed helpful to append a chronology of
his life.

St. Olaf College   E. CLIFFORD NELSON
Northfield, Minnesota

Contents

APPENDICES

List of Illustrations

Introduction

The purpose of these introductory words is to provide an orientation for the reader as he peruses and studies the following documents. Those who are not acquainted with the general subject would find, not unexpectedly, many puzzling historical references to religious and social conditions in both Norway and the American Midwest. In order to provide this orientation it has been deemed best to do the following: (1) to describe in general terms the nineteenth-century background against which the Norwegian emigrant is to be seen; (2) to depict briefly the American circumstances in which the immigrants sought to establish their church life; (3) to provide a concise biography of J. W. C. Dietrichson as a supplement to the biographical references in the documents themselves; and (4) to make an assessment of Dietrichson's contribution to the immigrants' life in the New World.

I

When the typical Norwegian emigrant embarked for America, he was torn between ardent love for his native land and bitter dissatisfaction with the social, economic, and even religious conditions it had imposed upon him. Although he left part of himself in the motherland, he carried with him a cultural and religious heritage that was an integral part of his being. Moreover, even though he reacted negatively to his Norwegian environment, his general outlook upon life had already been shaped in large measure by the milieu from which he emigrated.

When the nineteenth century dawned, Norway had been united with Denmark for several centuries, but undeniably she occupied a subordinate position. Copenhagen was the capital, and public officials (church-state-military) were almost entirely Danish. The end of the eighteenth century and the beginning of the nineteenth

1

witnessed a rising Norwegian nationalism and desire for auton-
omy. The Napoleonic Wars both hastened and hindered this development. In 1814 a liberal national constitution providing a
monarch and a parliament (Storting) was adopted. Norway's
hopes for complete independence, however, were not to be realized for almost a century, because at the same moment it obtained
a national constitution it became a victim of the political maneu-
verings of European powers, who punished Denmark and rewarded Sweden by transferring Norway from the hegemony of
one to that of the other. Between 1814 and 1905, Norway and
Sweden were united under a common sovereign who ruled from
Stockholm but abided by Norway's constitution. Again as the
junior partner, Norway found the union basically distasteful and
experienced both real and imagined infringements of political and
economic rights. Fortunately the friction never developed into
open hostilities and, finally in 1905, the union was peacefully
terminated.

This political awakening was accompanied by a social trans-
formation. Lacking a hereditary nobility, Norway nevertheless
possessed class distinctions. The public officials (*embedsmenn*)
and wealthy businessmen constituted an upper class whose origins,
education, and culture were largely Danish. Their official language
was Dano-Norwegian, which differed in large measure from the
language of the common folk, chiefly farmers and fishermen, who
made up ninety percent of the population. The Norwegian
farmer, or *bonde*, owned his own farm and possessed a proud and
independent spirit even though he seldom achieved wealth. At the
bottom of the rural social scale were the cotters, or *husmenn*, who
occupied cottages on the landlord's property and had the use of a
small tract of land for which they paid rent or did a specified
amount of work. It was not strange that the threat of hunger and
a feeling of inferiority produced social agitation among them.

Most of the people who left for America were from this rural
society, both *bønder* and *husmenn*. The upper class, including the
clergy, seldom migrated; almost from the start, they regarded the
emigration movement as a national catastrophe. An episcopal letter
sent by the bishop of Bergen, Jacob Neumann, warned the "emi-
gration-smitten" farmers of his diocese that forsaking the motherland for America would bring frightful consequences.[1] This

J. W. C. Dietrichson

Photo by W. R. Ferman, Stoughton, Wisconsin

admonition did not stop the movement, however, as Norwegians and Swedes at about the same time were gripped by what was called the "America fever." This reached epidemic proportions as a result of "America letters" written to friends and relatives by those who already had made the daring transatlantic crossing.

Norway's religious life was shaped by many factors. Two of the most important were the established Lutheran church and a succession of religious revivals, especially among the common people. The adoption of Lutheranism by the Danish-Norwegian kingdom in the sixteenth century was largely a change imposed by authority. It took many years before the people were indoctrinated in the Lutheran faith. One major contribution was made by the age of orthodoxy in the seventeenth century. The eighteenth century in Norway, as in other Western European lands, was marked by the so-called ages of Pietism and Rationalism. Pietism brought to Norway a conventicle type of Christianity which stressed the gathering of the "regenerated" believers for mutual edification and gave impetus to mission work. Bishop Erik Pontoppidan, a Pietist, wrote an explanation of Luther's Small Catechism entitled *Truth unto Godliness* (*Sandhed til gudfrygtighed*), a volume that became a layman's dogmatics. It was a remarkable blend of Lutheran orthodoxy and Pietism, setting forth emphases that characterized Norwegian Lutheranism, both in Norway and America, into the twentieth century.

The eighteenth century also saw Rationalism make inroads on the clergy and the leaders of intellectual life. Laymen, however, were for the most part unaffected by the new ideology. Instead, they continued to nurture their religious life by emphasizing the traditions inherited from orthodoxy and Pietism. Before 1811, Norway's pastors were educated at the University of Copenhagen, with the result that Danish ecclesiastical policies and practices were simply extended to Norway. In 1811, however, the Royal Frederik University in Christiania was established. Henceforth all Norwegian pastors were required by law to receive their theological education at the new university. But the form of church doctrine and practice—the liturgy and regulations governing pastoral and congregational activities—remained quite as before.

By this time Rationalism was on the wane, and a major new religious awakening brought vital spiritual impulses to Norway. The

THE DIETRICHSON FAMILY COAT OF ARMS
Source: David Dietrichson, *Stamtavle over Slægten Dietrichson*
(Kristiania, 1882)

latter movement, associated with the life and work of a lay evangelist, Hans Nielsen Hauge (1771–1824), left a deep imprint upon
Norwegian Christianity, especially among the rural population.
Hauge's message of repentance and conversion, arising out of his
own transforming religious experience in 1796, brought the awakening to the whole country. His activities as a preacher and writer
soon met opposition from the authorities of the state and the
church. A neglected law, the Conventicle Act of 1741 which was
originally designed to restrain Moravianism, forbade itinerant lay
preaching and required that public religious meetings should be
held only under the supervision of a pastor. Hauge was arrested in
1804 and was kept in prison until 1811 while his case was being investigated. Finally, in 1814, he was judged guilty of violating the
Conventicle Act, of encouraging others to violate it, and of de-
nigrating the clergy. His punishment was limited to a fine and
court costs. His health, however, was broken by the long im-
prisonment, and consequently his activities were curtailed. The
revival, which had languished for a time, nevertheless received
new impetus upon his release and soon reached into the lives of
some of those who had previously opposed him. Many prominent
pastors, professors, and bishops came over to his side, and when he
died in 1824 his fame was nationwide.

The tension between Haugeanism and officialdom, however,
was only temporarily eased. The conflict that swirled around
Hauge was more deep-seated than the antitheses of lay preaching
versus state-imposed order, or lay Pietism versus clerical religion.
It also involved a social conflict between the merchant class and
officialdom, on the one hand, and the religiously awakened common people, the *bønder*, on the other. Although Hauge had no
thought of being a socio-political reformer, the movement that he
began had wide-ranging implications. Many Haugeans, for example, were among the representatives who drafted the Constitution
of 1814 and others became members of Parliament. When it is
remembered that the vast majority of Norwegians who emigrated
to America were from rural Norway and, as such, often deeply
influenced by Haugeanism (although only a minority were
Haugeans by personal conviction), it is small wonder that they
brought a spirit of independence and personal resourcefulness to
the task of shaping their lives in the New World.[2]

TRONDHJEM

SLIDRE
• PARISH

NORWAY

BERGEN •

CHRISTIANIA (OSLO) •

DRAMMEN •

NERSTRAND

TØNSBERG
PORSGRUND FREDRIKSTAD
LANGESUND •

STAVANGER

HOLT •
ØSTRE •
MOLAND

LINDESNES • CHRISTIANSAND

SWEDEN

• GÖTEBORG

DIETRICHSON'S
SCANDINAVIA

DENMARK

• HELSINGØR

• COPENHAGEN

HAMBURG •

KEIDAR DITTMANN, JR.

One of the more controversial disciples of Hauge, Elling Eielsen (1804–1883), found his way to America and sought to mold immigrant religious life into an Eielsen form of Haugeanism. The sharp differences between Eielsen and J. W. C. Dietrichson in the New World are prominently displayed in the literature of the forties, not least in the two documents that follow.

In addition to understanding the clash between the advocates of a state-church order and the proponents of Haugeanism, one must be aware of at least one more factor in Norwegian ecclesiastical life during the first half of the nineteenth century: the influence of the Danish religious and cultural leader N. F. S. Grundtvig (1783–1872), whose thought, like that of his contemporary Søren A. Kierkegaard (1813–1855), has radiated out from Denmark to stimulate theological, philosophical, and historical judgments universally into the twentieth century.

It should be pointed out that Grundtvigianism, alongside of but hardly compatible with Haugeanism, was one of the ingredients causing Norwegian religious ferment in the nineteenth century. A mild form of it was represented in the theological faculty; its most vigorous proponent, however, was an influential Christiania pastor, Wilhelm Andreas Wexels (1797–1866).[3]

What were the tenets of Grundtvigianism that made it distinctive? The Danish theologian began his career as a strong opponent of current and popular religious indifferentism and rationalism. A thoroughgoing advocate of biblical Christianity (in fact, a biblicist), Grundtvig came in due time to the conclusion that biblicism was too subjective: what one finds in Scripture depends too often on one's personal preference and interpretation. This reasoning led, in 1825, to what he called his "matchless discovery," which was to be the essence of Grundtvigianism. He had a growing conviction that there was a need for an unfailing key to interpret the Bible. This, he now believed, was to be found in the historical fact of the church and the sacraments. Questions regarding Christianity's nature and doctrine were not to be answered by a legalistic use of the Bible (biblicism) nor by a dogmatic use of the Lutheran confessions (confessionalism). Rather, Christianity and its doctrine were to be understood historically. This was not to say that Christianity was a feather carried on the winds of history; it was not vitiated by the relativities of the past or of the present. To the

DETAIL OF MAP OF CHRISTIANIA AND ENVIRONS, 1816

contrary, Christianity rested on solid, objective, historical reality: the existence of the church and the sacraments (especially baptism) through the centuries. He even wrote a hymn about it saying, "*Kirken den er et gammelt hus*" (The Church is an Ancient House).[4]

To be a Christian, therefore, one must be baptized into the church. The Apostles' Creed had always been a part of the baptismal formula; consequently, belief in this creed marked one as a member of the Christian community. Through it, the voice of the church had remained unchanged down through the centuries. The creed, therefore, was the key to understanding the Bible. Did not the church exist before the New Testament scriptures? Did not the church confess its faith before it inscripturated it? Had not the church always been confessional? To these questions Grundtvig answered yes. In fact, the Bible, to him, was a book of faith, a product of the Christian faith as confessed by the church in the words of the creed. Therefore, the Apostles' Creed (or the confession of faith) was primary, and the Scriptures were secondary. The words of the baptismal formula, together with the words of institution of the Lord's Supper and the Lord's Prayer, said Grundtvig, are "the Living Word" direct from the Lord. Although Grundtvig's thought included the Lord's Supper and the Lord's Prayer, it is clear that his chief emphasis was on baptism and the creed. Scripture was invaluable as a source of information, but it was not to be equated with the life-giving Word. This Grundtvigian view was soon dubbed "the churchly view" (*den kirkelige anskuelse*).

It is not strange that Grundtvigians came under attack in both Denmark and Norway, and later in America. Their exaltation of tradition over Scripture led Lutheran orthodoxists and Haugeans to charge it with being at least crypto-Catholic. Moreover, its generally optimistic and happy view of man irritated the somber Norwegians, who felt that Grundtvigians did not emphasize adequately man's original sin and propensity to evil, and that they were too indulgent regarding such matters as drinking, theater attendance, card playing, and dancing. Finally, most Grundtvigians were charged with holding the view that there existed the possibility of conversion after death.

J. W. C. Dietrichson, whose theological views and ecclesiastical

Opsloe Church, circa 1825

Artist Unknown
Source: Riksantikvariatet, Oslo. Used with permission.

practices are clearly discernible in the accompanying documents, was a Norwegian state-church cleric who had been introduced to Grundtvigianism as a student and who remained within its general theological frame throughout his ministerial career.

II

The Norwegians who migrated to the New World before 1850 settled primarily in the Upper Middle West, especially in the state of Illinois and the territory of Wisconsin.[5] In the last half of the century and up to World War I, the immigration movement spread out to include Iowa, Minnesota, the two Dakotas, and the broad expanses to the Pacific Coast, in both the United States and Canada.

When Dietrichson arrived in America in 1844, there were five main colonies of Norwegian immigrants: the Fox River settlement in Illinois, southwest of Chicago; Jefferson Prairie, on the border between Illinois and the territory of Wisconsin; Muskego, southwest of Milwaukee; Rock Prairie (later Luther Valley), near Beloit, Wisconsin; and Koshkonong Prairie, near Madison.

Although the Church of Norway and other arms of the state showed very little concern for the religious fortunes of the emigrants, at least one group of the latter had interested a candidate of theology, one Peter Valeur, to accompany them in 1838 as their spiritual shepherd. By the time the Norwegian Department of Ecclesiastical Affairs had investigated the qualifications of the candidate and had discussed the propriety of ordaining a man without a call from an organized congregation and whose ministry in far-off America could be supervised only with extreme difficulty, the emigrants, weary of bureaucratic red tape, shoved off for the New World without a pastor.[6]

It was not until the autumn of 1839 that a religious leader appeared among the immigrants. He was Elling Eielsen Sundve (the surname was later dropped), the Haugean lay preacher mentioned above. "The coming of this restless, forceful, uncompromising lay chieftain of religion," writes Theodore Blegen, "symbolizes in special degree the transfer from Norway to America of the Haugean spirit. For he represented in pre-eminent degree the Lutheran low-church point of view, pietism, puritanism, the concept of the congregation as a body of the 'awakened,' the belief in the rightness of lay preaching."[7]

Led "by the Spirit," Eielsen finally reached the Fox River settlement, where a handful of lay preachers had kept the embers of religious life burning. Forthwith he took charge, erected a combined hospice and church (*forsamlingshus*), and began religious services, thus averting the danger of the colony's being overrun by sectarianism and secularism.

Eielsen was much too restless and zealous to confine his ministry to Fox River. He soon visited the other colonies in Illinois and Wisconsin, gathered the "awakened" or those "on the way to conversion" around him, and brought a semblance of Lutheran religious life to the settlements. Although many of the communities were peopled by farmers of the Haugean persuasion, some of them, especially at Muskego, found Eielsen's personality and religious views (notably his anticlericalism) repugnant. They had retained, despite their own displeasure with the Church of Norway, a modicum of affection for Lutheran church order and the office of the pastor. They favored lay preachers, to be sure, but Elling Eielsen—well, he was a bit too much!

Moreover, lay preaching in America—whether in Wisconsin or in Illinois—was a quite different enterprise from its Norwegian counterpart. In Norway, Haugeanism was a movement, not an organization, within the church. It was the church that cared for what some considered externals—baptisms, marriages, confirmations, burials—while the Haugeans supplied "the spirit." In America, Haugeanism had no church organization to tend to sacraments and rites. Thus it turned out that the Muskego Haugeans eventually called and ordained a Danish schoolteacher, Claus Laurits Clausen (1820–1892). Suffering from tuberculosis, the twenty-two-year old Clausen had undertaken a walking trip in Norway at the urging of his doctor. There, among the mountains and streams of the Northland, he not only recovered his health but met Grundtvigian Pastor W. A. Wexels in Christiania and Haugean layman T. O. Bache in Drammen. The latter, a comfortably well-off businessman, had received a letter from his son Søren in Muskego, Wisconsin, enclosing a call, signed by thirty individuals, for a teacher of religion. The elder Bache persuaded Clausen to answer this plea. He did so, and arrived in Muskego with his wife in August, 1843.

The chief religious problems facing Clausen seemed to be Eielsen, Baptists, and Mormons, in that order. Eielsen, hovering on the edge of the Muskego colony, continued his condemnation of churches and churchmen. Although Clausen made overtures of friendship, he was repulsed by Eielsen. Moreover, he discovered that religious life was in a deteriorating state. Despite the efforts of earnest laymen to nurture Christian faith and life, it was soon evident to one and all that the community required the ministry of an ordained pastor. Hence the Muskego congregation requested a neighboring German Lutheran pastor, one L. F. E. Krause, an "Old Lutheran" from Prussia, to examine and ordain Clausen, whom they now officially accepted as their pastor. Thus a little more than two months after his arrival, Clausen, a Dane, was ordained by a German to serve a Norwegian congregation in America.

Meanwhile, Eielsen and his friends suddenly began to feel the need of an ordained minister and quickly arranged with Pastor Francis Alex. Hoffman, "secretary of the Ministerium of Northern Illinois," to conduct the rite of ordination. This was done on October 3, 1843, ten days *prior* to the Clausen ordination. Although the validity of the act was challenged by his contemporaries—notably by Clausen and J. W. C. Dietrichson (after the latter arrived on the scene)—Eielsen stoutly maintained that he was properly ordained. Although his examination was informal, he reasoned it was better than most. He had been tested by the Holy Spirit, "under persecution, wakefulness, nakedness, and hunger."[8]

Frontier dissension, both hidden and apparent, was present in the Norwegian settlements. Not only was there disagreement between Eielsen and Clausen; there was also a spirit of divisiveness present among the people. Some were drawn to Eielsen, others to Clausen. How else could it be? In less than a year, however, a giant personality was to stride into these swirling currents of Norwegian-American religious life. He was Johannes Wilhelm Christian Dietrichson, "a barrel-chested proponent of ministerial authority and ecclesiastical order." His coming did not diminish the dissension on the frontier; if anything, it intensified it.[9]

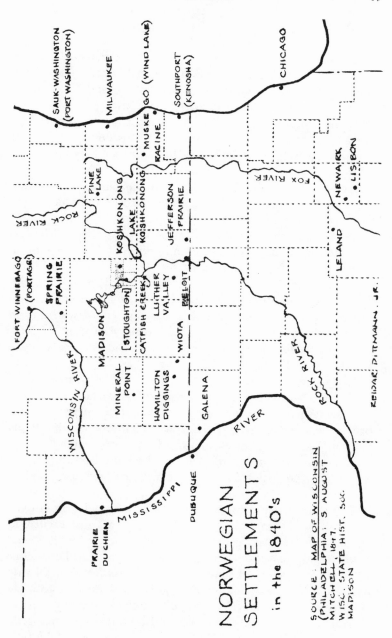

NORWEGIAN SETTLEMENTS in the 1840's

SOURCE: MAP OF WISCONSIN (PHILADELPHIA; S AUGUST MITCHELL, 1847, WISC. STATE HIST. SOC. MADISON

REIDAR DITTMANN, JR.

III

In the 1840s Wisconsin was still a territory; statehood was to come in 1848. Its largest city, Milwaukee, boasted 7,000 inhabitants. Madison was a village of 700. Muskego and Koshkonong Prairie—the former near Milwaukee, the latter near Madison—were gradually being settled by immigrants from Norway and by Norwegian-Americans who came to these Wisconsin communities from the Norwegian settlement in Illinois in the hope of finding better land and richer opportunities. It was soon evident that Koshkonong especially was destined to be both populous and prosperous. In 1844 it became the headquarters for a new campaign against frontier irreligion.[10]

Søren Bache, the Peer Gynt-like son of T. O. Bache who had sponsored C. L. Clausen's mission to Muskego, kept a diary of his American experiences. The entry for August 7, 1844, describes Dietrichson's arrival in Wisconsin. It reads: "We expected this day to pass as quietly as the others, but . . . this morning I met a strapping young man down by the road. His tall, powerful build and rosy cheeks reminded me of some young giant from the Norwegian mountains. We shook hands and introduced ourselves, and I then learned that he was J. W. C. Dietrichson."[11]

Dietrichson had arrived at "Musquigo" (as he was to spell it later) from Milwaukee the previous evening. Bache now led him to Clausen's parsonage and heard him inform the surprised pastor that his coming to America had been prompted by the "Holy Biblical Word" and the desire to visit his countrymen in the New World "in order to maintain among them the Lutheran faith." Bache confided to his diary, "Time will tell how successful he will be."[12]

What was it that came to the settlement that day in August, 1844? What was there about this "young giant" that excited attention and provoked comment? Surely it was more than physique; it was a spirit—and an unwelcome one at that. Dietrichson was the embodiment of something that the settlers thought they had left behind in Norway: the old-country caste system, the Norwegian "aristocracy," the State Church. The immigrants believed that they had rid themselves of these things by crossing the sea; but now, in a moment, the cultural dichotomy of Norway

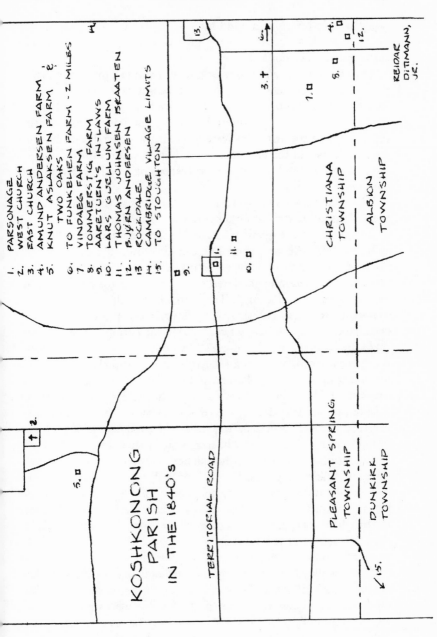

KOSHKONONG PARISH IN THE 1840's

1. PARSONAGE
2. WEST CHURCH
3. EAST CHURCH
4. AMUND ANDERSEN FARM
5. KNUT ASLAKSEN FARM
6. TWO OAKS
   TO FUNKELIEN FARM - 2 MILES
7. VINDAEG FARM
8. TOMMERSTIG FARM
9. AARETUEN'S IN-LAWS
10. LARS GJELLUM FARM
11. THOMAS JOHNSEN BRAATEN
12. BJÖRN ANDERSEN
13. ROCKDALE
H. CAMBRIDGE VILLAGE LIMITS
15. TO STOUGHTON

TERRITORIAL ROAD

CHRISTIANA TOWNSHIP
ALBION TOWNSHIP

PLEASANT SPRING TOWNSHIP
DUNKIRK TOWNSHIP

REIDAR DITTMANN, JR.

was glaringly brought to mind by a young preacher who stood in their midst. Who was this young man whose presence was so disturbing and unwelcome?

The Dietrichson family was originally from Denmark, imported in an earlier day to help form the bureaucracy that ruled Norway. Erasmus Dietrichson (1673–1737) received his name according to the prevailing law of patronymics. The family was prominently represented in the army (at least three major generals and several lesser officers), in the church (one bishop, one professor of theology, several pastors), and in the professions of banking, law, medicine, and the civil service.[13]

Johannes Wilhelm Christian Dietrichson was born April 4, 1815, in Fredrikstad, where his father, Fredrik Dietrichson (1787–1866), was a captain of the guard who later became military commissary at Stavanger.[14] According to Dietrichson's own *vita* recorded in the Koshkonong parish register, he chose the study of theology as a result of enthusiasms engendered while preparing for confirmation under his minister, Pastor J. Tandberg. In the absence of a local *gymnasium* (junior college), he was privately tutored and then certified to the university, where he took the entrance examination (*artium*) in 1832, and the so-called "second" examination in 1833, receiving in both instances a relatively low grade. He entered immediately upon his professional studies, however, and received his theological degree in 1837 with a somewhat better academic rank, despite the fact that during the oral examination the examiner repeatedly found it necessary to "help" the candidate in his efforts to find the right answers.[15] The next year he successfully sustained a "practical" examination in homiletics and catechetics, receiving the same grade. Although Dietrichson did not excel as a student, it should be noted that he was not thereby prevented from entering a professional career. Clearly the standards in the middle of the first half of the nineteenth century were considerably less rigid than today, when the University of Oslo would hardly judge such a record a sufficient qualification for a career.

It was while Dietrichson studied theology that he came under Grundtvigian influence. How this occurred is not clear from his own writings. Those members of the faculty who were Grundtvigian in outlook were only mildly so.[16] Extracurricular interests, however, may have been the decisive factor in drawing Dietrich-

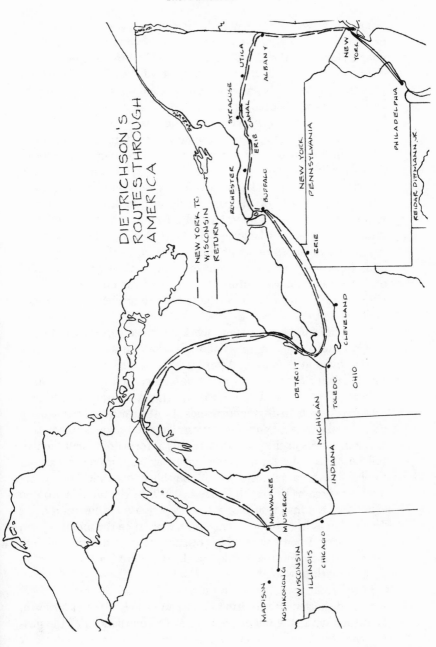

DIETRICHSON'S
ROUTES THROUGH
AMERICA

NEW YORK TO
WISCONSIN
RETURN

son to the views of the Danish theologian. While he was a student, he served as an assistant teacher at an *asyl* (a charity school for poor children) in the Grønland section of Christiania. The director of the school was Erik Nicolai Saxild, one of the driving forces in a program to provide Norway with folk schools in the later Grundt-vigian pattern.[17] Moreover, as a student Dietrichson may have been caught up in Grundtvig's romantic attack on the use of Latin in lectures and examinations at the university. Grundtvig's roman-ticism led him to urge the Danes and the Norwegians to glorify their Nordic past. One way to do this was to use the vernacular. The native language was an expression of a people's history; it was the "Living Word" of the past. Latin, on the other hand, was a symbol of classical tyranny. Should a country permit itself to be tyrannized by a dead language? If the students of the 1830s were anything like the students of today, it is not difficult to imagine how appealing Grundtvig's romanticism was. In any case, Die-trichson was a student during the height of the controversy over Latin. And he emerged from the university an incipient Grundt-vigian.[18]

Upon finishing his academic work, he received an appointment as a private teacher at the Vallø salt works near Tønsberg, the oldest town in Norway. After a year he returned (1839) to Christiania for further study at the university. Joined by two other students, C. A. Lütken and Theodor Thode, he opened a private preparatory school for confirmands. In 1840 he was retained by the city's Board of Penal Institutions to give religious instruction to the prisoners in the local (Grønland) reformatory each Sunday and holy day. We learn something about his attitudes regarding the purpose of penal institutions from his first publication, a ser-mon delivered at the reformatory in 1839. In the introduction he expresses his conviction that a *Redningsanstalt* (an institution for "rescue") ought to be concerned with more than the moral reform of prisoners. A genuine *redning* (rescue) means that men's eyes are opened to their spiritual needs and that they are led to conversion by hearing the gospel.[19]

In the same year Dietrichson married Jørgine Laurentze Brock, who died shortly after bearing him a son in 1841.[20] Grief-stricken, he turned with new understanding to the consolations of the gos-pel, and as if to give himself time to adjust to his loss, he undertook a trip through Denmark, Germany, and Switzerland in 1842. Returning to Norway in the spring of 1843, he received an episcopal appointment as an unordained assistant to the prison chaplain in Christiania. He held this position until his departure for America.

With deepened religious convictions, he had become active in the recently born foreign mission movement (the Norwegian Missionary Society had been formed in 1842), serving as one of four delegates of the Christiania Mission Society to the first general assembly of the national organization at Christiansand in 1843. It was on this occasion that Hans Paludan Smith Schreuder (1817–1882), one of the foremost figures in Norwegian mission history, was chosen to be the first missionary of the Society to Zululand, Africa.[21]

Dietrichson records that it was during that same summer that he met another mission enthusiast, a layman by the name of Peter Sørensen. Sørensen, a dyer by trade, was a devout layman and close friend of Grundtvigian Pastor W. A. Wexels. As a consequence of this relationship, Sørensen, too, had become a Grundtvigian, and he complained that the Haugeans, whose mission interest appealed to him, refused fellowship with him and other Grundtvigians.[22] While Dietrichson and Sørensen conversed, they recognized their common interests in Grundtvig and the Schreuder mission to Zululand. Dietrichson reported, moreover, that it was only natural that their conversation turned to the religious needs of their countrymen who had emigrated to America. At this point Sørensen asked Dietrichson if he might be interested in undertaking a journey to investigate the situation in America, to establish congregations among the immigrants, and at least to lay the foundation for a solid "churchly order" among them. If he could undertake such a mission, Sørensen would subsidize the enterprise. Dietrichson listened sympathetically and, after later consultation with ecclesiastical officials, was convinced that this was a divine "call." He applied shortly for royal permission to be ordained. Some months later, on February 23, 1844, the rite of ordination was performed by Bishop Christian Sørenssen at the Opsloe church in Christiania.[23]

Dietrichson's eagerness to make the journey to America sprang from the conviction that religious life among his countrymen in the New World was desolate, and that the way to remedy the situation was to transfer as far as possible the Church of Norway to the woods and prairies of Wisconsin and Illinois. Therefore, he looked upon his "call" not as the task of serving some specific congregation but as an opportunity to bring order out of the religious and ecclesiastical chaos in the American wilderness. This attitude accounts for his frequent references, in both *The Parish Journal* and *The Travel Narrative*, to the fact that his call was to bring "the true saving doctrine" and "the edifying church order" to Norwegian-American communities. With this accomplished, he would feel free to return to the motherland.

Dietrichson left Norway on May 16, 1844, and arrived in Wisconsin, as we have noted, in August. It is at this point that *The Koshkonong Parish Journal* and *The Travel Narrative* provide a detailed account of his life and work in America. The first year, he reports, was a busy one, but by the spring of 1845 he felt the desire to return to Norway to seek out suitable pastoral candidates to carry on the work in America. He promised that should he fail in this, he himself would return.

The year in Norway was full of activity. He wrote and published the account of his American experiences in *The Travel Narrative* (*Reise blandt de norske Emigranter i "De forenede nordamerikanske Fristater"* [Stavanger, 1846]); he remarried; he appealed to young theologians to go to America as missionaries; and he requested and obtained financial assistance from the Norwegian government to defray the costs of a second trip to America. The publication of *The Travel Narrative* and the continuing record in *The Parish Journal* (C. L. Clausen kept the record up to date during Dietrichson's year in Norway) were to provide posterity with valuable sources of information regarding social and economic conditions among the Norwegian immigrants, as well as an account of the emerging church. Charlotte Josine Omsen Müller, the young lady whom Dietrichson married and whom the gossipy Søren Bache describes as the "sweetheart back home who tugs at his [Dietrichson's] heartstrings,"[24] was to become the first in a long line of heroic women to leave Norway's social aristocracy to take up life with a ministerial husband in the rough and crude circumstances of the American frontier. Dietrichson's urgent appeal for volunteers was motivated by a profound religious concern for the plight of the immigrants, and the genuineness of this concern was demonstrated by his own return to America when his plea did not bring immediate results. The financial subsidy from the government (about a hundred dollars) was granted apparently on the condition that Dietrichson would transmit regular reports setting forth conditions in America "in the right light." Thus, it was reasoned, "the disturbing and frivolous emigration desire" would be counteracted.[25]

By September, 1846, Dietrichson, together with his bride, was back in Koshkonong to fulfill his call to serve the parish until April 1, 1850. *The Parish Journal* indicates continuing vexations, some successes, and an untiring and ofttimes uncompromising sense of duty. His troubles led him in a moment of hopelessness to request release from his contract in order that he might return to the peace and quiet of his homeland; but he was persuaded to remain. Subsequently he extended his ministry beyond the Koshkonong parish. For example, he organized a congregation at Spring Prairie, north of Madison, Wisconsin, and arranged for it to call its own pastor, the Reverend H. A. Preus, who was to arrive in 1851. This new recruit remained in America to become one of the leading churchmen and theologians among nineteenth-century Norwegian-Americans.[26] Dietrichson's activities also included the writing of what were to become virtually model constitutions, both for congregations and for a synod of congregations. The far-reaching significance of these two documents will be discussed below.

By 1850, Dietrichson was quite ready to return to his native land. Although he had been unsuccessful in his last major effort, namely, to form a synod, he left behind him the impress of his powerful and colorful personality and the basic structure for the yet unborn church body that in a short time was to become the largest and most vigorous of the early Norwegian-American churches. Later it came to be known popularly as the Norwegian Synod, a union of congregations expurgated of Dietrichson's Grundtvigianism but nonetheless committed to a churchly tradition, especially in the pattern of seventeenth-century Lutheran orthodoxism.

Significantly, Dietrichson's farewell sermon, based on St. Paul's words to the Ephesian elders (Acts 20:25–27) was a sort of *apologia pro vita sua* in which he reminded his flock that he had not shrunk from declaring the whole counsel of God and was therefore innocent of the blood of all men.[27] Behind him in America, there remained loyal friends, bitter enemies, and an utterly unique missionary ministry. Perhaps it is fortunate that he returned to Norway, for this stormy petrel of the pulpit hardly possessed the tact and patience for a successful ministry in the free and democratic conditions of the American frontier. In fact, as it turned out, he continued to have difficulties even after his return to Norway, thus indicating that there must have been some traits of personality that militated against warm cordiality between pastor and people, whether in America or in Norway.

The royal resolution granting permission for Dietrichson's ordination in 1843 had contained the qualification that the ordinand was not to be given "the right to perform ministerial acts in Norway" until he had received a regular appointment to a parish in his homeland.[28] This was forthcoming shortly after his return, when he became pastor in Slidre, Valdres, where he remained until August, 1851. Subsequently, in the same year he was named to a similar post at Nerstrand in Ryfylke near Stavanger; this he held until 1862. The years, however, were characterized by people-pastor abrasiveness. One report said that Dietrichson was a "contentious and hot-headed fellow" (*ein strid og hissig kar*), and that difficulties reached the point where parents refused to send their children to the pastor for religious instruction. The record continues: "One of the most religious men in the community, armed with a stick, chased those children home again."[29]

The precise nature of Dietrichson's problems was made clear by the fact that the parish had many supporters of Elling Eielsen. These pietistic lay people knew that Dietrichson had sharply opposed Eielsen's activities in America. Quite naturally they sided with Eielsen and received their new pastor with open distrust. Moreover, the latter's decidedly Grundtvigian views (he had reprimanded the congregation for a widespread neglect of the sacrament; 600 of the 2,500 members had not communed for several years) led the parish leaders to draw up a list of complaints to present to the bishop. The bishop sought to defend Dietrichson by pointing out to the people that he was a good preacher, a diligent pastor, and an effective teacher of young people. (He did not mention nor did not know that Dietrichson had also alienated the local youth.) Despite the minister's obvious strengths, the bishop had to admit that the pastor was unyielding in his catholic (Grundtvigian) views. It was patent that Dietrichson had outlived his welcome—if he ever had one—at Nerstrand.[30]

Dietrichson was next appointed to the parish at Østre Moland in southern Norway, assuming his duties in June of 1862. Meanwhile, he had strengthened his ties to Grundtvigianism, which had received no little publicity and broadened support as a result of three Scandinavia-wide Grundtvigian conferences: Copenhagen in 1857, Lund in 1859, and Christiania in 1861. The first meeting had been addressed by Grundtvig himself (on his favorite theme, "The Living Word") and by Bishop Christian Kierkegaard, the brother of Grundtvig's opponent, the late Søren A. Kierkegaard. Bishop Kierkegaard (1805–1888) took the Copenhagen meeting by storm, and many of those who had previously been unfriendly to Grundtvigianism "were won over to the [churchly] view."[31]

Dietrichson was one of four Norwegian delegates to the second meeting, at Lund, indicating that he remained a prominent member of the diminishing Grundtvigian circle in Norway. He agreed with his friend W. A. Wexels that Grundtvig's "churchly view" was rooted in the early church fathers and in Luther. All had the same emphasis on "the natural, the human, the folk, the individual, and the importance of emotions in human life [*livsrørelse*]."[32]

It was hardly unexpected, considering Dietrichson's consciously cultivated convictions, that the earlier pattern of parish problems would soon be evident in Østre Moland. By 1866 Dietrichson had applied unsuccessfully for transfer to the Cathedral Church of Our Saviour in Christiania, where his friend Wexels was assistant pastor until his death the same year. Forced to remain in Østre Moland, he became increasingly the target of attack by local lay preachers, whom Skrondal describes as having Methodist and Baptist leanings. An already unpleasant situation was exacerbated by a visit to the parish by a voluble advocate of lay preaching, Pastor Lars Oftedal of Stavanger. His appearance brought the parish brouhaha to a boil and Dietrichson was presented with the following bill of charges: (1) he refused to conduct baptisms according to the ceremony prescribed in the altar book; (2) he taught that the Bible was valuable only for enlightenment; (3) he denied that there was a literal "hell fire"; (4) he practiced self-communion by consuming the bread and wine following the administration of the sacrament to the people; (5) he was an enemy of inner missions; and (6) finally, his reprehensible actions were driving people out of the church.[33]

Dietrichson was not slow to defend himself. He replied that he had used the same baptismal formula for eight years and nobody had complained; why now?[34] With regard to communion practices, he was only following the regulations laid down by the revered Bishop Erich Pontoppidan in his officially accepted *Collegium Pastorale Practicum*, chapter 37 (1757 edition). With regard to his view of the Bible, he could not follow biblicists like Lars Oftedal, who demanded that the people read the Scriptures from cover to cover. Regarding "hell fire," he admitted that he had tried to de-literalize people's understanding; moreover, he admitted to being no friend of those inner mission people who opposed the folk-school movement. Finally, the charge that he was driving people from the church could not be statistically demonstrated. During the eight years of his ministry, the official state records showed that only 72 persons, mostly unstable [?] women, had asked that their names be removed from the membership register.

Despite this rather dispassionate, honest, and documented answer, the already intense conflict only worsened. Dietrichson sought to mitigate at least one charge—the one regarding self-communion—by receiving the Lord's Supper in a neighboring congregation at Holt. In 1873, when he presented himself to the recently appointed pastor, Adolf Carl Preus, he was refused communion on the grounds that he was "heterodox."[35] When this information became known, his own parishioners, instead of defending him, looked upon this judgment as further evidence that they had been right all along in questioning his qualifications as a minister.

The discussion had long since been brought to the attention of the Norwegian Department of Ecclesiastical Affairs, but officials were reluctant to transfer him to another parish. Moreover, it would be fruitless to bring the case to trial, because the Supreme Court had recently sent down a judgment in the famous "Gunnerus Case," in which the issues were similar. (Like Dietrichson,

Gunnerus was a Grundtvigian.) The Department would have preferred that Dietrichson be removed from the ministerial office, but felt it did not have sufficient grounds for such drastic action. If the situation were to be resolved, therefore, the pastor himself must "loose the knot." Between 1873 and 1876 Dietrichson sought a way out by applying for a civil service position. Finally, he was appointed postmaster in Porsgrund (1876); he demitted the ministry and continued in his new office until he retired on a pension, April 29, 1882. He died suddenly during the night of November 14, 1883, while on a visit to Copenhagen.[36]

Thus a complex and amazing life came to an end. The sadness, pathos, and silence of the last years hardly stilled the voice of one who had been both a prophet and a priest, an unyielding visionary and a practicing churchman, a kindly Christian pastor and a stubborn architect of order. For any pastor in the nineteenth century to demit the holy ministry for other than doctrinal or moral reasons was an action taken only in an extremity. Moreover, to move from the office of a pastor in the Church of Norway to that of a postmaster in a provincial town—well, that required some explanation. True to his nature to the end, Dietrichson opened to public gaze his inner motivations and his personal reflections on the rather dismal conclusion of his ministry in the church. His last writings were a compilation of the official documents relating to his move from ecclesiastical to civil office and a pamphlet containing his farewell sermons at Østre Moland. In the former he laid the blame for the difficulties largely on the Department of Ecclesiastical Affairs, which he felt had taken a vacillating position regarding the use of the baptismal formula. As a result, the weaker pastors responded to the whims and demands of parishioners, sometimes using the correct form, at other times the wrong. The result was that those pastors of solid convictions (among whom Dietrichson naturally reckoned himself) were made to suffer because they held to the belief that the creed was "the Word of God inseparable from baptism." The tone of the farewell sermons is muted. He did not wish, he said, to use the occasion to dig up the past, to accuse anyone of causing trouble, or to defend his own actions. Rather, he would depart without bitterness, wishing God's peace and blessing on each member of the congregation.[37]

IV

There is an air of genuine tragedy about the conclusion to Dietrichson's public life. The tragedy lies in the fact that he became the victim both of a religious clash between two ways of interpreting Christianity and of a conflict between two social classes in Norway. In that age there seemed to be no way of bridging either of the clefts, the religious or the social.

Dietrichson's Grundtvigian view of Lutheranism simply could not be understood and appreciated by those whose pietistic convictions made them myopic to the somewhat more subtle and profound insights of the Danish religious genius, who to them could only be seen as an enemy of the true faith. In fact, it has taken a century for Christians in general and for Lutherans in particular to strip away such Grundtvigian crudities as the nonhistorical view of the Apostles' Creed, the simplistic identification of the creed and sacraments with "the Living Word" in contradistinction to the Bible as an inscripturated "dead word"—from such basic insights as the relation between the oral confession of faith ("the Living Word") and the church both as the creation of the Word and the bearer of the Word in lively continuity with tradition (*"Kirken den er et gammelt hus"*), the relation between creation and redemption, between "the folk" and the church, between humanity and Christianity (one is a human being first, a Christian second), between the secular and the sacred, between history and eschatology (the "already" and the "not yet"). Much of what Grundtvig, and disciples like Dietrichson, strove to communicate to a generation that was tone deaf to anything but Pietism or Orthodoxism, or a combination of the two (Pietistic Orthodoxism), was like casting seed upon an unprepared soil. There was no way for a meeting of minds and hearts in the religious milieu of Norwegian Lutheranism, either in America or in Norway.

But the social cleavage seemed equally unbridgeable. The farmer-fisher folk of Norway and the immigrants in America were unquestionably a product of and a witness to a stratum of society that was "separate and not equal" to the *embedsklasse* (official class) of which Dietrichson was a resented representative. Perhaps only those Haugean preachers whose roots were among the common people could hope to get a sympathetic hearing from their social peers, and thus eventually to bridge the gap between the official church and the commonality of men.

A major factor in Dietrichson's successes and failures was certainly his personality. A complex man who eludes easy analysis—he could be authoritative and unyielding in one situation, warm and self-critical in another—this Norwegian clergyman made both lasting contributions and lasting enemies. On the one hand, it was said that no other man did so much in such a short time to influence the Norwegian Lutheran church in America. Yet, on the other hand, wherever he went, in America or in Norway, controversy and ill will invariably accompanied him. Such a paradoxical person may perhaps be best understood simply by an evaluative account of the man's personality, his theological views, his ministerial and social concerns, and his relations to and observations about others whom he encountered on the American frontier.

No one will deny that at times Dietrichson's personality was correctly described by the layman in Nerstrand: he was "a contentious and hot-headed fellow." The farmers in southern Wisconsin undoubtedly thought of him as "strict and overbearing," "avaricious," "an aristocrat of the aristocrats," and "imperious." At the same time they would laugh quietly at a man who took himself and his office so seriously that he could never once let himself forget that he was an ordained clergyman of the Church of Norway. A local tradition had it that he even did the parsonage farm chores dressed in his cassock and collar.[38]

True though these characterizations may be, they alone do not describe fully the man's personality. In fact, the careful reader of *The Parish Journal, The Travel Narrative,* and the letters that he sent back to Norway cannot escape the impression that here was a man of warm and earnest piety, a true minister with profound pastoral concerns, a thoughtful and careful theologian with keen churchly sensitivity. He looked upon ecclesiastical irregularity and insubordination as highly reprehensible, but at the same time exhibited graceful and penetrating ability for self-criticism. His letters, for example, reveal that he wondered whether he was equipped by temperament to be a frontier pastor. He wrote only a few months after his arrival in Koshkonong: "As far as I know myself, it is . . . very likely that I am better suited for breaking the ice, for plowing and hoeing and rough-planing than for harrowing and filing, for guiding and maintaining."[39] Frequently, he betrayed concern about his personal effectiveness as a pastor and would ask the church officers whether or not people were satisfied with his ministry. This "feeling-his-pulse" betrayed an underlying insecurity that was quite in contrast to his usual confident and authoritative bearing.

Yet despite his changing moods—his humble misgivings and his imperious confidence—he was convinced that the religious needs of the immigrants overshadowed everything else. He confided in one letter: "If I could follow my bent, I would rather accept the most miserable calling in one of the most desolate places in Norway than a position in any other country." The reference, of course, was to America, to which he was never fully acclimatized. Nevertheless, since God had called him to service in the New World, there he would remain, at least until he was convinced that his mission was accomplished. He wrote to friends in the homeland: "The Lord will place me and use me where He chooses." This is why he came a second time, after unsuccessful efforts to persuade others to take over the work he had begun at Koshkonong and elsewhere. Had he remained in Norway all his life, it is doubtful that he would have been known beyond his homeland. But acting upon what seemed to him to be a divine vocation, he had set himself the task of planting the church among the Norwegian diaspora in the New World. Brand-like, he would do God's will at all costs.[40]

Dietrichson's theological and religious beliefs, it has already been noted, were a combination of traditional Lutheranism and Grundtvigianism's "churchly view." These presuppositions must constantly be borne in mind while recounting and assessing his concept of the ministry and his attitudes toward other people— congregational reprobates, frontier ministers, non-Lutheran denominations, and quasi-Christian sects.

It is evident that Dietrichson was in some respects a "high churchman," but at no time did he look upon episcopacy as a divine order in the Roman or Anglican sense. For example, in his defense of C. L. Clausen's non-episcopal ordination, he wrote: "He possessed all the essentials for the ministry: the call, the examination, and ordination. The fact that he was ordained by a pastor and not by a bishop has no bearing upon the validity of his

ordination, according to Lutheran doctrine. . . . Pastor Grundtvig has often pointed this out clearly and thoroughly." But there
were at least two areas in which his views could be judged "high
churchly." One was his concept of ordination; the other was his
elevation of the liturgy to what was virtually a *nota* or mark of
the church. Writing in both *The Parish Journal* and *The Travel
Narrative*, Dietrichson said that, if he were "to accomplish anything among the immigrants," he would need "the authority that
only ordination could give." When he described the beginnings of
Clausen's ministerial career, he wrote: "Clausen saw that, although
he was rightly called, he could never dare to accept this ministry
unless, through the church's regular ordination, he had been given
the Lord's power and authority to be a steward of the good things
of God's house."[41]

Dietrichson's view that ordination conferred "authority" has
been generally rejected by Lutheran theologians, who relate authority not to ordination but to the "call" or commission of God
mediated through the church. The church, in turn, sets apart the
"regularly called" person for the office of the holy ministry by
the rite of ordination. Lutheran theology, therefore, looks upon
the locating of "authority" in the act of ordination as a high-
churchly aberration, and of this Dietrichson was no doubt guilty.

The second hint of high churchism lay in Dietrichson's understanding of the role of the liturgy, order, and discipline. Throughout both documents the reader will note the frequent appeals that
are made to the "edifying church order" and/or "the Ritual"
(*Ritualet*) of the Church of Norway. The latter did not simply
mean ritual or liturgy, but the officially approved manual including the main liturgy, the forms for occasional services such as baptism, confirmation, marriage, etc., together with regulations governing church life. Dietrichson's "orderliness" was shaped almost
entirely by a sense of obligation to govern the church according
to *Ritualet* and the generally accepted guide for pastoral and
parochial practices and discipline by Bishop Erich Pontoppidan of
Bergen, *Collegium Pastorale Practicum*.[42]

The problem of "high churchism" arose, not from Dietrichson's
scrupulosity regarding liturgical forms and parochial regulations,
but from his elevation of such matters to the position of virtual
marks (*notae*) of the church. Lutheranism's primary confession

(the Augsburg Confession, 1530) asserts that the only marks of the church are the gospel and the sacraments administered according to the gospel. The confession clearly rejects human traditions, rites, and ceremonies as essential marks of the church: "It is not necessary that [they] should be everywhere alike." Dietrichson, however, laid down "order" as one of the conditions for the unity of the church. He wrote regarding Clausen's ministry that a true church had come into existence at Muskego because "the Word of God is preached and the sacraments are administered *according to the order of the church through a lawful ministry* [italics added]." At a later date, when he was concerned about the formation of a synod, he wrote that "an organic union of all congregations having the same doctrine *and order* [italics added] must be brought about." Thus it is evident that Dietrichson had moved beyond Lutheran ecclesiology to an essentially Catholic position.[43]

In addition to regular ministerial duties at Koshkonong—such as preaching, teaching, administering the sacraments, conducting home visitation, and officiating at marriages and funerals—Dietrichson was a tireless missionary. He traveled to near and distant communities where Norwegians had settled. There he offered his pastoral services, often organized congregations (some of which became "annexes" of the Koshkonong parish), and generally exhibited a compassion for "the sheep without a shepherd."

Of more than passing interest were his observations about American blacks and Indians. In his travels it was inevitable that he encountered these peoples. While in New York he was both amused and disturbed by the Negro "revival meetings," but it was the white man's attitude toward the blacks that upset him. One Norwegian's denunciation of the Negro was described by Dietrichson as "only a coarse echo of that hatred and loathing which many Americans even here in the North . . . have towards the black people. And neither do they enjoy equal citizenship in these free states where people are constantly shouting about equality and the rights of man. . . . One will never see a white man walk with a black, and I often heard them talk contemptuously about the Negroes, as if they were animals."[44]

The American treatment of the Indians was another object of his critical eye. He observed angrily that they had been driven "by deceit and force" from land coveted by the white man. Despite the predatory acts of Americans in general, he had noted that the Indians often demonstrated kindness and helpfulness to the immigrants. This led him to say that "these examples of a grateful and loving disposition put many a Christian to shame!" There was no excuse for the shameful manner in which Americans displaced the Indians. He commented: "The manner in which this is done should at least be humane." In both instances of prejudicial treatment of the nonwhites, Dietrichson had put his finger on a sore spot that was to develop into a gaping wound in American society.[45]

One of his most enduring contributions to Norwegian-American church life lay in the area of polity or church government. No other man did so much in such a short time to give form to congregational and synodical life in the early churches. This was achieved by the drafting of model constitutions for congregational use and for synodical organization.[46]

The congregational constitution, although embodying Dietrichson's Grundtvigian views (later excised by his successors in America), was a document of far-reaching influence. Prepared originally for the Spring Prairie congregation north of Madison, it became in time a model for other congregations, Swedish and Danish as well as Norwegian.[47] Although it is difficult to establish a documentary link between the Dietrichson-authored constitution and Danish or Swedish constitutional efforts in America, internal evidence seems to indicate that one of the sources of the congregational constitution of the Swedish Augustana Lutheran Church, for example, was the Dietrichson draft. This was most evident in the definition of and distinction between deacons and trustees.[48] Dietrichson had given "spiritual" responsibilities to the deacons, while trustees were to have charge of money matters and other "material" things. He had failed to recall that, according to Acts 6, the "deacons" were precisely charged with "material" or "temporal" affairs. Thus he slipped into the Gnostic dichotomy that pitted the realm of material things, the evil, against the realm of spiritual affairs, the good. Later "orthodox" churchmen vigorously denounced Dietrichson's Grundtvigian "heresies" but failed to detect this incipient Gnosticism, which was quite as reprehensible to orthodox Lutheranism.[49]

The synodical constitution reveals a keen sense of balance between the inherited traditions and the demands of the new American situation. Convinced that the scattered congregations ought to be united into a single church body, Dietrichson in 1849 took the initiative in inviting pastors and laymen to consider such action. Although his efforts were not immediately fruitful, he nevertheless had prepared a careful draft for what he called a "Constitution for the Church of Norway in America." The document, again cleansed of Grundtvigian impurities, became in time the basis for a synodical organization in 1853. The constitution proper was divided into thirteen articles that made the customary provisions for name, doctrinal stance, liturgical practices, and church government. The latter was a peculiar combination of congregational, presbyterial (synodical), and episcopal polity. Earlier statements indicated a rather tight congregational polity, but this instrument insisted on the authority of the synod, the role of the "presbyterium" or church council, which was given power to act between synods, and the prerogative of the superintendent. (The word bishop was not used.) All of this was combined with the implication that basic authority rested in the congregation. Significant was the provision that the clergy controlled decisions in the synodical convention and in the church council.[50]

Where did Dietrichson obtain his model for such a constitution? The three most likely sources for doctrinal and liturgical provisions, all of which he had access to, are Pontoppidan's *Collegium Pastorale Practicum; Dannemarkes og Norges kirke-ritual* (1762); and *Forordnet alterbog udi Danmark og Norge* (1688). The provisions for church government were most probably borrowed from English- or German-speaking Lutherans already established in America, and from the American Presbyterian and Episcopal church constitutions. Dietrichson himself gives no hint as to what helps he may have had at hand.

Accompanying the constitution was a document called "Regulations for Internal Government of the Church of Norway in America." This consisted of twelve "canons" dealing in large measure with pastoral duties and relationships to the synod and the presbyterium. It should be noted that the canons included detailed instructions for the trial of clergymen charged with offense "against the church, its constitution, or its regulations, in doctrine or in conduct." Once again Dietrichson gives no indication of the source of these obviously American-influenced "canons." The use of the word canon—perhaps the only time ever proposed in American Lutheranism—might imply that Dietrichson's Episcopal acquaintances in Wisconsin, especially Gustaf Unonius and J. Lloyd Breck, may have provided him with their manuals. At this point, however, this interpretation must remain pure conjecture.

Dietrichson's associations with other frontier ministers of the gospel were naturally limited. Among the Norwegians there were three—C. L. Clausen, H. A. Stub, and Elling Eielsen. Clausen and Stub he recognized as fully accredited Lutheran clergymen. Eielsen, however, he regarded as improperly ordained, a highly irregular and questionable preacher whose activities and words he was not slow to challenge. Among the Swedes he encountered a John G. Smith, who posed variously as a Lutheran and as a Baptist preacher. He caused no little difficulty in the Koshkonong community, but was finally exposed as an impostor.[51] Another Swede, Unonius, worked closely with the Reverend Breck, the founder of Nashotah House, the Episcopal seminary at Pine Lake.[52] Serving as Breck's interpreter when the latter traveled among Swedish and Norwegian settlements, Unonius soon enrolled at Nashotah House and became an Episcopal priest. Henceforth he sought unsuccessfully to convince the Lutheran immigrants that there was no essential difference between Anglicanism and Lutheranism. Dietrichson felt obliged, when they were together in August of 1844 and later at the dedication of the Muskego Church in 1845, to point out his errors. Later Unonius received similar challenges from Swedish Lutheran pastors, and in 1858 he became disenchanted with America and returned to Sweden.[53]

Most aggravating of all to Dietrichson were the presence and methods of a new American cult called the Mormons, the Church of Jesus Christ of Latter Day Saints. Devoting a large section of his *Travel Narrative* to an exposition of Mormon history and teachings, he warned the immigrants lest they be seduced by the new movement.[54]

It was no doubt Dietrichson's experience in the ecclesiastically undisciplined atmosphere of the American Midwest, and especially his encounters with men like Eielsen, Smith, Unonius, and of course the Mormons, that caused him to emphasize increasingly the necessity for properly qualified Lutheran ministers in the immigrant settlements. The carefully prepared congregational and synodical constitutions and the "canon law" all express concern for the great importance of the ministerial office. Dietrichson sought to establish a frontier church with built-in defenses against vagrant ministers and ecclesiastical charlatans who might lead the very elect astray.

Dietrichson did not mean to imply that the "elect" under his shepherd's staff were sheep without blemish. The truth is that *The Parish Journal* reveals quite the opposite. "The Affair Funkelien" and the Braaten episode, recorded in some detail, were only two instances of the unregenerate character of many. Einar Haugen has called attention to the energy with which Dietrichson commented on the foibles and vices of his parishioners. One man was "a big-nosed and rebellious fellow"; another "a sweet-tongued, hypocritical individual." Others were evil-minded, stingy, and degenerate. A few cases of illegitimacy, one of prostitution, one of stealing, one of witchcraft filled in a catalogue of sins ranging from drunkenness to marrying an American.[55]

Despite a continuing barrage of frontier problems, Dietrichson's spirit was not destroyed. Undismayed and even hopeful, he went about his regular parish tasks with vigor and enthusiasm. His interests and talents extended beyond the normal parish ministry. We have seen how he concerned himself with organizing the common life of the Christian community by providing constitutional structures for congregation and synod. He realized, however, that these forms, though important, were not adequate for all frontier contingencies. What good would these be if the young remained uneducated and if the intellectual level of the adults was not raised?

Actually, from the very outset of his American ministry, Dietrichson had busied himself with establishing parish schools and soliciting financial support for them in Norway. The parochial schools were intended primarily for religious instruction. They were not to take over the entire educational task. As a matter of fact, only when the "common" or public schools failed to provide the three "R's" adequately, were the congregational schools to supplement their work with such instruction. One of the public institutions that Dietrichson judged to be carrying out its function acceptably was located in Grange, Walworth County, Wisconsin, where he had organized a congregation. Teaching in this school was a gifted Englishwoman, Mary Blackwell Dillon, who had mastered several languages, including Norwegian. A devout Roman Catholic, she carefully avoided insinuating her personal religious tenets into her classroom instruction and thus won the respect and admiration of the entire community.[56]

The religious needs of the children were further cared for by the introduction of a novelty—at least to Norwegians—known as Sunday school. The Sunday school movement, already under way among English-speaking peoples, owed its beginnings among Norwegian-Americans to Dietrichson.[57]

His educational and cultural interests were not restricted to instruction in religion and the three "R's." Music and adult education also claimed his attention. For example, he encouraged a movement to establish "singing schools." The immigrants tended to look upon these activities as unnecessary frills and therefore were reluctant to support them. Despite the pastor's good intentions, therefore, they never emerged as a significant cultural factor in the communities.

There was one educational activity, Dietrichson was convinced, that would win the support and enthusiasm of the people: the encouragement of reading good literature. Dietrichson thought it "good and profitable" to establish a community library—also a "first" among Norwegian-Americans. Moreover, he organized a reading society with an initial membership fee of twenty-five cents and annual dues of twelve and a half cents. When the library opened it contained 133 volumes.[58]

One additional fact should be mentioned: Dietrichson possessed a strong feeling for history. Shortly after his arrival at Koshkonong, he began the record herewith presented for the first time in English translation. The reader will note how frequently the pastor-author was writing more than a mere chronicle of events; he was consciously interpreting and selecting materials that were judged of value and interest for posterity. For example, at one point he parenthetically apologized for the seemingly excessive detail: "I have so thoroughly reported on these events in this journal because it seemed likely that in the history of the Norwegian Lutheran Church here in Wisconsin, long after my time, they will be of importance. It is precisely the details in a case that make it possible for an outsider to gain a somewhat clear insight into conditions of the past."[59] It is this kind of historical intelligence that characterizes both *The Parish Journal* and *The Travel Narrative*. Moreover, it has elevated the work of the editor and translators above a pedestrian, plodding enterprise to an exciting adventure. The readers of these documents will no doubt discover in themselves a certain ambivalence in their reactions to the central character, who, it must be admitted, repelled people by his lordliness and impatience and, at the same time, provided a genuine pastoral presence in the rough and tumble of a frontier American community. We are indebted to him for giving us a glimpse into the travail of body and soul experienced by the thousands of immigrants who forged a new life in the American Midwest.

St. Olaf College   E. CLIFFORD NELSON

Chronology

1815	April 4	Born in Fredrikstad, Norway
1832	Spring-Summer	Passed university entrance examination (*artium*)
1833		Passed the "second" (*anden*) examination
1837	February	Passed examination for theological degree
1838		Passed "practical" examination
		Teacher, Vallø, near Tønsberg
		Further studies in Christiania
1839	November 1	Marriage to Jørgine Laurentze Broch
1840		Catechist at Grønland Reformatory in Christiania
1841	May 25	Birth of son, Jørgen Laurentz Wilhelm
	June 16	Death of wife
1842	Spring	Trip to Denmark, Germany, Switzerland
1843	Spring	Return to Norway
	June	Unordained assistant to prison chaplain, Christiania
	June 15–16	Attended first general assembly, Norwegian Mission Society, Christiansand
	Summer	Conversation with Dyer Peter Sørensen about America
	October 12	Department of Ecclesiastical Affairs approved Dietrichson's application for ordination
1844	February 23	Ordained by Bishop Christian Sørenssen

1844	May 16	Departure for America
	July 9	Arrival in New York
	July 25	Departure from New York
	July 28 (?)	Arrived in Buffalo, N.Y. Visit with Pastor J. A. A. Grabau
	August 1 (?)	Departure from Buffalo
	August 5	Arrival, Milwaukee, Wisconsin
	August 7	Arrival, Muskego, Wisconsin
	August 11	Preached at Muskego, Wisconsin
	August 15–20 (?)	Visited Unonius at Pine Lake, Wisconsin
	August 30, September 1 and 2	First services, Koshkonong, Wisconsin
	September–October	Visited other Norwegian settlements in Wisconsin
	October 10	Organized East Koshkonong congregation
	October 19	Organized West Koshkonong congregation
	December 19	Dedication of West Church
1845	January 31	Dedication of East Church
	March 3	Dietrichson called by the Koshkonong parish to be pastor for a term of five years
	March 13	Dietrichson participated in dedication of Muskego Church
	March 21	Dietrichson answered call by announcing intention to return to Norway to seek a successor. If unsuccessful, would return as pastor
	March 31	Clausen accepted call to be interim pastor
	May 12	Dietrichson left Koshkonong for Norway
	June 7	Dietrichson sailed from New York
1846	June 24	Marriage to Charlotte Josine Omsen Müller
	September 23	Dietrichson's return to Koshkonong

1847	January	Organized Spring Prairie (Wisconsin) congregation
	February	Incorporation of the Koshkonong parish
1849	July 15–16	Constitution for a synod
	August 27	Constitution for the congregation
	September 6	Letter of call to Pastor A. C. Preus
	October 15	Constitution for Spring Prairie congregation
1850	May 29	Dietrichson left Koshkonong for Norway
1850		Pastor in Slidre, Norway
1851		Pastor in Nerstrand, Norway
1862		Pastor in Østre Moland, Norway
1876–82		Postmaster, Porsgrund, Norway
1882		Retired on a pension
1883	November 14	Died in Copenhagen, Denmark

The Travel Narrative

Original title: *Reise blandt de norske Emigranter
i "De forenede nordamerikanske Fristater"*
(A Journey among the Norwegian Immigrants
in the United North American Free States)

Translated by
MALCOLM ROSHOLT

CHAPTER I

Across the Atlantic

In the summer of 1843 I made the acquaintance of a devout Christian man in Christiania,[1] P[eter] Sørensen, a dyer. It was he who stimulated the mission to our countrymen in America which is the subject of these pages.

In our conversation, talk of our dear Schreuder's mission in Africa led naturally to the question of the religious needs of our fellow believers who had emigrated to a different part of the world. As this matter had been on Sørensen's heart a long time, he asked me if I did not feel called to sail to America to investigate the spiritual situation among the Norwegians, to establish congregations, and thus to lay the groundwork for a permanent church order among them. Along with this challenge, he offered to pay all expenses of the trip. The proposition stirred me the more since it came from one who, motivated by love, gave rather of the widow's mite than of the rich man's surplus.

I had often worried about the emigrants, exposed as they were to every wind of doctrine, but it had never entered my mind that I should undertake this task. The religious needs of the emigrants now aroused a much deeper concern in me. I was fully aware both of the importance and the difficulty of such a call. I pondered the matter seriously and conferred with several Christian men, whose judgment I valued far higher than my own, as to what they thought I might accomplish. Encouraged by them and with faith in the Lord who gives strength to the weak, I decided to accept the challenge, provided I might receive ordination in the Church of Norway. Both my advisers and I saw that if I were to accomplish anything among the emigrants, I would need the authority that only ordination can give. Only if this were granted me would I be able to regard the challenge as a call from God and dare to accept it.

45

I therefore humbly requested ordination and on October 12, 1843, it pleased His Majesty graciously to consent.[2] Together with J. Hansen, who had been called as assistant pastor in Rollaug Parish, I was ordained on February 26, 1844, in Opsloe church, by his grace, the bishop of the Christiania Diocese.[3]

At Langesund on May 16, 1844, I boarded the brig *Washington*, commanded by Navy Lieutenant H. Smith, bound for New York with iron and emigrants, and on May 21 the wind permitted us to weigh anchor; including crew, we were 112 souls altogether.[4] When the weather permitted, I conducted morning and evening devotions as well as Sunday and feast day services for this little congregation. Our good captain gladly endorsed this practice. I also instructed the children of the emigrants in religion. Thus we had both church and school on board. The quartermaster's cabin was our schoolroom and the ship's deck our church, the passage-way over the cabins a pulpit, the heavens above a roof, and the rolling waves a church mural. Our services began with the festival of Pentecost and our last was held on the fifth Sunday after Trinity. Although the journey bore out the old sailors' saying that there are always storms when a pastor is aboard (we had a stormy crossing and some pretty grave days), still I was able to preach every Sunday but one.

Our beautiful ship fought proudly through the sea, and already on the eighth day we passed the little mountain island "Fair Hill," on Scotland's north coast.[5] We were visited by fishermen there as well as at the Orkney Island of Stronsay. On the morning of St. Hans Day [June 24, Midsummer Day], the captain woke me with the words, "The banks, the banks!" which made me realize that we had reached *the great Bank of Newfoundland*. This meant that we were out of danger from icebergs. During our crossing we learned that several of these intruders had threatened us, as we had felt quick changes of wind and temperature. The fog, however, had hindered us from seeing them. The big blocks of ice tear loose at this time of year, drift around in these waters, and are especially dangerous in storm and fog. There was scarcely any wind and so we celebrated St. Hans Day by heaving to and fishing; we were rewarded by a fine catch of codfish and some huge halibut. Both passengers and crew were fed for a couple of days from this rich fishing bank.

On Sunday, July 7, a fine American gentlemen dressed in black came on board to act as pilot, and on Monday, the 8th, we anchored in quarantine outside Staten Island in New York, both ship and passengers in good condition. Although a journey can be very monotonous when one sees only sea and sky, the monotony can be a joy as well. What is more beautiful than a quiet night on the broad Atlantic, when the ship, without a care, is driven by the fluttering sails before an imperceptible breeze, the billows rocking the vessel like a child's cradle, the moon casting its shining silvery beam across the water's surface, the stars playing on the blue waves. And even when a storm comes up and roils the sea and the spray reaches the shortened topsail, there is majesty, beauty, and power. The ocean birds and, occasionally, a whale are our only guides when these storms come up. The more serious-minded person will learn from an experience like this to fold his hands in prayer, lift his heart to the Lord of heaven and the sea, and say, "He who rules over the storm and weather can say to the billows 'so far and no farther.' "

What a relief when the storm abates, the battle over, and the windward braces can be shortened, even though the topsail and mainsail are doubly reefed. How the soul is filled with gratitude when the ship's wake runs straight from the stern, and the white froth reveals increased speed. The vessel moves rapidly toward the rolling wave and leaps up on its foaming crest, which flings its spray across the onrushing waters.

Even in such a sea one finds much boredom among those passengers who would rather sit and dream than consider the serious possibilities of such a scene and raise their minds and thought to him, the Almighty One, who rules over all and without whose protecting hand this tiny ship would quickly be smashed to pieces with an offering of passengers to the hungry deep.

Look at the towering, wind-driven blue-green masses of water that could destroy any human structure, no matter how strongly built or how ably handled. See these masses of water throw themselves as if they would engulf the entire ship. See how this threatening monster rushes upon the frail structure, at one moment sneaking under the ship's keel, and in the next furiously throwing itself high up on the other side as though frothing in rage because it must bow before a human creation—because all its power has succeeded only in soaking a sailor's shirt.

When one realizes that this onslaught goes on endlessly and that ships can still resist its force, he has all the more reason to think of God, but also to be mindful of the inventive genius he has given to man whereby he becomes master over nature. Indeed, he must earnestly learn to thank and praise the Lord when he again sets foot on dry land, especially if, like us, he had one day seen a wrecked ship floating by. This ought to have convinced us how easily our own brig could have become a victim of the sea.

CHAPTER II

New York

On Friday, July 9, we debarked after having been at sea fifty-five days, during which time a ship had been our home. I took a ferry from Staten Island to New York, that capital of New Europe, where everything is *Leben und Treiben* [hustle and bustle]. New York is a big, beautiful, and rich city which has gone forward with giant strides. In 1696, about 75 years after the first settlers had arrived, the number of people was 4,500; sixty years later it was more than 16,000, and up until the year 1786, three years after the English withdrew, there were still no more than 23,700 inhabitants. After this date the influx of people increased. Four years later New York had more than 33,000 people. Since that time it has been growing by leaps and bounds. In 1800 there were 60,000; in 1810 about 96,000; in 1820 nearly 123,000; in 1825 over 166,000. In 1830 there were 202,000; in 1840, 213,710; and I have heard people say there are now between 400,000 and 500,000 people in the city.

If the growth continues at this rate, New York will be the most heavily populated city in the world by the end of this century. People pour in from all parts of the world, giving the city an amazing cosmopolitanism. If one stops half an hour on one of the congested street corners of Broadway, he can hear most of the world's languages spoken. Everywhere the visitor finds a spirit of industry which fills him with wonder. Clearly it takes time to orient oneself in this vast city, and a visit there is doubly time-consuming because one sees so many new things, which at least for the moment capture one's attention.

I found lodging in a boarding house on Liberty Street, located near both Broadway and the harbor. Ships without number fly their flags; sailors can be heard singing; and there is such a babble of tongues that it is enough to make one's head swim. If one walks down to the Battery, a pleasant and popular promenade, he gets a lovely view of the bay and of the surrounding territory of Long Island and New Jersey. Here I spent many a pleasant hour breathing in the fresh salt air, to get away from the heat of day in this stuffy city. To stroll up and down Broadway is surely interesting. It is the widest and most famous street in the city, frequented by the fashionable world en masse, especially on the West Side. The East Side does not share this honor and glory; to walk there is *malapropos* and contrary to the fixed rules of elegant society. But on the West Side, adorned with beautiful buildings and glittering shops, a person is so overcome that he does not know which way to look or which shop to peruse.

One building on Broadway is of special interest to the visitor. This is the well-known Astor House built by a German of that name who is reputed to be one of the richest men in the United States.[6] Part of the building is a hotel which rents for $2,000 annually. In 1843, Mr. Astor, it is said, sold his interest to one of his sons for one dollar, to evade a law which prohibits a father from giving anything to one of his children in preference to the others.[7] On the ground floor there are eighteen elaborate and excellent shops. The hotel, which has 390 rooms, was opened in June, 1836. At one time it is said to have housed 700 guests. The manager takes in $1,400 per day. I mention this fact only to indicate the extraordinary number of visitors. On the same side of the street there are some houses and another hotel called Franklin House, where one can see many gentlemen, Yankee style, sitting in easy chairs with hats on, their feet propped on the window sills, reading yard-long newspapers. A little farther up the street is the City Hall, a large building with a lovely park and also a delightful fountain. Time and money did not permit me to see all the great sights of the city.

I conducted two religious services in New York for Norwegians, Swedes, and Danes. On July 14, the sixth Sunday after Trinity, I preached aboard a Swedish ship whose commander was Captain Nissen from Gothenburg. Her captain belongs to a group of Swedish skippers who have pledged themselves to assemble their countrymen for devotions on holy days. That is why Nissen's vessel carries the "Bethel" flag, consecrated by the Swedish archbishop and raised whenever services are held on board.[8]

The next Sunday a German Lutheran minister, Stohlmann, graciously gave up his church, St. Matthew's, permitting me to hold Norwegian services and to administer communion.[9] We used Swedish hymnbooks, as there are more Swedes than Norwegians in the city. But naturally I used the Norwegian liturgy. About fifty persons came to communion from a congregation of about two hundred, most of them Swedes, as was also the case with the former service. On the whole, it seems that the Swedes living in New York, who greatly outnumber the Norwegians, are more interested in church affairs than are the Norwegians, and several of them attending the service expressed a desire for a resident Norwegian-Swedish pastor. It would seem to make more sense in this city than in London, where there is a Swedish minister but perhaps not as many Swedes and Norwegians as in New York.

The pastor of the German Lutheran church where I preached, Herr Stohlmann, is a fine Christian gentleman who showed great interest in my mission and a willingness to make arrangements for a Scandinavian service. He went with me to the organist, a Mecklenburger, who played for us gratis, while the president of the congregation secured the loan of *vosa sacra* for me.[10] In short, he did all he could to help us.

Several of my countrymen seemed to be stirred by the memory of the fatherland's beautiful church liturgy which I conducted at this Norwegian service, but the feelings of the majority were, sad to say, only lukewarm. Most of the Norwegians in New York belong to no congregation and have been dead members of the mother church which originally took them to her bosom. Many of them have become so Americanized in this "land of liberty" that they expressed annoyance when, at the close of my sermon, I urged everyone present (in accordance with the apostolic admonition) to pray for our fatherland and its newly crowned king.[11] Some of these Norwegians have joined the Reformed church and others I talked to have joined the American Lutheran Church,[12] which has been deeply influenced by the Reformed. Some of the more sincere Norwegians have gone over to the Methodist sect, which has such an appearance of spirituality.

After the services in St. Matthew's, I was approached by a young countryman who had been in America six years. Of pleasing personality and apparently a sincere Methodist, he seemed interested in all church work, as well as in my own mission. The Methodist and Lutheran doctrines, he said, were the same. I did not wish to get into an argument with him over this, because I knew it would be useless. When he was about to leave, he said, with deep feeling, "Perhaps we will never meet here on earth again. Let us therefore pray together." With this I readily agreed; we knelt down and he offered a long and well-intentioned prayer. After he had finished, he seemed completely exhausted. We parted in deep sadness and I saw that he had a pale, sickly look, but he assured me that he was at peace with himself and happy in his decision to join the Methodist church, where he had found what he had been looking for. "The upright in heart shall be blessed." God alone knows his heart! He spoke of several Norwegians who have joined the Methodists. A Swede who was a convert to Methodism once told me that he thought it was a sin to wear any kind of decoration, such as a brooch, a gold watch chain, or rings. When I called his attention to a mirror held in a gold frame and other items of elegant furniture in his room and then showed him my hair band with a gold lock on it, I asked him if he thought it was a greater sin to wear this than to have the other things in his room. He changed the subject! This manifestation of respect for external form, which the Methodists seek to incorporate into Christianity generally as well as into each convert, in the life of the Christian is especially evident among the Methodists in America, who are very numerous and attract many proselytes.[13]

That same Sunday evening I was in a German Methodist church, very plain and simple in its arrangements but brilliantly illuminated with gas lights. The preacher stood at the lectern which served as a pulpit; behind it was a sofa. He wore no vestments, as these are not commonly used by the leaders of the sects. This man was a tall, sincere, dark-complexioned South German who gave a lively sermon, using as his text Acts 2:37–38—"Men and brethren, what shall we do to be saved? Then Peter said unto them, Repent, and be baptized every one of you in the name of Jesus Christ for the remission of sins." The first part of the text he treated very well and thoroughly, showing clearly the Methodist pattern of conversion, but the latter part, dealing with baptism, he touched on only lightly.

As I wanted to visit a Negro Methodist meeting that same evening, I left before the service was over. Consequently, I saw only slight manifestations of the effect that this type of revival preaching often produces. It is revealed most often audibly and visibly during and at the end of the preaching, although not in the same crazy fashion among the whites as among the more uninhibited and emotional Negroes. I have never heard nor seen anything so insane as what I saw and heard in the hall where the Negro Methodists held their service. The noise of the meeting could be heard far out in the street.

After I and my guide, a German Lutheran pastor, announced that we were Protestant clergymen, a Negro guarding the entrance permitted us to go in, and we came into a big foul-smelling room, where there were 700 to 800 Negroes assembled—the ladies in the gallery, the men below. The first preacher was already in the pulpit gesticulating feverishly, screaming as if all his listeners were deaf, and grimacing like a man insane, wiping off perspiration every second and shouting about the condemnation his flock was facing. He even named some of the members of the congregation and pictured hell in the most realistic terms possible. The effect of his sermon was abundantly clear. As the congregation moaned and screamed, first one, then another, shouted, "No, no, I will not, I will not go to the devil."[14] Then the preacher shouted, "Be converted. Turn to God. Now is the time. Right at this minute," *etc.* His listeners became so exhausted in body and soul that they would fall into convulsions and then would jump up and scream, "Honor, praise, and thanks be to the Lord. I have been converted and have found grace!"

To see and listen to this was both comical and tragic, and one wonders whether to laugh or cry. The hair on one's head would stand on end at the thought that this performance could be called Christianity. Several began to jump and dance around and on the benches. Finally the speaker stopped; a song was sung and another of the two reserve preachers began to pray, at first very softly, but, little by little, in such a crescendo of screams that one could scarcely understand what he said. The congregation replied to the prayer's thoughts and wishes, "Save us from hell and the devil. Yes, yes, O Lord, save us," *etc.* The more luridly hell, the works of the devil, and the tortures of the damned were pictured, the louder and more frequent were the responses. Thereupon the

preacher began a long prayer in which he described the heavenly
Jerusalem with its golden gates and streets of silver. The congregation's screams of anguish gave way to shouts of joy. "Yes, yes,
we want to go to heaven," to which the preacher replied, "Amen."
Just as this was finished, the third preacher sang a song to a joyous
dance tune, while he and the audience beat time with hands and
feet. Toward the end, the dancing became general, old women
and young girls, who on such occasions become highly emotional,
hopping and jumping around.

Deeply distressed at seeing such an insane spectacle, of which
one could well say, "The Lord was not in the storm," we left the
meeting a little after ten o'clock. My guide, Pastor Brohm,[15] told
me the next day that some of his parishioners who lived in the
neighborhood had no peace or quiet until two o'clock in the
morning, owing to the noise that came from the Negro meeting.
One may put up with such carryings-on from crude Negroes,
many of whom are literally heathens, as they are not baptized,
and the rest of whom grow up without religious instruction except what they learn from these pulpit sermons, the main theme
of which is hellfire and brimstone. How much more difficult it
is to understand why Europeans, who have been instructed in
God's word, can be led into the same kind of absurdities, though
perhaps not to such extremes.

From reliable sources I have heard that the Methodist *camp
meetings*—gatherings held at certain times of the year under the
open skies—are still more disgusting, especially after darkness has
cast its veil over the scene. I have never attended any, but in Wisconsin I was present several times at English Methodist *Quartem-
ber* (quarterly meetings) where, at the prompting of the pastor,
people were urged to tell about their secret experiences. Before a
large number of people they revealed their innermost feelings,
which, although they might occasionally be confided to a pastor
or to a very dear and trusted friend, are, after all, a matter between
the soul and God.

In addition to the many other sects and cultist teachings which
naturally flourish in this heavily populated area, a sermon was delivered while I was in New York by a former Catholic, Herr
Ludwig. He appeared before a big audience with the worn-out
story that Christ was a bandit who was hanged for stirring up the

people, *etc.*, and that all the clergy should be destroyed to make way for a new order of things. Thus in religion as well as in politics, there is constant dissension, schism, and strife. To be thrown among all these sects from the wildest emotionalism to the most brazen atheism and not be taken in by them requires a religious stability few of the immigrants of our nationality possess.

I met a Norwegian in New York, now living in New Orleans, who was a strong advocate of the slave trade which, as is well known, is found in the Union of Free States.[16] He considered it an excellent and just law that Christian instruction should not be given the blacks, and with great triumph he told of a church in New Orleans which was burned by a mob because the minister had gathered some Negroes together and had preached to them. When I pointed out that this action was most ungodly, he became angry and accused me of being a hypocrite because I did not agree with him. His denunciation of the Negro was only a coarse echo of that hatred and loathing which many Americans, even here in the northern nonslaveholding states, have toward the black people. Moreover, the blacks do not enjoy equal citizenship in these free states, where people are constantly shouting about equality and the rights of man. In New York one will never see a white man walk with a black, and I often heard the whites talk contemptuously about the Negroes, as if they were animals. This contempt is evident even among men of various colors, so that a brown man will not mix with a black or the less brown with the more brown.

During the first time I was in New York, the foundation was laid for a Scandinavian fraternal society, where the Norwegians, Swedes, and Danes might meet together, subscribe to Norwegian, Swedish, and Danish newspapers, and establish a library of Scandinavian books, thus maintaining contact with the mother countries. The idea is very good and will be a means of uniting the Scandinavian brethren in New York if it does not, as with so many other things, go up in smoke. Only six or eight of some forty persons who got together to organize such a society were Norwegians.

CHAPTER III

From New York to Milwaukee

On July 25 [1844] I went by steamship from New York to Albany. The Hudson River, which one follows on this course, is truly deserving of the name used by the Americans, "the noble Hudson." Majestic and grand, it winds through a beautiful countryside and its banks are studded with farms. The river would not be unlike the Rhine if it had the grand ruins of castles which make the latter so interesting, and if the buildings along its banks were built in more regal style.

As one approaches Albany, the banks of the Hudson are especially fertile and lovely while the river itself is dotted with beautiful small islands. Albany, the capital of New York state with a population (census of 1840) of 33,721, has a thriving commerce, as it is linked both by the Erie Canal and the railroad to Buffalo and to the western states and territories, while the Hudson is the connecting link with the eastern states. Albany has some competition from Troy, New York, seven miles[17] away, with a population of 19,334.

After a few hours in Albany, where I arrived on the day after leaving New York City, I took the train to Buffalo. The route passes through several smaller cities—Schenectady, Utica, Syracuse, Palmyra, Rome, and Rochester—and we covered a distance of 300 miles in thirty-six hours. Buffalo, a beautiful city on Lake Erie, is a fast-growing community. In 1814, fire destroyed the city, and for a time it was only a spot on the map, but now it has over 20,000 people and an excellent harbor filled with ships and splendid steamers. The "Main Street," the city's chief avenue, is handsomely built and adorned with stores as nice as any on Broadway in New York.

The day after my arrival in Buffalo I attended a German Lutheran church served by a Pastor Grabau, to whom I had a letter of introduction from Pastor Brohm, whom I had met in New York.[18] In this church I witnessed a very edifying, genuinely Lutheran, service and heard a fundamentally Christian and, for this congregation, especially fitting sermon preached from the text for the eighth Sunday after Trinity—Matthew 7:15: "Beware of false prophets." The pastor spoke with clarity and power, and showed us (1) how to recognize these false prophets as they always attack the person of Christ or the works of Christ or his sacraments, (2) what forms these false prophets take, and (3) how to guard ourselves against them.

This sermon clearly revealed to me the nature of the sects and cults in this divided land, and made me realize the great work that lay before me, namely, to bring order out of the chaos existing among our religiously confused immigrants. Following the ritual of the German Lutheran church, a penitent woman sinner, who had offended the congregation publicly and had caused resentment, confessed her error and received absolution and holy communion with the other communicants. How useful and desirable it is to have discipline in the church, especially when the congregation is surrounded, as in America, by sects which claim for themselves a stricter discipline than even the Lutheran church! All this came to me most clearly at the service in Buffalo.

After the service was over, I sought out the pastor and found him to be a serious and sincere Lutheran who, with real German *Gemütlichkeit*, received me and invited me in to stay with him. After we became better acquainted, he pleaded with me to remain a few days in Buffalo and to preach once in his church. As I thought it would be important in my own work to form a closer liaison with this Lutheran congregation, I accepted his invitation.

At vespers one of the next days, I preached in German for the first time in my life. My text was Luke 10:43—"One thing is needful." Grabau is one of the Old Lutheran clergymen who went through the persecution which the Lutheran church suffered in Prussia when the Union Church (the Reformed and Lutheran) became dominant. He left Prussia with his congregation and came to Buffalo five years ago, after twice being imprisoned in Prussia because he refused to obey the royal decree banning all Lutheran clergymen from performing their ministerial functions if they did not join the Union Church. This Old Lutheran congregation now in Buffalo has come so far that its members have both a church and a school. The congregation consists of 500 communicants, and the Old Pomeranian ritual is used. In churchly affairs the clergy and officers have the deciding voice.

In addition to this congregation, there is another German Lutheran group not far from Buffalo, in Canada, served by a Prussian who emigrated with Grabau, namely, Captain Rohr.[19] The latter formerly acted as sexton in Buffalo, and was ordained a pastor after being examined by Grabau and another German Lutheran minister. This event took place after I left and I learned of it on my return. So he who had once been in military uniform was now wearing a new kind of uniform. Several other Lutheran clergymen and their congregations in Wisconsin, Illinois, and Missouri belong to this Old Lutheran group. A split occurred in these congregations over the question of the ministry and ordination. An attempt to heal the breach was to be taken up by a synod convened at Milwaukee in June last year, shortly after I left Wisconsin. I do not know how successful it was.

In Buffalo, I was told, a church was being built where services were to be held for Christians of all faiths. How an idea like that can be realized is beyond my power of comprehension.

From Buffalo I made a trip through the small town of Chippewa, in Canada, over to Niagara Falls, where I heard in the noise of the roaring waters a mighty sermon by the Almighty God. I find it impossible to describe this frightful and yet beautiful natural wonder.

When I returned from this trip, I was visited by six of my countrymen, one of whom had been aboard ship with me on the Atlantic, but as he had no financial means of going farther, he had remained here, where his wife died last year. One young man from Kragerø, who had been here for some time and had found work, was very sincere and, in an effort to learn truth, had gone over to the Methodist church to find peace of mind. He asked me what I considered wrong about the Methodist faith and wherein this sect differed from the Lutheran church. I tried to show him as well as I could, and had the good fortune a few months later of meeting him in Wisconsin, where he had settled at Koskonong*

---

* Dietrichson invariably spells Koshkonong without the *h*.

Prairie. He became one of the strongest members of the Norwegian Lutheran congregation established there. The other Norwegians I met in Buffalo were, it seemed, indifferent to everything religious.

After a stay of five days in Buffalo, I went on board one of the splendid steamers sailing the Great Lakes. These ships certainly look like floating palaces, so elegant and comfortable are they in their appointments; nevertheless, they are not seaworthy and the machinery is dangerous. But travel by lake steamer is inexpensive. I paid $15 for a first-class passage of about 970 miles from Buffalo to Milwaukee; this included food for the five-day trip. Food, drink, service, and the other accommodations were as good as one could ask for. So the trip in this respect was comfortable, even though steamship travel, as everyone knows, is monotonous. The places and regions one passes through do not offer much for the eye. In addition to smaller cities like Erie, Huron, Toledo, and others, the route passes by Cleveland, Ohio, a really beautiful city, and Detroit, Michigan. The route continues through (1) Lake Erie, which by way of the Little St. Clair Lake and through St. Clair River, connects with (2) Lake Huron, which in turn, via the Mackinac Straits, connects with (3) Lake Michigan, the largest of these lakes. When the railroad is finished—it is already halfway—one will be able to go from Detroit via Marshall to St. Joseph, directly through the center of the Michigan peninsula, thus avoiding the present way around. It will then be possible to go directly from St. Joseph via Lake Michigan, whether one wishes to travel to Chicago, Illinois, or to Milwaukee, Wisconsin.

When the paddlewheel on our steamer broke en route, our passage was delayed and we landed in Milwaukee on August 5, one day later than scheduled. Luckily escaping the numerous hotel agents who meet every ship that comes in and swarm all over it, I got accommodations in a tavern at the other end of town. There, in my miserable room, I threw myself on the straw mattress, thoroughly pleased to be getting closer to my destination. Poor as this lodging was, a Swedish man in New York had recommended it to me as a good and cheap place to stay. At least it was good for something, as I met a countryman from Drammen who gave me, a complete stranger, considerable information. I also learned from him that some immigrants had arrived that same day on a brig.

When I went out to look for these people early the next morning, I suspected correctly that they were former shipmates from Norway who had left New York fourteen days ahead of me but had taken the tedious journey via canal boat to Buffalo and sailing ship across the Great Lakes. They had met with many difficulties and had been both mistreated and swindled.[20]

When I met these people of my one-time little congregation at sea, I was deeply distressed and thought how much still lay ahead for them, even though they naturally hoped that the worst was over. I knew that their expectations of the promised land in many ways would end in disappointment. It seems that they, too, had begun to realize it. This was the more or less conscious reason for the tears which flowed when they saw me again—tears that fell no less from strong men than from women and children. They had separated themselves forever from the fatherland for a distant and strange land to seek their uncertain fortune. I could only comfort them to the best of my ability and admonish them to remain true to the Lord and to build their hope on him and he would also bring some good out of their undertaking.

I had now entered Wisconsin, which is known as the "far, glorious west," as the Americans in the eastern states call the region west of the Great Lakes. This suggests both the great pride they have in the area and the glittering hopes that attract eastern Americans in great hordes annually; it has also lured many Europeans, among them our own countrymen.

As it is especially in Wisconsin and Illinois that the Norwegians have settled, it would not be out of place to include at this point a short description of Wisconsin, and later on I will do the same for Illinois.

CHAPTER IV

Wisconsin Territory

Wisconsin or *Wisconsan* is one of the territories which has not yet joined the Union, but it is part of the North American Republic. In this, as in all territories, the president of the United States appoints a governor and other officials who are paid by the federal government. This arrangement continues until the territory is admitted to the Union as a state. It will not be long before Wisconsin becomes a state, an honor which, when it becomes a fact, will cost dearly because then all the considerable governmental expenses, now paid by federal agencies, will then have to be paid from the state's own treasury. The settlers will learn to appreciate the low taxes which, among other advantages, they now enjoy. Last year, when the question came to a vote, some of the Scandinavians in Milwaukee urged the Norwegian immigrants not to vote for statehood. This was not so stupid.

Wisconsin, which extends from 42½ to 46 degrees north latitude, is bounded on the east by Lake Michigan, on the west by the Mississippi River, on the north by a line running from the source of the Mississippi River northward to the Canadian border and then east to Green Bay. On the south it is bounded by the state of Illinois.

Indians still dwell in the western part of Wisconsin and in Iowa, which lies west of the Mississippi and was organized as a territory by an act of Congress in 1838. The colonists in the western regions are protected by troops and forts.

Not all the land in Wisconsin is surveyed. The areas already surveyed are partly forest and partly prairie, for the most part rolling and in some places swampy.[21] In addition to the Wisconsin River, the most important one, the Rock River also runs through the state. Smaller ones such as the Fox and Milwaukee flow into Lake Michigan.[22] The territories, like the states, are divided into "counties" and each county again into "townships." The area of each township is 36 square miles. Such a square mile is called a "section" and contains 640 acres, one acre being equal to 9,000 *alen*.[23]

The counties where the Norwegians have settled are as follows:

Dane—1,234 square miles, about one fourth of which is prairie, for the most part "rolling prairies." The northern part of the county is watered by the Wisconsin River and the southern by the Catfish River and Sugar Creek. ("River" means *flod*, and "creek" means a *bæk* or *aa*.) Four lakes lie near the middle of Dane County. Nearby is located the city of Madison, between the third and fourth lakes. Situated in a beautiful meadow, it is still insignificant in size but serves as the capital of the territory as well as the county seat.

Jefferson County—576 square miles, lies directly to the east of Dane County. Here there are more forests than in the above-mentioned and more swampy areas. The Rock River is the principal stream. Jefferson, though small, is the county seat. Watertown, still just a spot on the map about eighteen miles northeast from Rock River, lies on the border of Jefferson and Dodge counties. Koskonong Lake, a small body of water through which the Rock River runs, lies in the southwestern part of this region bordering Dane County on the west and Rock County on the south.[24]

Milwaukee County—800 square miles, lies directly east of Jefferson County and has forests and in several areas swampy land. Milwaukee, the territory's most important city with almost 7,000 inhabitants, has blossomed out extremely fast when you consider that eight or ten years ago it was merely a small settlement with a few houses. As this city lies on Lake Michigan, which forms its eastern boundary, it serves as the connecting link with the eastern states. Milwaukee is the county seat and here too is the government land office, where land already surveyed can be purchased at the minimum price of $1.25 per acre. The rivers in this region are the Milwaukee and branches of the Rock and the Fox.[25]

Washington County—675 square miles, lies to the north of Milwaukee County and is bordered on the east by Lake Michigan. The Milwaukee River is the principal stream and the land is heavily forested. A city called Sauk-Washington has been laid out on Lake Michigan but only a few houses have been built.[26]

Dodge County—756 square miles, lying west of Washington County with Jefferson County to the south, has some prairie with quite a bit of woodland and is very swampy.

Portage County—756 square miles, west of Dodge County, has a level terrain with alternating prairie and forest land. The Wisconsin and Fox rivers form the western boundary. Fort Winnebago, garrisoned with troops, stands as a protection against the Menominee tribe of Indians and others that live to the west. This is also the county seat.

Racine County—610 square miles, located south of Milwaukee County, has a rolling terrain and is rich in forests. The city of Racine on Lake Michigan, which forms the eastern boundary, is an up-and-coming town and serves as the county seat. Rochester and Waterford, a little farther north, both on the Fox River, are small towns.

Rock County—710 square miles, lies west of Racine County with Dane and Jefferson counties on the northern boundary. The land here is for the most part prairie. It is watered by the Rock River and its tributaries. Rockport, on the west bank of Rock River, is to be the county seat; presently Janesville, a little town on the east bank of the river, performs this role.[27]

Iowa County—1,300 square miles, lying west of Rock County with Dane County to the northeast, consists of large prairies. The Pecatonica and several smaller streams flow into the Wisconsin River, which forms the northern boundary of the county.[28] Mineral Point, almost in the center, is the county seat. This region, including Dodgeville to the northwest and Wiota to the southeast of Mineral Point, as well as several other places, is rich in lead and also some copper ore.

In addition to these eight counties where Norwegians have settled, there were, up to last year, so far as I know, eight other such districts, but I do not consider it necessary to describe them. Racine, Rock, and Iowa counties, together with Walworth County lying in between, and Green County, lying between Rock and Iowa counties, and Grant County to the west of Iowa County, are all bounded on the south by Illinois. The Norwegian colonies already established in these areas I will discuss below.

The Norwegian Settlement at Muskego

Now I will return to my journey. In mid-morning of August 6 [1844], the day after my arrival in Milwaukee, after making the necessary arrangements, I continued onward. I was accompanied by the son of the gymnastics teacher, Hansen, from Fredriksvern, who was kind enough to show me the way to the Norwegian settlement nearest Milwaukee.[29] Our route led over a poor road and we traveled in just as poor a vehicle. We arrived late in the evening at the home of my escort's parents, who are among the Norwegians living closest to Milwaukee. In this Mr. Hansen I recognized, after I had collected myself, my childhood dancing teacher. I reflected how strange are the ways of life. Above the bed in his hut hung Hansen's old violin and bow. I recalled vividly how, because of my boyish pranks and tactlessness, I had received many well-deserved smart raps from this bow on my spindly legs, adorned with white socks and dancing shoes. I learned to the tune of that same violin the rhythm of the waltz as practiced in the dancing school of Fredrikstad. It seems rather far-fetched that a score of years later this boisterous young boy should meet with his old teacher and expect hospitality in a log house in the woods of the New World where, when we last saw each other, hardly anyone had set foot except Indians who now, by deceit and force, have been driven farther west.

After a visit with my countrymen, I went to bed and woke in the morning very much eaten up by mosquitoes and bedbugs—insects which seem to have established a permanent home in these oak-log huts. Next morning I left on foot for Clausen's, four miles from Hansen's place.[30] He knew that I had come from Norway and seemed to be anxiously waiting for me, and therefore he welcomed me with open arms. I established a temporary home with members of his friendly, enjoyable, and hospitable family.

The Norwegian settlement in Muskego lies partly in Milwaukee and partly in Racine counties, near and around some small lakes, of which Muskego and Wind lakes are the largest. The nearest cities are Milwaukee, about twenty miles northeast, and Racine, which is about the same distance to the southeast. In addition, there are a couple of small spots like Waterford and Rochester lying quite near the Norwegian colonies.

The land here is low and swampy, covered with quite heavy forest. In the opinion of most people, it was a most unfortunate choice of location for a settlement. The soil is not nearly so fertile as in other places. Also from the standpoint of health, it has proved to be a poor choice. Especially the fall of 1843 there was much illness among the Norwegians, and a great many died. But the autumn of 1844 was uncommonly healthful, as also in most of the other colonies. As the land is low, there are more rattlesnakes than on higher ground, and I know of two Norsemen who were bitten last year but who recovered after a long and painful illness. The first Norwegians to arrive five years ago were Søren Bache and Johannesen.[31] Others came from Voss Parish, some from Numedal and Telemark. The number of colonists is estimated at around 600. Their economic condition is on the whole about average. Those of the immigrants who are better off have purchased land, but precious little of it has been cultivated because it is hard to clear. With few exceptions, the people live in small, poor huts built of oak logs which have not been decently hewn. The logs are laid one on top of the other and chinked with clay. The huts consist of a single room where everything is packed together. Few have decent out-buildings. It is thus a sad fact that the immigrants have not done well economically, at least for the present.

In the autumn of 1843, steps were taken to organize a Norwegian Lutheran congregation when the colony called Clausen as its pastor. As it is of much importance and interest with respect to the religious conditions among the Norwegians, I wish to speak in more detail about this man. Claus Lauritzen Clausen, now about twenty-six years old, was born on the island of Ærø in Denmark. From his earliest youth, he was awakened to an understanding of Christian truths, but was confused for several years by pietistic and Anabaptist errors; God in his mercy gradually brought him around to a firm ecclesiastical point of view. He was influenced by several Christian pastors in Sjælland, namely, P. A. Fenger, F. Boisen, and especially Grundtvig and his writings.[32]

For a long time Clausen had a strong desire to become an instrument in the hand of the Lord and to preach the word of life to his fellow man. This longing received fresh impetus and even greater vigor when he heard about Pastor Schreuder's Christian decision to go as a missionary to the heathen. He therefore went to Christiania to talk with Schreuder about accompanying him [to Africa]. In the various obstacles that arose, he thought he saw a sign from the Lord not to take this course. While he was in Norway, he received an invitation to come to America to work as a schoolteacher among the Norwegians. This invitation he accepted for several reasons.

When he arrived at the Muskego colony in August, 1843, it soon became clear to him that it would be wrong and wasteful to work as a schoolteacher under circumstances which, from an ecclesiastical point of view, had become so confused among the immigrants. He realized that the parish school in which he intended to work had no firm basis and never could have one so long as there was no church to back it or to assert its authority over it. At this time, therefore, he confined his activity to reading sermons from various books on Sundays and holy days for the people who gathered to hear him.

The need and longing for a pastor now became clearer, especially among several of the Norwegian leaders. Since they believed that there was little chance of ever getting an ordained pastor from Norway, they conferred with some of the other pioneers nearby and finally turned to Clausen with a written call for him to serve as their pastor. Clausen saw clearly that, although he was rightly called, he would never dare to accept this ministry unless, through regular ordination, he had been given the Lord's power and authority to be a steward of the good things of God's house. He explained to the people that, only after he had been examined and found qualified and ordained by a properly called and regularly ordained minister in the Lutheran church, would he accept their call. The colonists then turned to a pastor of the German Old Lutheran church, who, as previously mentioned, had left Germany over the question of union in the Prussian church. He was L. F. E. Krause, pastor of a so-called German Old Lutheran congregation in Washington County near Milwaukee.

Even though Clausen did not actually have a degree, Krause thought, under the circumstances, that it was his duty to do as he was asked by his Norwegian brethren-in-the-faith. He therefore examined Clausen and found, according to his written report, a deep insight into God's Word and good knowledge especially of church history. He ordained him on October 18, 1843, according to the Norwegian Lutheran ritual, and administered the oath of office to him. Clausen is therefore a rightly called and properly ordained servant of God, in accordance with the manner that the Lord has prescribed, by a person qualified to perform this act with prayer and the laying on of hands. Thus he has been given the authority "in the church publicly to preach and teach publicly and to administer the Lord's holy sacraments" and to perform other duties. Naturally there can be no doubt about this when a person considers the essence and meaning of ordination in accord with our church's practice.

Because Clausen had not become a pastor in the ordinary way, as had we who were examined by the state church and (as a rule) ordained by a bishop, he cannot, because of the existing law, be recognized as a minister in the state church of Norway. Nevertheless, he must be regarded as a true minister of the Lutheran church, if we put aside the concept of a state church and recognize that he possesses all the essentials for the ministry: the call, the examination, and ordination. The fact that he was ordained by a pastor and not by a bishop has no bearing upon the validity of his ordination, according to Lutheran doctrine. Even according to the regulations of the Norwegian state church, ordination, although administered generally by a bishop, in some cases may be performed by a pastor or a rural dean; with respect to the higher clerical order, this amounts to the same thing. Moreover, when we consider this case from a strictly ecclesiastical point of view, Lutheran bishops, even though they have a higher rank in the state church than the pastors, nevertheless have not taken a higher ordination than the pastors. Pastor Grundtvig has often explained this fact clearly and thoroughly. After an inquiry from Clausen on this point, the theological faculty in Christiania, too, has declared that an ordination performed by a pastor and not by a bishop is not invalid.

I have seen fit to write at some length about this matter because there are some, both among the Norwegian immigrants and the people at home in Norway, who have confused notions about ordination as an act of the church entirely independent of the power of the state. Naturally considerable disorder and confusion would be created in Norway as in America if it should become the common rule that persons who have not studied theology and about whom one has no guarantee of their qualifications should be called and ordained. But in Clausen's case, the circumstances and the special situation were such that his ordination was desirable. In truth, the Norwegian immigrants have the greatest reason to rejoice that Clausen has been ordained, as he is surely a noble servant of the Lord with a sound churchly view, possessing zeal for his calling together with a humble and unpretentious Christian faith, and what he says is a living witness to the Lord.

Another person who settled in this colony and who has played an important role in church work among the Norwegians here as well as in other settlements should be discussed at this point. I refer to Elling Eielsen Sunve, a man from Voss Parish, who maintains that he is a rightly called and ordained Lutheran pastor.[33] How justified this claim is will soon become clear. When he came to America, Eielsen followed the same line of work he had carried on in Norway for many years; that is, he went about and preached, insisting that he was called by God, but he provided none of the evidence which the church naturally requires of anyone claiming the right to teach. It was not long before he expanded his self-appointed evangelistic role and ministry even further, and acted as if he were a full-fledged pastor, not only preaching the word of God, but also administering the sacraments. He offered as his authority a call from a few Norwegian immigrants but was still lacking the ordination that he later claimed to have.

The same fall that Clausen was called, examined, and ordained, Elling Eielsen stepped forth, saying that he had as much right to be called a Lutheran pastor as did Clausen. At several places he read a document in English which he claims to be his ordination certificate. It was some time later that I found an opportunity to talk with Elling and to see this paper. This took place about Easter, 1845, and I finally asked him by what right he called himself a pastor. He replied by citing Christ's command to his disciples to go out into the world and to preach the gospel. I called his attention to the church's rule concerning a call, examination, and ordination for everyone who considered himself a proper pastor of the church, and asked him if he did not, since he called himself Lutheran, accept the Augsburg Confession, which says that "no one may teach publicly in the church or administer the Lord's sacraments without being regularly called." He replied that he was both called and ordained, and, after some hesitation, showed me the document in English which he said was his ordination certificate. This paper quotes Francis Alexander Hoffman, who calls himself "secretary for an association of Lutheran pastors in northern Illinois," that "Elling Eielsen, on October 3, 1843, has been ordained a pastor in the Lutheran church."[34]

When I now asked Elling how he was examined and pointed out the apostles' directive in I Timothy 3:10 and II, 2:2, that those who seek to teach should also be tested for aptitude, he replied that he had been examined as a Christian more thoroughly than either Clausen or I: he had been tested by persecution, wakefulness, nakedness, hunger, etc. In short, he wanted me to know he had gone through almost an apostolic trial-by-fire. I tried to make it clear to him that the apostles, in the above reference, naturally meant one examined and thus qualified, and that whoever professed to be a teacher had to be able to teach others. I asked him several times whether he had undergone such an examination. He avoided answering this question and I got no further with him. Nor could I then make out what connection his explanation had with the matter of a call and ordination.

A month or so later I went down to the Norwegian colony in La Salle County, on the Fox River in Illinois, where I again met Elling. I tried to impress on his heart how improperly he was acting and how much confusion in church affairs he was creating among the immigrants by assuming the office of minister. Since a foundation was being laid for an organized church among the Norwegians, and there was reason to hope that it would continue, I asked him in the future to quit calling himself a pastor and especially to stop assuming the responsibility of administering the Lord's sacraments. I tried to convince him that if he wanted to work for the upbuilding of the church, it would be proper and correct, both for himself and for the Norwegians—even those in his own little groups, whose churchly notions were being increasingly confused by his actions—not to continue as before. He replied that he could not act otherwise because he was called both by God and man, called before either Clausen or me, and that it was in reality he who was the Norwegian immigrants' pastor. Clausen and I had come to worm our way among the people; it was we who confused and perverted them with false and papistic teachings, etc. He continued to insist that he was forced by the settlers in this colony to become their pastor and shepherd, that it was upon their request, with a call from them, that he had turned to a Lutheran minister to be ordained, although he actually did not consider ordination necessary for the ministry. Such comments, together with much vulgar criticism of the clergy in Norway and of the Norwegian church by him and a couple of his followers—in whose house I had dinner in order to have an opportunity to meet Elling—were the substance of the conversation on the day I saw him.[35]

One of the most honorable gentlemen in the settlement on Fox River is Christen Olsen Hole (?) from Stavanger County, one of the few Norwegians in this religiously confused settlement who has held fast to the Lutheran church.[36] From him and from others I learned how the call to Elling had come about. He explained that in the fall of 1843, when the Muskego settlement called Clausen to be its pastor, Elling had circulated a piece of paper on which he asked the Norwegians who wanted to cling to the Lutheran church to write their names; Elling would then do whatever he could to help them preserve its doctrines. A great number of persons signed their names, and among them was this Christen Olsen. A short time later he realized that Elling had gotten another Norwegian to write some additional lines in English on this paper stating that the undersigned had called Elling to be their pastor, and that Elling, with document in hand, had gone to a so-called Lutheran minister and requested ordination. On the strength of this document, the aforementioned Hoffman acceded to their request. Olsen wants to tell Elling the next time he sees him "that he has stolen both his name and that of several others as well."

A day later I met Elling at Christen Olsen's place, and it gave me an opportunity to talk with him. I told him that, while on the day previous I had hoped that he was honest and truthful, I had now learned how deceitfully he had acted. Earlier he had put on a sanctimonious air and declared that he was called to the ministerial office both by God and man, but here was a man who would tell him to his face how little truth there was in what he had described. Hole affirmed this and said straight out, "You have stolen both my name and that of others."

When I called Elling's attention to how displeased God must be with such a procedure and told him I considered it a duty wherever I went to expose him and his doings, he merely replied: "Then be a barbarian!" Whereupon I left him and have not seen him since.

I have found it necessary to describe this situation at length because when I returned to Norway I learned that many of "Hauge's Friends,"[37] whom I know to be earnest and good Christians and whose good opinion I esteem, felt that I had written too harshly and too hastily when, in a letter to a friend, I said that Elling, without a call, had forced his way into the ministry. I now want to ask everyone who may be interested in this point to study carefully what I said, and he will learn, without comment from me, whether or not I have passed unfair judgment on Elling in my letters. Nor are the teachings of this self-made pastor pure. Beside the fact that he has no idea what makes us Christians, what the baptismal covenant or baptism itself signifies, he completely confuses justification, regeneration, and sanctification, and on these, as on several other points, he is tainted with Methodist and pietist errors.

I have heard Eielsen preach twice and both times the content of his sermon was the same; in fact, he even repeated many sentences verbatim. He departed from the text that he read almost at once, and preached about conversion without clearly and coherently showing how it came about, or how it was related to sinful man. For that matter, Elling turned upside down the basic teachings of the very church whose pastor he professes to be. He holds that no minister has the right to give absolution, which he therefore has done away with. He has thus broken the staff, not only over the head of our Luther, but over those of the church's apostles—yes, over the head of the Lord Christ himself, who has given the church, through its ordained ministers, the power to be ambassadors with authority either to loose or to bind, to forgive and to spare the sinner. By encouraging women as well as men to get up and pray and preach at his meetings, he goes contrary to the apostles' admonition, which states that everything shall be conducted for edification and that women shall not be heard in church.

After he has been preaching, Elling proceeds to ask one, then another, in the audience, "How do you feel now? Did you feel the spirit working in you?" In this respect he sounds like the Methodists, who regard conversion as something that can come about in the twinkling of an eye. He accuses the old Lutheran church as we have it in our fatherland of being papistic and false, and proclaims that a new church in harmony with the union principle in Prussia has established itself in America, which, not only in ritual but also in doctrine, is created after the Reformed style; this, he maintains, is the legitimate church. Thus he destroys the unity of the Lutheran church. In short, I would never finish if I were to describe all the points on which he departs from the Lutheran church and perverts its order. Such is his public and churchly conduct as a teacher, which it is necessary for me to expose if I am to give a factual picture of conditions among the Norwegians. His private life, according to several reliable sources, is less than Christian. I am not going to judge that. But it is not only my right, it is also my duty, to state, as I have done in my letters, my conviction that Elling Eielsen, by his conduct, has been an important tool in corrupting the childhood faith and churchly sense of several of our compatriots and thereby has made them easy prey for the sectarians. I am sure every honorable person will agree with me in this.

It appeared at the time I left America that Elling's apostolic role was running out its course. In Muskego he still has a few admirers, and among them was one who served the holy sacrament of the altar in the following manner: he set out bread and wine on a table, and, after saying a few words to the audience, asked the people to come up and help themselves since they knew what it meant.

To demonstrate how Elling's followers, like other sects of this sort, believe that they have the power to test men's hearts and minds, I will relate the following: When I met Eielsen the second time in the Fox River settlement, it was at the home of a Norwegian family, and the wife asked me what I thought about him. I replied, in Elling's presence, as I had already told him, that it was inexcusable and improper in the highest degree for him to assume the office of minister without a call. She replied, "I can see now that you are worldly and that Elling is spiritual."

"My good woman," I said, "you certainly must have unusually sharp eyes when, in such a short space of time, you can judge whether or not I am worldly or spiritual. Forget not the words of Christ: 'Judge not lest ye be judged.' "

Elling himself, as well as his zealous followers, have tried in every way possible to slander Clausen and to defame him. They condemn his most innocent acts. For example, he occasionally takes his gun and goes hunting for recreation. For this he is accused of being ungodly and un-Christian. I am condemned by Elling's followers as a drunkard because I stopped at a tavern to rest on a hot summer day and drank a little wine mixed with water. Another time [they said] I broke the Sabbath when I asked the members of the congregation at Koskonong Prairie to meet in the afternoon after services for the purpose of deciding on conditions for calling a minister.

I write this only to show the pietistic errors in the warped and unloving condemnation of others which permeates this sect. This group also believes strongly in dreams and visions. A short time before I left, one of Elling's followers had a dream in which he talked with the Lord and saw the saved and the damned. The Lord had revealed to him that among the world religions the Lutheran church was one of the best but that it too, as it existed in Norway, was papistic and false; the Methodists therefore represented the real communion of saints. This dream was written up and circulated as a revelation from the Lord.

This incident reveals a remarkable similarity to the judgment these people passed upon a sermon I preached many months earlier on the text in Revelation 3:11—"I come quickly: hold fast that which thou hast, that no one take thy crown." After first attempting to impress on the hearts of the audience what it is that we as Christians and members of the holy Christian church must cling to, I reminded them that we, as members of the visible church, should, for our own edification cling to the noble church order we have from our forefathers. This last point especially was meant for the Ellingians, several of whom were present at the service to twist my words and to suck poison from them.

They interpreted my sermon as instructing the people to hold fast to sin and misery inasmuch as our church order is false. Moreover, it seems that this group shares with most of the sects the belief that they have established a pure and holy community.

Shortly before my departure, a relative of Elling, a man from Voss Parish, Niels Colbeinsen Fjeldbye, who was a member of the Norwegian Lutheran church at Koskonong, left the congregation. In a letter to me, Fjeldbye gave as grounds for his leaving that it was impossible for our congregation to belong to the true church of Christ, because there were so many unholy people in it. In conversation, I tried to convince him that the Christian church on earth, according to the Saviour's own words, was bound to have tares among the wheat. True, it is and always will be the church's right, yes its duty, to exclude from the congregation the openly ungodly; yet, by the nature of things, there were bound to be many unholy ones left who cannot be excluded, under the rule that a congregation cannot judge its members except on the basis of what it sees and hears. The man remained unconvinced and withdrew from the congregation. Elling had worked on this relative, and it is also clear that if Eielsen did not openly teach that his own church body was the pure one, at least his followers got that impression. This will have to be enough about the Ellingians who, having formed their own sect, rightly can be called by their own special name.[38]

As mentioned earlier, when the Norwegian settlement at Muskego called Clausen, and after his ordination, the first step was taken in October, 1843, toward formal church organization among the immigrants. From that time on, Pastor Clausen preached the Word of God, administered the sacraments, and performed the other essential pastoral duties in the homes round about. To that extent, certainly, a congregation was organized, because where the Word of God is preached and the sacraments are administered as prescribed by the church through a lawful ministry, there a true church exists.

In addition to other churchly matters, there was one especially which had to be straightened out before these small beginnings could achieve any degree of permanence. When Clausen accepted the call to the ministry, those persons who wished to join the congregation naturally should be required to adopt a formal statement of belief—a declaration that he or she wanted to be a member of the congregation under conditions that had been agreed upon. It must be borne in mind that in the United States there is complete freedom for everyone to join or not to join any religious organization, and it is clear that the Norwegian immigrants in America were of the same mind. Despite an admission in their call to Clausen that in this foreign land they wished to remain Lutherans, it did not follow that they were Lutherans as prescribed by the Norwegian *Ritual* and ordinances.[39] This point had to be cleared up. They would have to agree first on whether or not theirs was to be a Norwegian Lutheran congregation. If they agreed that it should be so and wished to hold fast to the fatherland's church order, it was absolutely essential that proper conditions be laid down. This had not happened the year before and the results were evident.

While I was attempting to organize a congregation at Koskonong Prairie, Clausen wrote to me concerning a bitter controversy that had broken out in Muskego. Clausen discovered that some of the members who had been considered part of the congregation were now seeking to go their own way and did not wish to abide by Norway's ecclesiastical order, to which Clausen, by his oath, was bound and to which he considered it his duty to adhere. He issued a declaration to the congregation stating that if he was to be their pastor and shepherd, the members would have to make a promise to observe the order of the Dano-Norwegian church *Ritual*. Among other points, he declared it to be absolutely essential that the discipline laid down for the state church in the *Ritual* (though now neglected and unused) should be enforced.

He therefore had to require that each person who wanted to attend holy communion should come to him the day prior, not for private confession, which he regarded as less important; but for an opportunity to talk about the seriousness of going to the Lord's Supper. It was over this last point that the struggle primarily raged. The leaders of the settlement, particularly those who originally were the most anxious to call Clausen, regarded this as a papistic yoke laid upon their conscience. They said that if he were to continue in this way, they were not going to belong to the church body he represented.

As often happens, the leaders of the opposition attracted a large number to their position, and at first it appeared as if only a few persons would abide by church order. Little by little, truth won out and eventually many joined the church on the conditions which had been adopted, while the original opponents and many with them remained outside the congregation until I left. A confession should have been required of those who, by calling Clausen, in a sense constituted a congregation. Had this been done, then naturally those who were unwilling to join under the terms agreed upon would not have become members. The scandalous controversy which so shook and divided the infant congregation would thus have been avoided. As mentioned earlier, in the fall of 1844 a confession of faith and order was required. From the old congregation a small new one was thus formed, committed to the regulations of the fatherland's church *Ritual*.

As early as 1843, Tollef Bache from Drammen and several of his relatives and friends kindly donated 420 specie dollars for the building of a church.[40] This edifice was so nearly completed that it was dedicated on March 13, 1845. In addition to Clausen, who gave the dedication sermon, Krause, the German Lutheran pastor, and I were present on this solemn occasion.

In compliance with Wisconsin statutes, a school has been organized to which the Norwegians, together with their American neighbors, may send their children. They are instructed in English, writing, arithmetic, etc. The law states that where a settlement has been established containing a certain number of families, it can make a request to "the board of school commissioners" of the county for permission to organize a school district. From the eligible voters of each school district, three "trustees," one "clerk," and one "collector" are elected to the board. The county school treasury annually pays a portion of the cost, according to the number of children required to attend (or rather eligible to attend, since there is no compulsory attendance). If this sum is not sufficient, the remainder is assessed the landowners of the district. The teacher is selected by the district directors, who also determine his salary. As there can be no religious instruction in public schools according to the constitution of the United States, which prohibits the teaching of any denominational doctrine, naturally such schools cannot be parochial institutions for the Norwegian

Lutheran congregations. Parish schools must therefore be organized and supported by the congregations. Such a school has not yet been established in Muskego, but, to meet this need, Clausen's good Christian wife, at great sacrifice and without pay and on the whole with little thanks, has instructed the children of the congregation.

I once visited an American public school of the type described where a few Norwegian children attended. A young American lady was hired that year to teach. The schoolhouse, here as in many other places of this new land, is a small and poorly built log hut.

Among the Norwegians in the settlement near Muskego who have not joined the Lutheran congregation, some are followers of Elling Eielsen and a few have joined the Mormons.[41]

CHAPTER V

The Norwegian Settlement at Koskonong Prairie

As mentioned earlier, I had taken up temporary residence with Pastor Clausen. From there I was able to visit the Norwegian settlements with a view to selecting a central location for my work. This was the first step necessary for the success of my mission, which was to acquire an understanding of the religious needs of the immigrants and to work for church order among them. Clausen intended to go with me on the first trips, but became ill, and so I had to go alone.

Fifty miles to the west of the Muskego colony lies the Norwegian settlement at Koskonong Prairie. It was the first place I visited on my tour. This colony lies near the middle of Wisconsin in a region called "Koskonong Prairie," after a lake of the same name lying to the southeast of the colony's center. It actually is made up of five smaller settlements separated by short distances from each other. Four of them lie in Dane County and the fifth, the easternmost, in Jefferson County, all within a radius of about twelve to fourteen miles. The nearest towns are Wisconsin's capital, Madison, about twenty miles northwest, Jefferson to the northeast, and Janesville in Rock County to the south. Catfish Creek to the west and Koskonong Creek to the east both flow into Lake Koskonong and water the land around.

The terrain is mostly "rolling prairies," but there is a dearth of trees; it is for this reason that the settlements are scattered. The first Norwegian settlers have been here about three or four years; the colony began to grow in 1843, when seven to eight hundred Norwegians could be numbered, most of them from Telemark, Numedal, and Voss, and some from Sogndal. On my first visit, I held services three times, the first two in a barn and the third on a beautiful grass-covered slope under a big oak tree.[42] At this last

78

service, where about 60 people came to communion, I used as the text for my confessional address the words from a psalm [78:19]: "Can God furnish a table in the wilderness?" And for my sermon, Christ's words: "Come to me all ye who are heavy laden." It was a clear and beautiful day and for me an unforgettable one. On this first visit, I was asked by a great many of the settlers to come and work among them, and this request was later made in writing.

Visits to the other Norwegian settlements convinced me that it would be expedient to make this colony my headquarters, both because at present it is the largest and also because it is somewhat centrally located among the settlements in Wisconsin and Illinois, where I hope to establish the church. Therefore I decided to accede to their request. After I had returned from my first journey, I remained for a time at Clausen's and then went back to Koskonong, where I established my residence in a little hut that belonged to one of the first of the Norwegian settlers.

Now I was ready to begin work, and the first item on the agenda was to bring about orderly church life. On my first visit here, as in the other colonies, I confined myself to holding services for all who wanted to take part, in the hope of awakening a conscious longing among the immigrants to maintain a relationship with the fatherland's true church and its edifying order. However, it was clear to me that in order to organize congregations among the immigrants, it was absolutely necessary to get a definite statement from them whether, in this land of the free, they intended to depart from the Norwegian Lutheran church and its discipline or to stick to it. I soon realized that certain basic rules had to be adopted for the organization of a congregation; the form in which this should be embodied now became the subject of my earnest deliberations. As a result, I drew up the following questions: [Editor's note: Dietrichson here states the four points found in *The Parish Journal*, p. 153.]

The reasons which led me to adopt these regulations in this manner were as follows: It was plainly apparent to me that it was my duty to gather and bring back the scattered and, in part, confused members of the Norwegian Lutheran church. Consequently, the first question for the immigrants, who in America have complete freedom to organize a church body by whatever method they deem best, is whether or not they were willing

voluntarily to declare themselves members of a Lutheran congregation.

It was also clear to me that in the formation of such a congregation by a pastor, bound by the ministerial oath of the Norwegian
church, and by a people for whom the church order of the fatherland must be precious, there can be no thought whatsoever of
creating a new system. We must build upon the *Ritual*. This was
the reason for bringing in the second question in the manner
cited.

The reason for the churchly confusion is for the most part a
lack of appreciation of the meaning of the call, examination, and
ordination to the holy ministry. Since they longed to share in the
blessings of the church, they turned to self-made preachers who
only further confused their sense of order. This fact led me to
phrase the first part of the third question in the manner given,
while the need for church discipline in each congregation, and
especially in one under such conditions, prompted me to include
the second part of question no. 3.

I am well aware that a pastor is a servant of the congregation.
But I also know that, correctly understood, it is not being papistic,
as some American sects like to assert, to demand that a member of
the congregation regard his shepherd as his ecclesiastical superior
and show him obedience within those limits by which he, as a
servant of the church, is bound. What else is this except the
apostle's admonition, "Obey your superiors in the Lord?"

Furthermore, I sought to call the attention of my dear countrymen to the fact that if they want to enjoy the great blessing of
church orderliness, they must accept certain rules. While these do
restrict religious freedom, they are nevertheless indispensable to a
congregation. The last question was put with the thought that the
minister might be compelled to go back in the records to show
individuals in the congregation the conditions they had willingly
accepted.

After I had established the fundamental rules for the organization of a congregation, I called together, on October 10, the
pioneers from the eastern part of the settlement. I told them first
in a simple and straightforward manner how I had arrived at the
decision to go to America and the purpose of my coming. I asked
them not to believe I had come to take their money, and assured

them that through Sørensen's Christian sacrifice, I did not need to ask anything of them; I could manage my own needs while I worked among my countrymen to bring order into their church affairs. I then asked my listeners if any among them were serious about remaining in the church in which they had been baptized and retaining its order in this foreign land. I asked them again to reaffirm the intention stated in the request they had made of me to arrange their religious affairs, and they all answered together, "Yes." I reminded them in a few words of their childhood faith and read to them several excerpts from the Augsburg Confession and also from our church *Ritual*, showing them again the rules mentioned above relative to the organization of a congregation. I requested that those who voluntarily accepted these rules should acknowledge them by answering each question and signing their names. In this manner forty families, in addition to a few single persons, signed that day. I followed exactly the same procedure at another meeting held on October 13 in the western part of the settlement; on this occasion about thirty families and some single persons signed. This was the beginning of a congregation to which more members are being added daily. I never tried in any way to persuade anyone; theirs had to be a free choice.

Church affairs among the immigrants continued to be confused. A person who calls himself John G. Smith, pretending to be a minister from Sweden, attracted a large number of Norwegians to him.[43] He administered the Lord's holiest sacraments and performed all ministerial functions, until his many lies opened the eyes of several and enabled them to see for themselves that he was only a self-made pastor. When the Norwegians also learned that he had openly ridiculed and blasphemed his own holy infant baptism by permitting himself to be rebaptized and converted to the Baptist sect, in which he was also supposed to have received a kind of ordination, most of them left him. Some thought of calling a Norwegian businessman as pastor and having him ordained, which in America is an easy matter.

Clausen had been there a couple of times and had preached and administered the sacraments before I came, but there was no organized congregation. A great deal of grace and wisdom from God was needed to bring order out of this confusion. A beginning had been made, as stated, and for those who were now joining the congregation I began to preach the Word, to administer the sacraments, and to officiate in other churchly matters according to our liturgy. Of course, everyone has the opportunity to attend our services and to hear the Word of God, but it lay in the nature of things that those who remained outside the congregation could not participate in such special blessings as the reception of the sacraments and other ministerial acts.

Immediately after the organization of the congregation, Ole Knudsen Trovatten was unanimously elected precentor.[44] He was from Laurdal Parish, where he had once served in the same capacity. Then, by another vote, eight deacons were elected, four from the eastern and four from the western part of the settlement. Each got his ward to care for and later, at another meeting, each was told his duties as the pastor's assistant according to the rules cited in Pontopiddan's *Collegium Pastorale*, pp. 587 ff., with the changes made necessary by New World conditions.[45] Each took an oath and shook hands on his pledge to live up to the rules as the pastor's assistant and, as the congregation's representative, to help the pastor to arrange everything for the best. The precentor later was also sworn in as *degn*,[46] according to the *Ritual* of the church.

As the congregation and I both felt the unpleasantness of gathering for worship in small cabins, a decision was made to begin construction of two simple buildings that could be dedicated and used exclusively as churches. One acre of land was purchased for each, and every member of the congregation supplied free lumber and labor; an assessment was also made for a small sum of money. The people worked with diligence and sacrifice, and God blessed their work with exceptionally mild weather for that time of year. To the joy of the congregation, as well as to me, and with thankful hearts, prayer, and meditation, we were able to dedicate a log house as a church in the western part of the settlement on December 19, 1844, according to the Norwegian *Ritual*. I was assisted by my co-worker in the Lord, Pastor Clausen, who offered a prayer from the chancel (*sit venia verbo!*)[47] while I preached from Hebrews 10:19–25 on the theme, "Having therefore, brethren, boldness to enter into the holiest by the blood of Jesus."

A short time later the church in the eastern part of the settlement was ready, and the dedication was held on January 31,

1845.[48] Clausen was unable to attend this dedication, and so I had to do everything alone. I preached this time on Genesis 35:2–3, using the theme "Let us arise, and go up to Bethel and I will make there an altar unto God; (1) what we in this respect have to discard; (2) what we must put on, (3) what we must build there." Heretofore we had held services in poor cabins, where I was pushed and shoved around against the clay-chinked logs and where big chests[49] served as pulpit, baptismal font, and altar table, all particularly inconvenient when administering the Lord's Supper. You can imagine how cozy and wonderful it was, both for the pastor and for the congregation, when our simple houses of God were completed.

It was self-evident that there was neither time nor money to build anything but the most economical structures. Both churches were made of logs and plainly furnished. A table covered with a white cloth, topped by a black wooden cross and surrounded by a kneeling bench, served as an altar. On the south side stood an equally simple lectern which served as a pulpit, and on the north side an oak log topped by a tin pan served as a baptismal font. The congregation sat on loose benches. The buildings are identical in size, 36 by 28 feet; and as the distance between them is about one Norwegian mile, none of the members has much more than that distance to church. I alternated services between the two every Sunday and holy day.

With the assistance of the deacons, I sought to arrange the religious affairs of the congregation and struggled to start a school. This was by no means easy, as there was little money to pay the expenses involved. We did manage to organize an American public school, which by law is supported by county funds—a school that all children in the district may attend—but this was no help in setting up a school where religion might be taught. As I have already pointed out, religious instruction cannot be given in the district school, which means that it can only be offered in a parochial school. If we were to have such an institution, it would have to be organized on a different basis, as it was important for the children of the congregation to be instructed in the pure doctrines of our church. In the hope of securing the necessary assistance from the fatherland, I, on my own responsibility, hired the precentor to teach at a salary of ten dollars per month, for three months in 1845. In this parochial school, instruction was given only in religion and hymn singing, as the children would learn the other subjects in common school.

Before I left Norway, I had received some books from the publisher Grøndahl of Christiania, and others from the "Society for the Publication of Christian Manuals and Devotional Books," also of Christiania. I gladly accepted a number of these books for free distribution. This collection laid the foundation for a small library in the congregation. The other books were distributed to individual members locally and in other settlements as well; Pastor Clausen also received a copy of each book. For these gifts Clausen, as well as the members of the congregation, asks me to express a hearty thanks to the donors.

After the congregation was partially organized, I called their attention to the fact that the call I had received from the colony was only for the purpose of bringing order to the affairs of the church. Since this had now been accomplished so far as I, the organizer, could go, the time had come for the congregation to hold a meeting, first to agree on the conditions for calling a resident pastor and shepherd and, when this matter was settled, to issue the call.

The deacons met and approved these arrangements and then brought the subject before the congregation. At this point, dissension arose and, when the members failed to agree, I was urged to intercede. Prior to that time I had considered it best not to have anything to do with the problem. As a result of the impasse, it was arranged to hold a general meeting after the service on Sunday, February 2, when the question could be settled.

With respect to remuneration for the resident pastor, it was found that there were three parties; one thought that the pastor's salary should be fixed at 200 dollars annually; a second party, led by a Swedish nobleman, felt that the pastor should receive no fixed salary but that each member should give according to his own discretion; and a third party, represented by the deacons, whose proposal was most acceptable to the congregation and so was adopted. There were a few dissenters, and among them the Swedish nobleman, who left the congregation.[50] The conditions, formulated by the precentor on behalf of the deacons and adopted at this meeting, were as follows:

"Conditions for Electing a Resident Pastor for the
Norwegian Lutheran Congregation at Koskonong Prairie

"Led by a sincere longing in this foreign land to hold fast to
our evangelical Lutheran church's true saving doctrine and our
fatherland's edifying church order, we, the undersigned Norwegian settlers in Dane and Jefferson counties, Wisconsin Territory of North America, have resolved to organize a Norwegian
Lutheran congregation and have for that purpose in October,
1844, given to J. W. C. Dietrichson, the Norwegian Lutheran
pastor who arrived the year before from our fatherland, the
responsibility of organizing our church affairs.

"Of our own accord and with heartfelt desire we have all, by
hand and mouth, declared our willingness to belong to the local
Norwegian Lutheran congregation, and to that end will accept
the church order which our Norwegian *Ritual* requires. We
acknowledge together that in the future we will not call or accept
anyone as our pastor and shepherd unless he can clearly establish
his credentials as a regularly ordained pastor of the Norwegian
Lutheran church. Furthermore, we promise compliance in all those
things which our pastor requires of us in accordance with Norway's *Ritual*. It is essential that he, as our spiritual leader, be given
that obedience that a member of a congregation owes to his pastor.

"As the said Herr Pastor Dietrichson has now accomplished
what he was commissioned to do, so far as it can be done for the
time being, it is now up to us to determine those conditions which
in the future will guide us in the selection of a resident pastor.

"As Christians, we recognize the Lord's command in I Corinthians 9:14, 'Even so hath the Lord ordained that they who
preach the gospel should live of the gospel,' and we are also
ready, as far as our ability goes, to observe these words of the
Lord.

"The conditions on which we are now agreed, and which form
the basis for calling our pastor, are as follows:

1. That the congregation will buy 40 acres of land for the use
   of the pastor, located, if possible, centrally between the two
   churches. A simple residence, consisting of a living room,
   two bedrooms and a kitchen, will be built on this land for
   the pastor. Ten acres of the land shall be plowed and fenced.

2. That in the next five years a sum of 300 dollars per year be paid as salary to the pastor in three installments.
3. That for ministerial services such as the churching of women [*barselkvinders indledning*],[51] baptism, confirmation, weddings and funerals, all fees shall be paid on a voluntary basis.
4. That on each of the three main festival days—Christmas, Easter, and Pentecost—the pastor shall receive a free-will offering.

"The expenses which devolve upon us in carrying out these provisions shall be administered by eight representatives elected for three-year terms. They will place an assessment on each adult member in the congregation in a manner they can defend before God, their own conscience, and us. The pastor must look to them for the fulfillment of these conditions.

"That this is our will and resolution, we hereby declare with our marks or our names.

The Norwegian Lutheran Congregation at Koskonong Prairie, Dane and Jefferson counties, Wisconsin Territory, North America, February 2, 1845."

Under these resolutions appeared 227 signatures. In addition to these families and unmarried adults in the congregation, more were added later and when I left there was a total of 575 souls.

After the congregation had drawn up the conditions for the election of a resident pastor, there was still the question of calling one. With this in mind, I pointed out that there were two ways of doing this: They could call a pastor from Norway, or they could call Clausen or myself, the only truly ordained Norwegian Lutheran clergymen in America who, for the moment, could be recommended. As for myself, I had often mentioned to the deacons, as well as to members of the congregation, that they would be doing me a big favor not to call me, as, for various reasons, I wished to return to the fatherland. I reminded them of what I had said, that the real purpose of my mission was only to organize the church affairs of the Norwegian immigrants, and, since this had been somewhat accomplished, that I considered my vocation in America completed. I said straight out that, even though God gives to each individually as he wills, so far as I knew myself, I had possibly succeeded in plowing and rough-planing and thus in awakening and establishing order among them, I now thought that others could much better harrow, nourish, and guide an ordered congregation. Despite my remonstrances, they nevertheless extended a call to me a short time later. The reason they did not call another theologian or clergyman from Norway was that they did not believe any competent man would come, and, moreover, that they did not have the financial means to bring one here.

The reason they did not call Clausen was partly that they did not wish to deprive Muskego of this man, and partly, as I learned later, that although they loved, respected, and were personally acquainted with him, some of the members were not quite certain whether he could be considered a fully ordained pastor. He had not been ordained by a bishop, something they found difficult to adjust to after having been brought up in a state church. I often tried to show them, as I have already said, that the fact that a pastor is ordained by another pastor and not by a bishop in no way nullifies the validity of the act. I now have reason to assume that most of them understand this.

As the letter of call sent me by the congregation gives some indication of the spirit which now seems to be stirring in the newly established congregation, I do not hesitate to enlarge this little book by including the text of it. The letter was drafted by the precentor in consultation with the deacons and is their own, in style and form, together with several expressions touched up by Clausen to whom it was sent for this purpose. It reads as follows:

"Most Highly Honored Herr Pastor J. W. C. Dietrichson:

"When you, in September last year, first visited us at our request and decided to make this settlement a starting point for your temporary church work, we left it up to you in October last year to unsnarl what was then a most entangled church relationship, and to try to found a Norwegian Lutheran congregation among us in line with our fatherland's church order—a responsibility which you accepted to our heartfelt joy. You have, so far as possible, done everything toward creating a correct church order. Now that your call is completed and your work in this connection is coming to an end, we feel that it is both a duty and a necessity to initiate action toward calling a resident pastor and shepherd who can continue the work begun among us in the same spirit and order, so that what has been built up shall not be torn down and split asunder.

"Because of your work which the Lord has so richly blessed among us, we have already learned to know you as a man who in every respect has those qualities we know should be found in every ordained servant of the Lord, especially in this land and under our conditions; we have found in you a ready zeal for the glory of God and the advancement of this congregation's true welfare paired with wisdom, patience, and love. We have found in you determination and stability in your work, together with a certain tenacity, which for a pastor is so necessary to hold the respect of the congregation. You have preserved and enlarged our esteem through blameless Christian conduct and qualities which, with the Lord's gracious help, establish you as a highly worthy and blessed man to work in this holy office. We do not say this in a spirit of flattery, but to cite the most obvious reasons why we hereby humbly extend this call to Your Reverence to accept the ministry to the established Norwegian Lutheran congregation at Koskonong Prairie, Dane and Jefferson counties, Wisconsin Territory in North America.

"As Christians, we must necessarily require of our shepherd: (1) that he preach God's word in truth and purity, that the holy sacraments be administered, and that all ecclesiastical acts shall be performed in complete harmony with our fatherland's church order to which every pastor, by his ordination and pastoral oath, is bound; (2) as we have already experienced how necessary it is to maintain church discipline, we therefore request that the pastor strictly apply this according to the church *Ritual;* and (3) that the personal conduct of our shepherd shall be blameless, according to the apostle Paul's admonition in I Timothy, chap. 3.[52]

"Sincerely wishing and hoping that you, Herr Pastor Dietrichson, will accept our call, we repeat what we have already pledged ourselves to in joining the congregation: to show our pastor and shepherd, as members of the congregation, due obedience in all that he requests and does in harmony with our fatherland's church *Ritual.* In like manner, we promise to be prompt and scrupulous in fulfilling the conditions agreed upon earlier with regard to salary for the resident pastor.

"With a sincere prayer to God that he, our father in Jesus Christ, will grant our pastor the power of the Holy Spirit and gracious support to strive and suffer as a true and worthy soldier of God, we hereby send you this, our unanimous election, to be our pastor and shepherd, and we enclose the conditions to which the pastor of the local Norwegian Lutheran church is bound.

"The above represents our will and determination, and we hereby affix our names in testimony thereof.

"The Norwegian Lutheran congregations at Koskonong Prairie, Dane and Jefferson counties, Wisconsin Territory, North America, March 3, 1845."

Under this were the same 227 signatures.

For a time I was uncertain about accepting this call. When I thought of the many privations, hardships, and sacrifices of being away from my homeland, which holds so much of what is dear to me, of the difficulties connected with the call, and of the churchly insight and strength required to lead and direct a congregation in sect-splintered America, it was seldom that I could say from the heart: "I am the Lord's to do as he wills!" On the other hand, when I thought of the possible consequences for this congregation, now grown so dear to me, if it were left without ministerial help, I saw no other way out and felt conscience-bound to promise, as I did, "that if it is God's will that I return to you, I am sure that he will clearly show the way through future circumstances. If there are no other competent and Christian men capable of continuing the work already begun who will take over the congregation in my place, then, after a trip back to Norway to make the necessary arrangements for a longer residence in America, I shall return."

This was the substance of my written reply to the congregation's letter of call. When it was read following the service on the first Sunday after Easter, all said they were well satisfied. I shall certainly keep my promise, no matter how hard it may be for me, rather than see this dear congregation left without a pastor and shepherd.[53]

CHAPTER VI

The Challenge to Authority

The first Sunday after Easter was a festival day in one of our newly dedicated churches; twenty-two of the young people, after instruction of two or three days a week for three months, reaffirmed their baptismal vow in the rite of confirmation.

But, together with the joy that both pastor and congregation felt in seeing that the church organization was developing little by little away from the above-mentioned confusion, we were forced to take an action that caused us much sorrow. It is true that a deep longing drove many to join the congregation, a longing they were made aware of by a longer or shorter period of doing without the great blessing of an organized church. But as the hope of temporal gain had originally prompted them to leave home, it was natural that many people who gave only lip service to the Christian gospel would also join, and that the congregation would become a net that gathered in all kinds of fish, as the church has been throughout the ages. We had some sad examples shortly after the congregation was organized. There was one member who made it absolutely necessary for us to enforce the strictest discipline if this church was to survive the threat of those who openly contradicted it.

An ungodly drunkard, Halvor Christian Pedersen Funkelien from near Kongsberg, who like the others had voluntarily joined the congregation and thereby had submitted to its rules and discipline, caused open scandal by his habitual drinking, fighting, and blaspheming the most holy of things, not only in the congregation but among outsiders living in the neighborhood.[54] He refused to listen to repeated loving admonition from pastor and deacons, and by his conduct openly rejected his holy baptismal vow, which constitutes the condition for admission to and continuance in the church for all Christians. Therefore, according to the *Ritual*, he had to be judged and punished by the congregation (following I Corinthians 5:1-13, and chapter 7, article 1 in the *Ritual*).

The offender sought in many ways to frighten both pastor and congregation, but fear naturally did not hinder us from doing our duty. After I had consulted with Clausen as well as with representatives of the congregation several times, it became necessary to follow the course which the *Ritual* specifies in this situation. On the first Sunday after Easter, the same day the young people confirmed their baptismal vows, we had to excommunicate this scandalous sinner who, by persisting openly in ungodliness, had broken his baptismal vow and refused to repent. It was indeed painful for everyone that such action was necessary. In its own way this action served to strengthen the congregation, and, similarly, it revealed even more clearly how absolutely indispensable was a strong discipline.

Our American neighbors are all members of sects; among them are many Methodists, who are characterized by a strict discipline. They would now truly have reason to criticize us Lutherans— which they are generally so ready to do anyway—for receiving and retaining all kinds of ungodly people, in the event that the congregation failed to use "the power of the keys" [*bindenøgle*].[55] Although they continued to represent our action in an odious light, it is clear that because of it they have since looked upon us with a little more respect.

Partly as a result of sectarian bitterness and partly because of the hatred and vindictiveness of the excommunicated, an event occurred that was least anticipated in America, where the state permits the church to shift for itself. This affair led to a legal action that has to be described, as it concerns the congregation's position. While Halvor Pedersen was being placed under the ban, in accordance with the church *Ritual,* and especially afterward, he carried on worse than ever, threatening to burn the building, kill the pastor, and inflict harm on the deacons—empty threats that did not worry us, even in a land where the laws do not help us much. During one of his drunken sprees, threatening and cursing me, he headed toward my cabin but was diverted by two women who got him to go home. During such bad spells, in which it was evident that his banishment from the church has a deeper significance than mere outward punishment, he often threatened to come to our services with a whisky bottle in his pocket and, instead of taking the back pew reserved for the excommunicated, to seat himself in front of the altar and pulpit to create a scandal. But we did not take these threats any more seriously than his other talk, at least so long as he did nothing about it.

Meanwhile, Easter passed and Pentecost came. During this time, Halvor cultivated the friendship of John G. Smith who, as already mentioned, functioned as pastor for the Norwegians before I came. For some time this man had been bitter, both against the members who had left his flock and against Clausen and me because we had explained to the Norwegians that it was impossible for him, a Baptist, to be a *bona fide* pastor in the Lutheran church. I especially offended him when, in response to his request that I ordain him a Lutheran pastor, I replied that the apostle's admonition, "lay hands hastily on no man,"[56] caused me to move with care in this matter. For I would never, without authorization, make use of the right that is, of course, given by ordination to confer what I have myself received. And the same admonition, especially in regard to one whom I considered absolutely unworthy and unqualified to be a pastor, forced me flatly to deny his request.

In addition to this denial, I had brought Smith's wrath down upon myself by occasionally warning several of the colonists to beware of one who alternated his role of self-made pastor with that of self-made doctor and practiced quack medicine upon their bodies. Probably in the hope of finding a better opportunity to avenge himself, he joined a group opposing the congregation, and he once conducted a service for them in company with Elling Eielsen. Both men entertained their audience by reading from Spener's *Spiritual Priesthood*[57] and applied all the expressions used about Catholic monks and priests to Norway's "papistic" clergy, "in whose long robes the devil dwells."

Smith won over the excommunicated Halvor Pedersen from an enemy to a confederate. What the two men discussed in their confidential chats I naturally cannot say, but the fact is that on Pentecost Sunday Halvor came to our church, from which he had previously stayed away.[58] It would certainly have been gratifying if he had come to hear the word of God, but the real purpose of his coming was soon evident. The service had not yet begun. I had arrived early, as usual, and was sitting behind our little altar when the precentor told me that Halvor had come into the church and was sitting in a pew among the other members of the congregation. I asked the precentor to tell him that he would have to take the place reserved for him. To this request Halvor answered defiantly that he would sit where he pleased and would remain there. When again advised that he would have to move to the assigned pew if he wished to remain in church, he gave the precentor a still more abusive reply.

While we waited for the deacons to arrive, Halvor moved from the seat on the men's side of the aisle to the front pew on the women's side nearest the altar, and sat there with an insolent and defiant look. Meanwhile the congregation assembled, but several women left the church in fear of Halvor. When the deacons arrived, I went over to Halvor and reminded him that he, like the others, had voluntarily joined the congregation on the understanding that he would observe the conditions implied in the rules of the church and would submit to the requirements of the *Ritual;* I repeated what a deacon had told him shortly after his exclusion, namely, that he had been banned publicly on the first Sunday after Easter because of his ungodly conduct and that I, therefore, had to ask him either to take the assigned place or leave the church. When he replied that he would sit where he pleased, I turned to the congregation, particularly the deacons, and asked them to escort Halvor out of the church. As if by magic, the entire congregation rose, a determined look on every face, as the precentor and two deacons took Halvor out despite his opposition and threats. When quiet was restored, the service began and continued without further interruption from him.

Pentecost Sunday passed without my hearing any more about Halvor, who I assumed was at home behaving himself. On the Monday after Pentecost, I rose early to go to the West Church which, as mentioned earlier, lies about one Norwegian mile from the East Church, near the parsonage. I gave my farewell sermon in the West Church that day and wound up some ministerial affairs and duties preparatory to leaving on my trip back to Norway. I got home late, tired and upset at the thought of leaving the congregation and of what had recently taken place among us, when who should be waiting at my door but Herr Halvor and two constables (policemen). One of them served a writ from the justice of the peace ordering him, "in the name of the United States, to bring me before him forthwith to answer to a charge of assault and battery."[59] The precentor and the two deacons who had removed Halvor from the church were also under arrest. When I had taken off my vestments and declared myself ready to leave at once in response to the law's demands, one of the constables remarked how tired I looked. I had not eaten since I left home in the morning and it was already dark and late. They agreed that they could overlook the "forthwith" wording in the order if one of them remained with me overnight as a guard while the second sought out the others. This was done, and I slept that night as a prisoner under guard.

Early next morning, we, the defendants, led by two lace-adorned constables, moved off to the justice of the peace, who lived five or six English miles from my residence. Some Americans and Norwegians had gathered there, and among them were several of our avid opponents, one of them a Norwegian Mormon pastor who happened to be passing by, peddling small wares. It was well into the afternoon before the witnesses for Halvor were assembled and the hearing could begin. The justice of the peace read the complaint and a jury was sworn in.[60] Halvor had selected an American farmer named Brown to represent him.[61] This man had been a member of a Methodist congregation until it banned him. Halvor had found in him a kindred spirit after his own dismissal, which only goes to prove the old proverb, *"lige Børn lege bedst."*[62] These two excommunicates had become good friends in their common hatred of our congregation and its pastor.

This hatred was revealed during the proceedings, when Brown urged every free-born American and true friend of the United States Constitution to resist papist control with all his might. He referred not only to those who openly called themselves Catholics, but also to the more dangerous kind who, despite the name Protestant, had revealed in ritual and policy that they, with Jesuit cunning, seek to smuggle papism into the church. It was as clear as two and two make four, he said, that the action initiated against the "gentleman" (Halvor) was a shocking injustice which the law must punish as an example for the future, and that it could correctly be called "assault and battery." Most guilty was the instigator, "the pope" and "blackcoated gentleman"—names he honored me with—but the three who carried out the misdeed were also guilty. He therefore proposed to the honorable jury that I be held most guilty in order to deter all like-minded persons from committing acts that threaten civil rights. In his opinion, I had so much authority over the honest and less educated Norwegians that it could amount to a threat if not curbed. This time I had only given orders to throw the man out, but what if I had ordered his head off? Who could be sure it would not happen? This was the substance of Mr. Brown's case against us.

Another American farmer, Mr. Parmer, a Presbyterian whose wife belonged to the Episcopal church, was quite interested in our case, as he and his wife felt a deeper religious fellowship with our congregation than with the neighboring sects, especially as his father—who had been a Presbyterian pastor—had had a similar experience with an ungodly member who had mounted the pulpit and tried to grab the Bible out of his hands.[63] He therefore kindly offered to plead our case and became our defense counsel. He showed the jury that United States laws, as well as Wisconsin statutes, clearly dictate that the state has no right whatsoever to interfere in church affairs. Civil laws can not hinder any religious community from exercising discipline so long as this does not conflict with the law. In fact, it is the duty of the state to protect the congregation from such incursion. Every church or meetinghouse is the private property of the congregation. And just as a man has rights in his own home, so a congregation or its representatives can assign each one his place and refuse to let him remain if he does not stay there. He thought it clear that the pastor was innocent, as he had not laid hands upon the plaintiff (essential to assault and battery). Nor could the ejection of a defiant person who refused to keep his proper place be called assault and battery.

Consequently, Parmer asked that the case be dismissed because the hearing had no jurisdiction in the matter. He tried, further, to convince the jury how unwise it would be for citizens of an enlightened nation, known for its liberal institutions, to judge a pastor lately arrived from a distant land guilty of civil transgression because he regarded the church as a holy institution according to the apostle's admonition, "remove the evil from your own midst," and, following the rules of the congregation, had suffered a stubborn drunkard and brawler to be taken from the church. The offender had not complied with the discipline he had earlier agreed to accept. He asked the jury to consider that a member of any church, no matter how different from ours, ought to rejoice when a congregation, its pastor, and deacons worked vigorously to check godlessness and promote virtue and fear of God. Finally, he said that if anyone were to be punished, it should be Halvor Pedersen, who had defiantly disturbed the worship of the congregation; for this offense, he should be convicted under Wisconsin law and fined. This was the substance of Parmer's defense. He then rested his case with complete confidence in the outcome.

Witnesses for the prosecution—among them, oddly enough, Halvor, who testified in his own behalf even though the same privilege was denied us—naturally stated that they had seen Halvor taken out of the church, though several mentioned that they had earlier heard him say often that he was going to church that day to test the pastor's authority to throw him out, to cause as much trouble as possible in order to delay his departure for Norway, and to persuade him never to return to America. Through the testimony of other witnesses it was clear that Halvor's actions were premeditated. He had hoped to provoke our action. The service that Sunday was held in the eastern part of the settlement, where Halvor was a member. He came to church on the Sunday that he knew was to be my last before leaving for Norway.

The verdict of the jury should not have been in doubt, but when the judge asked, "guilty or not guilty?" the verdict was "guilty", "guilty of assault and battery." The judge, who according to law determines the punishment, fined each of us $5, the minimum under Wisconsin statute. He said that "in respect of the circumstances" he ought not to give us a stiffer fine. We also had to pay court costs of about $12 or $13, if I remember correctly.

This, then, was the judgment of an enlightened and sworn jury of Dane County, Wisconsin, which they thought to be in accordance with territorial statutes, that expressly uphold freedom of religion and separation of church and state as one of the basic tenets of the law. It was evident that the verdict, a victory over our congregation, was being enjoyed by Halvor Pedersen and his friends, whose well-laid plans had now been achieved. In passing, it may be noted that the judge and most of the jury were "Seventh Day Baptists," and that some of them, together with other Americans had attended our church on Pentecost Sunday, contrary to their custom.[64]

It is not necessary to be a lawyer to know the reasons for this judgment. Its injustice is manifest. I shall not speculate whether it was Mr. Brown's brilliant argument playing upon the jury's unconscious ill-will toward our congregation, or whether the judgment resulted from a pardonable misunderstanding of law among uneducated jurymen—most of them quite young—or, what is more probable, both of these together.

Meanwhile, for our own sake and for that of the congregation, we could not be satisfied with a verdict in which the state, without any right whatsoever, interfered in churchly affairs, which in America are independent of government authority. This fact was clear, and so we decided to enter an appeal to "the District Court," a sort of diocesan court, which sits in the principal city of each county. It was at Madison in Dane County that our case was to be heard. We were told that, according to law, we had twenty-four hours from the time the verdict had been handed down to make an appeal and to have the necessary legal papers in order. Despite the fact that the judge and the jury tried to persuade us not to appeal, on the grounds that the judgment would be the same in a higher court and that we would simply incur further costs to no purpose, we decided to do so anyway.

Though the time was short—judgment was pronounced at 11:30 P.M. on the third day of Pentecost [Tuesday, May 13] and our appeal had to be in by the same hour the next day—the precentor and I hurried to Madison, twenty-three miles away, saw two able lawyers who, independently of each other, reviewed in greater detail the argument of our defender and advised us to appeal. They had no doubt that if the case had been heard by an impartial and knowledgeable jury, the verdict would have been the reverse. With the necessary papers in hand, we returned to the justice of the peace at nine o'clock that evening [presumably May 14]. He accepted the appeal despite his visible displeasure and opposition. As the district court in Madison has two sessions annually and as the time for appeal in the first session had already passed, the case could not be heard until the next session scheduled for November

1, 1845.[65] The case rested until that time. Pastor Clausen, on my behalf, was to meet and engage defense counsel in Madison, where there are lawyers who have studied and know the law.

This is the way matters stood when I left for Norway a couple of days later. If, during the time this little book is being printed, I should receive word from Clausen on the verdict in the appeal, I shall publish it as a postscript.

As I describe the act by which the Koskonong congregation undertook to exclude from its midst an open scoffer, I beg the reader to consider seriously the authority vested in the congregation by the Lord himself, as well as the practice of the church from ancient times, and the right and duty it has, even in our Lutheran state church, to exclude the openly godless. Every Christian lover of truth will see that this is a purely ecclesiastical act; everyone who considers the position of the Norwegian Lutheran congregations in America will realize how necessary discipline is for a church in such circumstances.

The congregation at Koskonong realized this fact immediately after its organization, and in its letter of call required that "the pastor shall maintain strict church discipline according to the *Ritual.*" The objection that one often hears against too strict a discipline is that it loosens, rather than strengthens, the bond between pastor and congregation. This proved to be entirely unfounded, at least in my experience. During the time that the case of Halvor Pedersen was being discussed, and after his excommunication, I heard the clearest testimony that the action helped the congregation internally as well as in its relation to the sects. Likewise, I received from the most serious and Christian-minded members the clearest testimony that the bond between pastor and congregation was not loosened but was made closer and more heart-warming.

Furthermore, the *Ritual*, in Chapter 7, Article 1, states that the excommunicated, if he comes to church, shall take a "special place in the back of the church." We did not regard this as a serious matter in itself, but we had to use force against deliberate defiance as a warning to others. The congregation had to make it clear that it would not, either through cowardice or fear, abandon a provision of the *Ritual* to which both pastor and congregation were bound. The decision, although it is not—like excommunication itself—essential, nevertheless has been accepted by our believing forefathers. Without permission from the church, we had no right to dispense with it.

When I saw the aims of my mission to America nearing fulfill-ment and was preparing to leave for Norway, the Koskonong congregation agreed with me that the best way to arrange matters was to call Clausen until I or someone else took over as regular pastor. Clausen replied that "he would accept the call and serve Koskonong as the main congregation, besides serving Muskego, and would alternately reside in both places." I took formal leave of my congregation on the second day of Pentecost. On my way back to Norway I passed through Muskego May 19, 1845; there I delivered the parish record and other congregational property to Clausen, who was to serve as interim pastor.

Between August, 1844, and the middle of May, 1845, events oc-curred at Koskonong Prairie as I have described them. During this period, I also traveled among the other Norwegian settlements, some located in Wisconsin and some in Illinois, and I did what I could to establish church order among them.

CHAPTER VII

Pine Lake and Rock River Settlements

About twenty-eight miles northwest of Milwaukee, lying mostly in Milwaukee County but partly in Dodge County, is the Norwegian colony usually referred to as the "Pine Lake Settlement," after a small lake of the same name—also known as the "Swedish Settlement."[66] This last designation stems from the fact that a Swedish student, Unonius, was, together with other Swedes, the first to settle there in 1841.[67] Only a few Swedes are left; the colony was enlarged by Norwegians with the arrival of Herr Gasmann from Skien and a number of others who arrived in 1843–44.[68]

The terrain is open and can be cultivated where it is not too heavily wooded. All the settlers, so far as I know, have taken land on "claim," i.e., they have taken it under the preemption law that entitles them to settle on government land and to cultivate it; each man has the first right to buy the land he "claims" when it is sold by the government. This land will probably not go on the market for some time, as a canal is being projected nearby. This matter is now in the courts and has to be settled before the land can be sold.[69]

A few days after I arrived at Muskego in August, 1844, I made a short trip to this settlement. I stayed with the Gasmann family and was received with great hospitality. Gasmann had not yet moved to the land he had bought a few miles farther north in Dodge County, where he owns a spread of 1,000 acres and has built a fine house and sawmill. There can be no doubt that a man possessing the insight and practical ability of Herr Gasmann—as well as the money and hired help he brought with him—will succeed in the New World.

With respect to church conditions in the settlement, most of the Norwegians have joined the Episcopal church. Not long after he came in 1843, Gasmann and the former Danish editor of *Dagen*, Herr Fribert, and a few others decided to join this church and elected as their pastor a Swedish student, Herr Unonius, who had studied *kameralvidenskaberne* at Upsala University.[70] If this move to another church was done with clear knowledge that a person in so doing cuts himself off from the paternal church body, it is a step to be regretted. In this connection, the archbishop of Sweden wrote a letter to Herr Unonius in which he said that, "if he, the bishop, did not call this a falling away then he certainly had to call it a downfall," but under no circumstances would he try to lure anyone who sincerely wished to be an Episcopalian to remain a Lutheran.[71] The Norwegians who had changed over had been told that there is no essential difference between the doctrines of the two churches, and that they can still be Lutherans in good standing even if they join the Episcopalians.

I had a talk with Herr Unonius about this matter and explained, as well as I could, the four main points which set the two churches apart—namely, baptism, communion, predestination, and the episcopacy. I sought to defend the doctrines held by the Lutheran church and to show the essential differences on these important points. When Herr Unonius stuck to the doctrines of his new church and insisted that the differences were only a matter of semantics among theologians—which it certainly is not, as the history of the church shows—it was plain enough that we could not agree, because the two churches have been in disagreement from the start. I tried to impress upon Herr Unonius that in a matter so important to both bodies, it was necessary to act openly and honestly, and to explain the differences between the churches in simple terms, letting the individual make his own choice. As this had not been done in the past, I considered it my duty to insist that it now be done, so that those joining his church would know what they were doing and would not persist in the false idea that they could continue to be Lutherans when they joined the Episcopalians. I thought that one of us had to inform the people. When he now gave me his promise to put the matter before the immigrants and to read a letter from the archbishop of Sweden wherein the latter points out the differences, I considered it wisest to let the matter rest. I was certainly not called to induce Episcopalians to become Lutherans, but to bring together the scattered members of our own church and to establish order among them.

As a courtesy and gesture of church liberalism, I presume, Unonius invited me to preach at his service the following Sunday, but for several reasons I begged to be excused. Unonius was not at that time an ordained pastor. He was attending a seminary in the vicinity. Although he was preaching, an Episcopal priest was administering the sacraments. Confirmation was conducted in the spring of 1844 by a bishop who, according to their rules, is the only one empowered to perform this rite.

I talked with Herr Unonius again at the dedication of our church in Muskego; he said that he had kept his word, but that the colonists nevertheless had decided to join the Episcopal church. He told me at this time that he intended using the Norwegian liturgy at his services, in the same way that he earlier had used that of the Swedish church. I called his attention to the fact that our church clearly teaches a doctrine of the Lord's Supper which is different from that of the Episcopalians. The latter hold that we receive the body and blood of Christ in a spiritual and heavenly way through faith; faith is the means by which we receive the body and blood of Christ. Our church, on the other hand, expressly states that the body and blood of Christ are present in the sacrament "as the words declare," and likewise at the distribution, when the following formula is spoken: "This is the true body of Christ, this is the true blood of Christ."

The Lutheran church definitely rejects any teaching which says that the presence of Christ's body and blood in the sacrament depends on the communicant's faith. For if the word of God is not the effective and creative agent on which the character of the sacrament depends, but rather something within me, then the concept of the sacrament as an act of God and not of men is destroyed. Christ's body and blood are present in the sacrament regardless of the faith or lack of faith of the recipient. The fact that the effect is determined by the faith or lack of faith of the recipient does not alter the essence of the sacrament.

I told Unonius straight out that I did not believe that he, as an honest Episcopalian and a pastor in that church, could defend the practice of conveying to members of the congregation a teaching that conflicted with their own doctrines, and that I also did not think that his superiors would permit him to use the Lutheran liturgy. Despite the fact that the phrase "as the words declare," which is found in the confessional address, did not exactly suit him, he still thought it permissible to use our service. He asked me then, and also later by letter, to secure for him a copy of the *Altar Book* and the *Ritual*. My personal feelings aside, I have not had a chance to get one for him. In any case, I want no part of this kind of churchly liberalism. In my judgment, no honest man can do what he is doing except at the cost of truth.

At Easter time in 1845, Herr Unonius was ordained by an Episcopal bishop, and he is paid, as far as I know, 300 dollars per year from the mission treasury of the Episcopal church.

In the autumn of 1844, a Lutheran pastor, Herr Böckmann, arrived from Sweden.[72] I have not seen this man but he replied to my invitation to attend the dedication of our church at Koskonong Prairie. In a fine Christian letter he wrote, among other things, "that in spite of efforts by the Episcopalian clergy and its followers to get people to join their church, [I have] succeeded in gathering all but two Swedish families into a small Lutheran congregation." This was the situation in the affairs of the church at Pine Lake when I left [for Norway].

Six or seven miles farther west, a few miles from the place called Watertown, on the boundary between Jefferson and Dodge counties, lies a small Norwegian colony on Rock River; the Episcopal church has also tried to extend its activities there.[73] This settlement consists of about 100 Norwegians, of whom the first, so far as I know, were Christopher Aamodt and Hans Uhlen, both from Modum's Parish.[74] They arrived in 1843. Most of the others came in 1844, chiefly from Setesdal and Kristiansand Diocese. The land is swampy, with fairly heavy wood lots consisting, in addition to oak, of some maple (like our *løn* tree), the sap of which makes a wholesome and very tasty sugar.

I had heard nothing about the colony—which I assumed . . . had joined the Episcopal church—until shortly after New Year's in 1845, when a man came to me at Koskonong and asked if I would go there and see what could be done to regularize church affairs.[75] This invitation was later repeated in writing. I therefore went in February and, calling their attention to the differences between the Lutheran church and the Episcopalian—which a large number of them were thinking of joining—I proceeded in the same manner as I had done at Koskonong and organized a small Norwegian Lutheran congregation; this attracted all but four families. This congregation was to be an annex of the Koskonong Parish, whose pastor they expected to visit them four times a year; he was to be compensated with a salary of twenty-four dollars a year plus free-will gifts for ministerial functions. I went back shortly before my departure for Norway, held services with communion, and also dedicated a cemetery. The congregation also plans to build a small meetinghouse that can be used as a church.

The settlement is about thirty miles northeast of Koskonong. As yet there is no road from Watertown. When I was there during the spring, I capsized in a "canoe" (a little Indian boat) in crossing the Rock River. I had to wade in swamps and crawl through the brush to reach my destination. The new road between Milwaukee and Watertown probably will be finished soon.[76]

Lying next to this Norwegian colony is a fair-sized settlement of Old Lutheran immigrants from Germany. Their fractured congregation is a sad example of what the spirit of sectarianism can do. They had not come in hope of temporal gain, but because of religious pressure exerted upon them in Prussia. One would certainly think that the grave conflict which had driven them, at considerable sacrifice, to leave their homeland would have made them hold fast to the church and its order which they had refused to give up at any price in Germany. They could have preserved loyalty to the old church in this free land if they had wanted to. But some of the more ambitious spirits among them had begun to preach about the spiritual priesthood which every Christian enjoys, and the spiritual freedom this brings, in such a way that they had begun to misunderstand and despise that special ministry of the regularly called and ordained servants of the church. With their ideas of freedom, they exceeded the limits of order. So many followed their lead that the settlement, formerly an annex of a German Lutheran congregation in Washington County, has now by its own authority called an unordained pastor. As a result, the community is split into several factions; only a few families still cling to the old church.

On my return journey from the Rock River settlement I met

some Indians. They frequently visit us during their hunting and fishing expeditions. Near the place called Astherland, my attention was drawn to a party of "red men" fishing at a small falls on the Rock River.[77] It was amusing to see how expertly they could handle their small tippy canoes and, with native-made equipment, spear the jumping fish. All of their movements revealed an elasticity of body and a liveliness unique to these half-wild children of nature. On the shore stood a number of elderly Indians and "squaws" (women) and children. They encouraged the fishermen with gestures and cheers. I conversed with them as best I could in English, of which they understood a few words, and also in pantomime. I had already won their friendship by giving them some snuff and tobacco, of which both men and women are inordinately fond. An old Indian thereupon came over to me, very friendly, and whispered in my ear: "Whisky, whisky!" meaning he wanted some of the liquor made from grain which they love so much. I replied in English: "No, whisky is not good for you," and took the opportunity to learn whether he had any conception of religion. I pointed at the sky, whereupon the Indian, with pious mien, folded his hands and looked upward saying, "Manitou! Manitou!" and then sat down disconsolate. He did not repeat his request for whisky. It was as though he realized that the condition he has probably often gotten into from drinking is not pleasing to his Manitou.

As is known, the Indians cannot be called gross idolaters, for they do worship one god, "the Great Spirit," which they call Manitou or, as an Indian from another tribe called it in his guttural language, "Manuach."

These Indians are Menominees, a tribe of four to five thousand, who have their lands near the northwestern boundary of Wisconsin.[78] Newly arrived immigrants usually fear the Indians, but without reason; they harm no one unless they are intoxicated or have been wronged. They are, on the contrary, good-natured and thankful for the smallest favors. A woman from Koskonong congregation came to me last winter and told how dreadfully frightened she had been when an Indian family came into her cabin one day while she was alone with the children. When the unwelcome guests saw bread lying on the table, they grabbed it eagerly and, after eating it, motioned for more. Fearing trouble, she gave them all the bread she had in the house. When they had eaten this, too, with great voracity, the Indian brave took the screaming and struggling woman by the arm and led her outside the cabin, where he pointed at a newly killed deer and motioned that this was to pay for the bread. With this gesture, the Indians nodded in a friendly fashion and left. The woman realized that the deer was worth more than the bread, but she assured me she "would not go through the anxiety she had experienced for ten deer."

Another Norwegian lost his way one winter night and came upon an Indian "wigwam" (tent); despite his fear, he decided to enter. He was warmly received and the Indians pointed to a place near the fire for him to be seated. A squaw took off his shoes, very carefully pounded the snow off, and placed them by the fire to dry. She then offered him venison and laid out a deer hide by the fire for him to sleep on. She banked the fire with more wood and everyone went to sleep. Despite their friendliness, this Norwegian was suspicious and afraid, and did not close his eyes all night. In the morning he was invited to eat again, but he was anxious to leave at once and tried to make them understand that he had lost his way. They nodded to him that they fully understood this, and one of them accompanied him for a way and put him on a road leading to an American living in the neighborhood. "They [gentiles] show that what the law requires is written in their hearts," says the apostle [Romans 2:15] and how these examples of a grateful and loving disposition put many a Christian to shame!

It is shameful the way the Americans treat the poor displaced Indians. True, culture and civilization progress, and it is in the nature of things that those who will not bow to them must yield; but the manner in which the Indians are dealt with should at least be humane.

Once a poor, hungry Indian who had had no success in his hunting, shot one of the many swine that are so numerous in the settlements, because they can feed on what they find in the woods. The American farmer who owned the swine heard the shot and saw the Indian in the process of dragging his quarry away. The farmer ran for his gun and shot the Indian. Other Indians belonging to the same tribe swore revenge on the man, which was only natural for these half-wild people. They vowed the death of two whites for that of one red man. The murderer escaped only by fleeing the countryside. The Indians' revenge would not be complete until they had kept their oath. Two innocent Americans paid with their lives for the guilty party, who in this case went scot-free. The government then entered the case and the military from Fort Winnebago drove the Indians farther west. The authorities did nothing to find and punish the farmer who had started it. This happened a short time ago near our settlements.

I must tell you about another incident that does not reflect credit on one of our countrymen. The Indians are, as mentioned, usually all too fond of the whisky bottle. Especially when they have had "blood on the tooth" and want more, they will offer anything, even their rifles—their dearest possession—which they handle with great skill. A half-drunken Indian goes by a Norwegian hut. The Norwegian knows the Indian's weakness and how to exploit it. He takes out a jug of whisky and shows it to the Indian, who convulsively grabs for it while the Norwegian tells him in sign language that he will get nothing until he promises to give him the rifle. The Indian forgets himself, sells the best thing he has for a drink, and leaves. After three weeks have passed, the Indian returns and takes out as much money as the whisky was worth and points to the rifle hanging on the wall. But the Norwegian pretends he does not understand, and refuses to give up the fine rifle for such a small price. When the Indian sees that being decent about it makes no headway with the man, he puts his hand on the weapon he is carrying, pulls back the hammer, and aims at the man, although he keeps his temper for the moment. When the Norwegian realizes that he is serious, he hurriedly returns the rifle, whereupon the Indian lays down the money and calmly leaves with his treasured possession.

CHAPTER VIII

Other Norwegian Settlements in Wisconsin

Approximately in the center of Iowa County lies the little village of Mineral Point, sixty to seventy miles west of Koskonong. Quite a few lead mines are to be found in this area, as well as at a place called Dodgeville a few miles north. A number of Norwegians are employed in these mining operations. Upon taking up residence at Koskonong Prairie, I had gone there and held services for a few countrymen not far from Mineral Point, in a beautiful wood, where the congregation sat on a grassy hillside and the stump of a newly cut oak tree decked with white cloth served as my pulpit. I have had invitations to visit them again but have not found the time to do so, nor can there be any thought of organizing a congregation, as the settlement is not large enough. I therefore advised the people who have a desire to become a part of an organized church to join the Norwegian Lutheran congregation at Wiota, which lies twenty to thirty miles southeast of Mineral Point in the same county. Some have already done this.

In and around the village called Wiota there are important lead mines, most of them operated by a man called Hamilton, after whom this region is usually called Hamilton Diggings. The name is also used to designate a settlement of Norwegians a few miles from Wiota on the Pecatonica River.[79]

Knud Knudsen, a man from Drammen, lives in Wiota.[80] He is a blacksmith who by unusual diligence has been quite successful in the New World. He is one of the deacons of the newly organized Lutheran congregation, which has a membership of about one hundred; most of them emigrated from Voss Parish in 1843. One of the first settlers in Wiota, Peder Davidsen from Voss, has voluntarily served as precentor in the congregation and also as a deacon. The land here is rather high rolling prairie.

Fifty miles or so to the southeast another small Norwegian colony was founded about the same time; it is usually called Rock

109

Prairie. It stretches across the great rolling country in the southern part of Rock County. The congregation has about two hundred members, who are for the most part people from Numedal.
All who emigrated from Land Parish settled here, and among them
is an exceptionally fine old man named Harald Ommelstad, who
has been elected precentor.[81] He has also given religious instruction to some of the children. On April 10 last year I dedicated
their cemetery. Gullik Halvorson Skavlem from Rollaug Parish
was, so far as I know, the first Norwegian to settle here in 1839.[82]
The immigrants have followed the same pattern of settlement as at
Koskonong, in that they live fairly well apart from one another
owing to the scarcity of wood lots.

Some sixteen to eighteen miles farther east in the same county is
a third small Norwegian settlement at Jefferson Prairie, a somewhat more level and rather treeless stretch of land, which is divided from Rock Prairie by the Rock River. The congregation has
about one hundred and fifty members, who also for the most part
are from Numedal. At these three settlements, the Swede, John G.
Smith, had represented himself as a pastor, as he had also done at
Koskonong. At Rock Prairie and especially at Jefferson Prairie,
Elling Eielsen has a number of followers. Among the latter is Ole
Nastad [Nattestad] from Rollaug Parish, who was one of the first
Norwegians in this area.[83] A good and able young man from Vinje
Parish, Aslak Olsen Gjerrejord, who had also attended Hvidesø
normal school, is precentor for this congregation.[84]

After my first journey among these three Norwegian colonies,
I made a second visit to them in the fall of 1844 and organized
congregations on the same basis as at Koskonong, all, for the time
being, to be considered annexes of Koskonong. The colonies
united with a small settlement on the Illinois-Wisconsin line, but
actually on the Illinois side. It was from the Norwegians in this
state that a call was sent to Norway in the fall of 1843 for a
clergyman. In February, 1844, the above-mentioned Knud Knudsen, who was the actual leader in the community, also sent an
appeal to the Christiania diocese. On behalf of the immigrants, he
asked the bishop to select an able clergyman for them, and promised an annual salary of $300 in addition to offerings and fees for
ministerial acts. Furthermore, they agreed to purchase 80 acres of
land, to plow and fence in whatever part of it was necessary, and
to build a parsonage upon it.

I knew nothing of this appeal until my arrival, but on my sec-
cond visit learned that the bishop got Knudsen's letter in July,
1844, and had replied to him. In his response the bishop referred
the settlers to me. They then requested me to become their pastor.

In the meantime, as mentioned earlier, upon the request made
by Koskonong, I decided to choose that settlement as the center
for my temporary church work and had already begun the organi-
ization of a congregation. Naturally I could not accept the other
call, as I did not come to America other than to investigate the
religious needs of the Norwegians, to help them get organized,
and to encourage them in the proper conduct of church affairs.
For this reason I could not accept any fixed position. I replied to
the people in the other colony that I could only attempt to establish congregations there and, while I had to consider Koskonong
as the focus of my activities, I would do what I could for them.

The congregations in that area then decided to call either a
pastor from Norway or Clausen, whom they knew from an earlier
visit. This was the situation when I left for Norway. It was their
hope that together they could establish a central congregation;
another smaller settlement in Illinois would have to be organized
as an annex. The pastor would live at the most central point between them. Such an arrangement meant an extremely burden-
some and widespread district, an area of between seventy and
eighty miles from northwest to southeast. For one pastor to cover
this parish would be exceedingly difficult, not only for providing
ordinary services but especially for individual soul-care, and also
for the establishment of schools in so many small and widely scattered places.

An American district school has been opened at Jefferson Prairie
during the past year and an application has been sent from Rock
Prairie as well. But as for parochial schools, which are absolutely
necessary for the existence of the congregation, I have done nothing owing to lack of funds. The children up to now have not had
regular instruction in religion except for the small start made by
Harald Ommelstad at Rock Prairie. Notwithstanding, I have confirmed seven young people in these congregations, whom I had
prepared and instructed so far as time permitted. Buildings for
services have been planned by these congregations and sites have
been chosen, but no work has been done. We have held services in
barn lofts, at times under the open sky, at other times in houses,

of which there are several very good ones at Rock Prairie and Jefferson Prairie.

In addition to the above-mentioned settlements—Hamilton Diggings, Rock Prairie, and Jefferson Prairie, which all lie in southern Wisconsin, the last two quite close to the Wisconsin-Illinois line drawn at 42½ degrees north latitude—there is also an insignificant colony about thirty miles north of Jefferson Prairie. It is halfway between Koskonong and Muskego, or twenty-four to twenty-five miles west of Koskonong.[85] This little settlement, named after a river, is called Skoponong and it lies in the southeast part of Jefferson County.

The first Norwegians settled here in 1843 and most of them came from Voss. The terrain is open prairie. Last fall a small congregation of about one hundred souls was organized, and a few miles away another small settlement was started in 1844; Pastor Clausen joined it to Skoponong and, for the present, it is served by him as an annex to Muskego. In this last colony there are a number of immigrants from Gjerpen Parish.

In Washington County, northeast of Muskego, a few Norwegians settled in the fall of 1844 at a small place on Lake Michigan called Sauk-Washington, which has been plotted for a town. Reimert [Reymert], a young man from Farsund who married a daughter of Hansen, the physical education instructor, settled there, and, in company with his father-in-law, he has started a business of supplying wood to passing lake steamers.[86]

Finally, a number of Norwegians in 1844 also settled in Portage County on a stretch of prairie north of Madison and northwest of Koskonong. As these small settlements are still in their infancy, neither Clausen nor I consider it justified at this time to divide our strength in order to establish congregations among them.

Quite a few Norwegians also live in Milwaukee, where they are engaged as artisans and household servants. I held services there twice on my way through town. Last year Clausen organized a small congregation and made it an annex to Muskego. In addition, a number of unmarried immigrants can be found in other small towns in Wisconsin. Those who are concerned about church affiliation have joined the nearest Norwegian Lutheran congregation.

CHAPTER IX

Norwegians in Northern Illinois

Illinois was admitted to the Union in 1818. It seems that before 1800 there were no settlements, but by 1810 the census showed a population of 12,000; in 1820, about 55,000; in 1830, about 157,000. After the census of 1840, there were 474,404. This is another example of how fast the population is growing.

The state of Illinois lies between 37 and 42½ degrees north latitude and is bordered by the territory of Wisconsin on the north, by Lake Michigan and Indiana on the east, by the Ohio river on the south—separating it from Kentucky—and on the west by the Mississippi River, which divides it from the state of Missouri and Iowa Territory. The state is 378 miles from north to south and 210 miles east to west, and it contains an area of 55,000 square miles.

The greater part of Illinois is flat country, except for some hills in the north and in the south. There is a dearth of forest land, but one finds vast stretches of prairie, much of which is flat and part of it wet. For this reason, the climate is regarded as less healthful than that of Wisconsin. During the heat of summer and also in the fall, many areas are afflicted with "fever and ague" and "bilious fever," which for persons coming from a northern climate may prove dangerous and often fatal. The principal rivers crossing the state are the Illinois and the Fox, both of which flow into the Mississippi.[87] For a state of this size, it has relatively few water resources. There are 87 counties in the state,[88] and Norwegians have settled in the following:

(1) Jo Daviess County, 650 square miles, where there are important copper and lead mines as in neighboring Iowa County in Wisconsin. Galena, the county seat, is situated on "Fever River," an Americanization of *"Fève"* or "Bean" River as it was called by the French. The corruption is not so illogical, as much sickness

and fever is prevalent in the area. The southwest boundary of the county is the Mississippi River, while to the east it is bounded by

(2) Stephenson County, 504 square miles. This is watered by the Pecatonica River and is bordered on the east by

(3) Winnebago County, 420 square miles. The Rock River and its tributaries water the land. Winnebago is the county seat, and to the east of it lies

(4) Boone County, 428 square miles. Belvidere, on the Kishwaukee River, which waters this area, is the county seat. To the east of it lies

(5) McHenry County, 425 square miles. The Fox River flows through this region and the county seat is located at McHenry.

These five counties, for the most part rolling prairie with occasional woods, link up with Lake County, which on its east side is bounded by Lake Michigan, while all their northern boundaries run along the Illinois-Wisconsin line.

(6) LaSalle County, 1,872 square miles, has a rolling terrain with tree-lined rivers. The Illinois River and its tributaries water this region. Ottawa, not an unimportant town, lying below 41½ degrees north latitude, is the county seat. Peru, a growing town, lies on the Illinois River at the outlet of a canal being dug between this river and Lake Michigan that will connect the Mississippi with the Great Lakes.

(7) Cook County, 1,000 square miles, has the same rolling prairies with some marsh ground and forest areas. Chicago, lying on Lake Michigan at the outlet of the Michigan-Illinois Canal, is the largest city, with a population of more than 20,000; Springfield, a city of about 6,000 on a prairie in Sangamon County about in the center of the state, is the capital.

About thirty miles southeast of the Norwegian settlement at Hamilton Diggings in Iowa County and eighteen miles nearly south of the Rock Prairie settlement in Rock County, Wisconsin, lies the Norwegian community commonly called "Rock Ground." The settled area lies partly in Stephenson County and partly in Winnebago County in Illinois, not far from the Illinois-Wisconsin line. The terrain is characterized by high-lying prairies alternating with forest. Clemet Torstensen Stabæk, a man from Rollaug Parish, who brought with him a considerable fortune, settled here in 1839 with others from the same district.[89] The majority of the approximately one hundred and fifty people are from Numedal. John Smith, the Swede, has acted as a pastor here too, but Elling Eielsen actually never had any followers in the area. As mentioned earlier, this settlement united with two others—Hamilton Diggings and Rock Prairie—that, through Knudsen, had written to the bishop about getting a pastor. On my tour of the colonies in Wisconsin, I also visited this settlement, where a congregation was organized and joined by almost all the settlers. In association with the three earlier-mentioned colonies, it will constitute a single congregation. On my last visit, I dedicated a cemetery. The intention is to build a house of worship as soon as possible. Christian Haraldsen, a son of Harald Ommelstad at Rock Prairie, was elected precentor for this congregation.[90]

Another small Norwegian community lies about twenty miles east in Boone County, which is near the Illinois-Wisconsin border, about eight to ten miles south of the settlement at Jefferson Prairie in Rock County [Wisconsin]. The Norwegians usually refer to this colony as Long Prairie after the prairie on which it lies. The terrain is mostly flat open country. Most of the settlers arrived in the autumn of 1844, chiefly from Viig Parish in the Bergen Diocese. They number one hundred twenty to thirty souls and are all members of the newly organized congregation. None of the sectarian preachers had made any headway among these immigrants when I visited them the first time in November, 1844. It was the intention that this group be made an annex congregation to the settlements at Hamilton, Rock Ground, Rock and Jefferson prairies. Aslak Olsen Gjerrejord of Jefferson Prairie was chosen precentor.

On my last visit, April 15, 1845, I dedicated a cemetery and on the same day confirmed a boy. For lack of funds it has not been possible to establish parochial schools in these two areas.

Farther east in McHenry County, there is another small Norwegian settlement, which was established about the same time as the above-mentioned ones. Most of the people are from Voss Parish. As I had no invitation from this group to visit them and as I had heard that most of the people were followers of Elling Eielsen, I did not wish to dissipate my energies by going there. Furthermore, the Norwegians are few.

A number of our countrymen reside in Jo Daviess County as

well as in Galena, some as household servants and some as workers in the neighboring lead mines. A few have joined the nearest congregation. There is no Norwegian settlement as such in the county.

The mining region, in which many of our people have found well-paid, strenuous, and unhealthful jobs, comprises a stretch of land—partly in Wisconsin, partly in Illinois—of about one hundred miles north to south and fifty miles east to west, from the Wisconsin River on the north to nearly twenty miles south of Galena. This territory was purchased from the Indians more than fifty years ago by the government, after lead was discovered by the Indians and sold to traveling merchants. The Indians profited very little, as will be understood, as all the work of digging and smelting was done by their women. The women also cultivate the land, as the male Indian considers it beneath his dignity to do this work and instead occupies his time in fighting and hunting, proudly carrying his rifle; his squaw must carry home even the game he kills and also perform other tasks for her man. The most serious charge a squaw can make against another is to accuse her of having "her man help to carry the burden."

After the land was purchased and surveyed, some of it was sold, but when the government learned that there were valuable minerals, no more land was offered for sale. Permission was given to mine or smelt on condition that the government should receive a percentage of the mineral. Consequently, a new form of speculation developed, namely, by *findere* (*finders*) who were on the lookout for "a good prospect," where there were signs on the surface of rich mineral veins. If they discovered such a vein, or if they could make people believe they had done so, they sold it to others who became the "diggers." Soon it was learned that nearly the entire area was one continuous mineral deposit. Ore was found, not only in the hills but also beneath the surface of the prairies, and everywhere one can find holes upon holes where the diggers have been.

A number of Norwegians have settled in Chicago, Cook County. On August 14, 1844, Pastor Clausen and I took a steamer on Lake Michigan from Milwaukee to Chicago, about eighty or ninety miles south of Milwaukee. During our stay there, we held services on two mornings and two afternoons in an unfinished church loaned to us by a *unieret* [*sic*] German congregation.[91] We did not organize a Norwegian congregation at this time, but Clausen on a later occasion formed one on the same basis as in the other places. It is served by him as an annex to Muskego, as it is not so difficult for him to reach Chicago by steamer from the nearest towns, such as Milwaukee or Racine.

While we were in Chicago we met many Norwegians, but most of them were newcomers passing through to settlements in Wisconsin and Illinois. There are about a hundred living permanently in the city, some as domestics, some as day laborers. Among those who have prospered to some extent is one Halstein from Stavanger County who, in his six or seven years here, has built a small house on the outskirts of the city. He is an industrious man, orderly and well thought of by the Yankees. Many of the other Norwegians, unfortunately, are drinkers who, by their disturbances and fighting, have brought our people into bad repute among the Americans. Under the nickname "the Norwegian Indians," they are frequently lampooned in the newspapers. Last winter, among other things, two were involved in a fight in which an Irishman was killed.

The settlement at Fox River takes its name from the stream by that name. It lies in La Salle County ten or twelve miles from Ottawa. The terrain for the most part is prairie, with relatively little forest along the river banks. This is the oldest Norwegian colony in the United States, an offshoot of a contingent who came in 1825(?) to a district near Rochester, New York. The oldest settlers on Fox River are those immigrants who came on the sloop which in 1824 [1825] left Stavanger for New York.[92]

In 1821, one Kleng Pedersen from Stavanger County emigrated and in 1824 returned to his birthplace. His reports on America aroused emigration fever in that part of Norway.[93] A company of about fifty persons purchased a small sloop, loaded it with iron, and left for New York. They sailed through the English Channel and landed in England, where they began to sell whisky, a forbidden import, and hurriedly set sail to escape paying a fine they would have been liable for had they been caught. On their passage they sailed too far south and wound up in the Madeira Islands, where they found a barrel of Madeira wine floating in the sea. They opened it and all got drunk. The ship drifted slowly into harbor, without command and without flag. A ship from Bremen was lying offshore in harbor, and one of its crew yelled to them that they had better hoist their flag on the double or they would be greeted by cannon fire. The flag went up at once.[94]

After such adventures, the sloop finally reached New York in the summer of 1825, after a passage of fourteen weeks out of Stavanger. On their arrival in New York, they again met with difficulties. The sloop had more people on board than American law allowed, and as a result the ship, its captain, and its cargo were seized. When the skipper was set free and the owners of the vessel got their cargo back, they sold both sloop and contents at a big loss.[95] While the captain and the mate remained in New York, the passengers, with the help of some Quakers, went farther upstate. Some of these immigrants, among whom there were Quakers, settled near Rochester, New York, where one of them by the name of Larsen still lives.[96] The others went about thirty-five miles farther to the northwest, where they found land for five dollars per acre. They suffered much and were homesick for Norway. Meanwhile, they managed to struggle along, and in 1834 some of them sold their land at a profit and moved to Fox River in La Salle County, Illinois.

In 1837, another group of Norwegians arrived in America, some of whom came to this settlement, while others went a few miles farther south to Beaver Creek, where Student Rynning lived and is buried.[97] When other Norwegians died because of the unwholesome climate, they returned to Fox River, which similarly does not have the best of climates. About four to five hundred Norwegians live here, the majority from Stavanger County and Bergen Diocese.

In the latter part of April, 1845, I visited this colony, although without much hope of establishing a church, as I had heard reliable reports of much religious confusion among our people. I wanted to see for myself what the situation was. The visit showed all too well what happens to the churchly interests of the unfortunate immigrants when there is no one from the church of the fatherland to guide them. Our dear countrymen, through holy baptism members of the Church of Norway, are with few exceptions scattered among a variety of sects here. Some are Presbyterians, others Methodists, Baptists, Ellingians, Quakers, and

Mormons. This is really the place where Elling Eielsen purports to have been called as pastor, although, as mentioned earlier, he actually lives in Muskego. He has erected a building that is used as a place of worship, and he also considers this his principal congregation, visiting it several times a year. The membership, so far as I can learn, has been reduced to only a few.

In addition to the colonies I have mentioned in Wisconsin Territory and the state of Illinois, there is a Norwegian settlement in the southern part of Iowa in Lee County, below the 40½ degree of north latitude. This settlement, in which the late Hans Barlien[98] was alleged to be one of the first immigrants, is now of no importance, as most of the Norwegians have left to escape its unwholesome climate. A Madam Lauman, whose husband died there some years ago, lives in the community.[99] A considerable number of the Norwegians are believed to be Mormons. As the settlement lies so far from those in Illinois and Wisconsin and, as mentioned earlier, is so insignificant, I have not visited it. I have been told that all the Norwegians there have taken land on "claim."

CHAPTER X

The Mormons

Since it is in the Fox River settlement of Illinois that most of the Norwegians have joined the Mormons, it is fitting that I should say something about this group. According to information I have received, I shall report what I know about its origin and teachings. This cult calls itself by the worthy name "The true Church of Jesus Christ of Latter Day Saints." Its real founder is an American named Joseph (abbreviated to Joe) Smith.[100] Joe's father was one of those people in the American West called "money diggers," people who roam about the country deluding others into believing stories about hidden treasure or where rich gold or silver deposits may be found. Joseph was his father's favorite son, and the father believed that, in his youth, he had seen visions and possessed the power of divination, and would one day become a great man. Joe had a good mind and became what the Americans call "a very smart fellow." While still young, he began to travel and often made lucky deals by selling good prospects of metal ore veins he said he had found. On one of these trips, he became acquainted with a like-minded person named Sidney Rigdon.[101]

Between these two men there grew up a warm and lasting friendship and they visited one another often. Rigdon, a genuine American adventurer, courted Lady Luck in many ways and had been at various times tavern keeper, clerk, merchant, newspaper publisher, and finally preacher. At the time he met Smith, he had begun to speculate along a different line. His sermons were filled with strange teachings and prophecies about great and wonderful things soon to come. At the same time, Joseph Smith's father circulated a rumor to the effect that a spirit had revealed itself to his son in a vision and had told him that, if he were to be dressed in black and ride a black horse on a certain day and to a place indicated by the spirit, there he would find buried two gold tablets. But he was never to look back or to lay down the plates.

A rich farmer, when told of this, offered to outfit Joe Smith with the black suit and black horse, whereupon he rode to the appointed place and found the tablets in a stone chest. But he did not obey the instructions: he put the tablets back into the chest, fearing that someone would take them, and he peered around. He saw that no one was looking, but when he tried to open the chest, a strange creature appeared before him gradually taking the shape of a person. This creature struck him twice. Smith fell to the ground and, in a trembling voice, asked why he could not receive the plates. The spirit answered, "Because you did not follow instructions. But come back a year from today and bring your oldest brother; then you will be given the tablets."[102] This spirit was the ghost of the prophet who had engraved the tablets.

The oldest brother died before the year was over. Joseph, according to the spirit's instructions, returned to the designated place, whereupon he was asked about his brother. When Joe answered that he was dead, the spirit ordered him to return again a year to the day and to bring along the person who meanwhile would be pointed out to him as the right one. This man turned out to be Sidney Rigdon, who accompanied Smith to receive the gold tablets.[103] They were inscribed in a language unknown to all the wise men of the world—one which Joseph alone could decode with the help of a clear shining stone which he received from heaven. When Joseph looked through this stone, the writing was translated and printed in a big book.[104]

This volume, which purports to be a supplement to the Bible and is written in biblical style, is said to give a historical account of America's aborigines. In it, the Indians are said to be descendants of the Israelites. The book also contains prophecies of the future. After it was published, revelation upon revelation followed. It was revealed to Smith that Christ's true church had been corrupted and banished "to the wilderness," and that the Lord had chosen Joseph to be the prophet by whom the church would be brought back to its former purity and apostolic form.[105] To accomplish this divinely ordained task, Smith was called directly by Christ and consecrated as his servant.

In this manner, Joseph, as the prophet of the Lord, established the cult whose first members were the persons who, together with Smith and Rigdon, had worked on the translation of the writings found on the two tablets. Their first endeavors were centered in the western part of New York state and in Pennsylvania, where they attracted many disciples.

In one revelation received by Smith, the Lord disclosed that the prophet and all his followers should move to Ohio, where Kirkland [Kirtland] became the headquarters of the church until 1838. This place, however, was not to become a permanent base, because the Lord had revealed in the book of the covenant "that he had hallowed this place for a short time only." Later they moved to Missouri, where they remained until early in 1839, when, driven out, they moved to Illinois, where most of them settled at a place on the Mississippi in Hancock County. They began to build, and within four years an important city grew up; its population is now said to be more than 20,000, all Mormons. The total membership of the cult is stated to have grown to the extraordinary figure of 200,000!

This city, the old name of which was Commerce, was renamed Nauvoo by the prophet; it is now the holy city of the Mormons and, for the time being, its main headquarters. The prophet resides in an elegant hotel called "the Nauvoo House," and a temple, a splendid building of stone, is being constructed with interior dimensions of 140 by 80 feet. Its baptismal font is designed like the molten sea in Solomon's temple (I Kings 7:23), and is supported by beautifully sculptured and gilded oxen. The sides of the font are engraved with various scriptural passages, and a fountain fills it with water. Every member of the Mormon church tithes toward the building of the temple—some with money, others with labor.

So much for the origin and development of this cult.

I do not believe that the peculiar teachings of the Mormons are to be found in any confessional writings, and I can only report what information I have received by word of mouth about them. They claim that their doctrines are based on the Bible, which they interpret literally and straightforwardly. As to the doctrine of the Christian church, they hold, as mentioned earlier, that it has been corrupted and lost. It had not been seen on earth from apostolic times in pure form until the Lord called Joseph Smith as his prophet. Wherever Christ's church is found, the order and customs of the original apostles must be maintained in every detail. The apostolic form, they maintain, has been recovered by Smith and is found in the church as restored by him. The priesthood, which had been lost because the succession from Christ and the apostles was broken in all the other church bodies, was reestablished by Smith after he was called and consecrated directly by the Lord; the true apostolic priesthood was restored by him.

At the head of the church, in place of the original apostles, are twelve elders. The same miraculous gifts, whose fullness was present in the apostolic church, are also found in this one: some have the gift of prophecy, others talk in tongues, and still others heal the sick, etc. These gifts will develop further as the time approaches for the advent of the Lord—and the time is not far off. Glorious promises are linked with the completion of the Nauvoo temple. The Lord will then come to reign for a thousand years on earth with his saints, the Mormons.

Like the Baptists, they teach that infant baptism is invalid and that baptism must be by immersion, not by sprinkling. Furthermore, a person shall be baptized not only once, but as often as he has grievously sinned; he can be rebaptized for the forgiveness of sins. Baptism of the dead at the grave of the deceased and baptism by proxy, as well as baptism for the spiritually dead (that is to say, all who are not Mormons), can save these people.

If I correctly understood one Norwegian Mormon, he said that the sacrament of the altar is received by them in the form of sugar and water, the latter being transformed by Christ to wine. The earth and all its fullness belongs to the Mormons, and will one day be transferred by the Lord from all the ungodly to them, who are God's saints.

This is what I have heard about the false teachings of this second Mohammed, who has deceived so many thousands of people. We can only marvel, and rightly so, that faith in this self-made prophet's "revelations" appeal to people. This phenomenon confirms again the experience which history clearly demonstrates, namely, that nothing is so insane but that fallen man cannot be led astray by it. It emphasizes the validity of the apostle's witness that those who will not accept the truth become the victims of falsehood inherent in the invidious errors that they listen to (see II Thessalonians 2:9).

Keep in mind, too, that Smith possessed all the qualities and knew all the tricks by which credulous hearts, turned away from the truth, are easily blinded. His speech was solemn and mysterious, as was his pretended ability to perform signs and wonders, all of which confirmed the people's belief in his God-sent mission. While most of his followers are uneducated, it is said that there are many learned and influential persons among them who work with great zeal to spread Mormonism. It does not seem reasonable to believe that the cult will fail even after the death of the founder-prophet. Smith was killed in the summer of 1844, in a riot against the Mormons, who naturally consider him a martyr to truth.

Sidney Rigdon, the real father of Mormonism, eventually fell out with the prophet and was thereafter placed under a ban by the church. In this way, the kingdom became divided against itself, and it is said that Rigdon gave information which exposed the entire fraud. From what I have heard, he explained the matter of the golden tablets in the following manner: In Connecticut there was a man by the name of Solomon Spaulding, a genuine Yankee who, like Rigdon, had tried everything from pastor to merchant, smith, and schoolmaster until in his old age he became an author.[106] The fruit of his last enterprise came out under the title *The Manuscript Found*, a historical novel about the first colonists in America; the author tries to show that the American Indians are descendants of the Jews. He gives a detailed description of their travels by land and by sea until, under the command of Nephi and Lehi, they arrived in America, where they divided into two tribes.[107] Evidence of their arts and sciences is found in the many strange ruins of cities; other objects of antiquity are found several places in both North and South America.

This novel was sold by Spaulding to a printer who died without publishing it. *The Manuscript Found* fell into the hands of Sidney Rigdon, who decided to publish it as a new revelation from God. When Rigdon considered the time ripe, he began to preach in order to prepare people to receive the book, but there were many difficulties to overcome before he could realize his plans. Then, as mentioned earlier, Rigdon became acquainted with Joseph Smith, in whom he hoped to find an effective instrument. But he misjudged Smith, who was far superior to him and made Rigdon his own helpless tool. These two men found the gold tablets, the text of which, with minor discrepancies, is said to be the same as Spaulding's manuscript. I have seen a treatise by a Mormon elder who seeks to refute the charge. The story must have some basis when one of the elders honors it with that much attention.

Among the many miracles allegedly performed by Joseph Smith, I heard of several that did not turn out so well. I will mention two. If Jesus could walk on water, so could his prophet Joseph Smith. On moonlit nights, along the banks of the Mississippi, people often saw to their astonishment a figure in white hovering over the river—the prophet, of course. One evening a great crowd gathered to witness this miracle. Joseph came forth, dressed in a long, white robe, but after he had walked a short distance, he fell in the water and had to be rescued. Some people discovered that the prophet had performed this trick simply by walking on some planks ingeniously placed below the surface of the water. They sawed the boards in such a fashion that they broke when Smith came out in the middle of the river. The Mormon explanation for the failure was that Joseph's faith was not strong enough. Meanwhile, some of his loyal followers removed the boards before the deception could be proved.

On a beautiful summer day, a well-dressed man came to an American farmer and asked for supper and lodging for the night.[108] The farmer received him kindly; supper was eaten and the two men talked, among other things, about the prophet Joseph Smith. The farmer expressed his disbelief; the stranger, who denied being a Mormon, said that one should be cautious about judging all that seemed strange, and related that he himself had been a witness to events so mysterious that they had left him wondering what to believe. While this conversation continued, a room was made ready for the guest. During the night the farmer and his wife were awakened by moans and cries from the guest room. The host hurried into the room to see what was wrong and found the stranger in the throes of death. All efforts to assist him were futile and he died after an hour of suffering.

Early the next morning, while the farmer and his family were still shaken by this unprecedented event, two persons approached the door and asked for breakfast. To them the farmer related the experience of the night before, and the two men became deeply saddened and dismayed and asked permission to see the body. As they followed their host to where the dead man lay, the strangers declared that they were representatives of the Church of Jesus Christ of Latter Day Saints, and that they had received from heaven the power to perform miracles—even to raising the dead. They were sure they could also raise up this man. When asked by the amazed farmer whether they were sure they had been given this power, they replied that he should not doubt, because the Lord had given them the power to work miracles and thereby awaken the people to faith in the true church recreated by the prophet of the Lord, Joseph Smith.

The farmer then told them to go ahead with their miracle-working, and in the meantime he sent word around to the neighbors who, anxious to see a miracle performed, flocked together. While the two Mormons knelt and prayed in front of the corpse, the farmer, who meanwhile had been outside for a few minutes, placed himself in front of the bed where the dead man lay and said nothing until the prayers were ended. When the two ministers were about to perform their miracle, the farmer asked them if they were absolutely sure they could raise the dead man and, if they were so sure, whence they had received this conviction. When they replied that they had just received a revelation from the Lord that they could so act, the farmer inquired whether their power was limited in any way by the manner in which the man had died, or whether they could wake him even if his arms and legs—or perhaps his head—were cut off. When the miracle workers replied that it did not matter how the man had died and that there was no limit to the power the Lord had given them in regard to the dead, the host stepped quietly forward. "As there is no limit to your power," he said, "I and the others gathered here wish to see the miracle performed in its full glory. Therefore, with your permission, since it does not matter whether the dead man's head is cut off or not . . .then. . . ." Whereupon he lifted an ax he had concealed under his coat and, to the great amazement of everyone, the dead man jumped up in terror and swore that he would not for any price have his head chopped off. The bystanders grabbed the Mormons and forced them to admit that this had been a plot to deceive them. The three got a sound thrashing and were chased away to try their luck some other place.

It is said that the two miracle workers were Joseph Smith and Sidney Rigdon, his worthy comrade. No doubt many stories have been fabricated at the expense of the Mormons, but it is a fact that their cult is built on deceit and that its leaders have practiced their deceptions in many ways, not always successfully.

It seems reasonable to assume that Joseph Smith was driven by political ambition. In Nauvoo he organized a home guard of several thousand men under the name of "the Nauvoo Legion," of which the prophet was the commanding general; and so, he, like a real pope, became the leader in church and military affairs as well as in commercial matters.[109] Anyone who had lived there for only six months was entitled to vote, and the presidency of the United States did not seem too high a goal for the prophet, especially as this position is said to have been mentioned in the songs that he heard in his cradle.

Smith is also reported to have his missionaries and agents among the Indians, probably for the purpose of organizing a group that could help the political ambitions of the church.

About 150 Norwegians have gone over to the Mormons, and most of them live in the settlement at Fox River, where, in addition to some young men who have become pastors, two older Norwegians have reached high positions in the church. One of these is Ole Heier, a man from Tinn, who is a bishop allegedly having the power to heal the sick.[110] The other, Gudmund Haugaas from Stavanger County, is nothing more nor less than "high priest after the order of Melchisedek in the Church of Jesus Christ of Latter Day Saints"; he is also "counselor" to the supreme Mormon bishop in secular matters affecting the church.[111] He possesses the gift of tongues.

Haugaas visited Koskonong while I was there and had with him a quite young Norwegian, Knud Pedersen, one of the seventy disciples who, as evangelists, have the responsibility of going about preaching and baptizing.[112] Both traveled around holding meetings in different places. I was present on one occasion. In a long introductory speech, the high priest made many apologies for his lack of education; he assured his listeners, however, that he did not despise, but respected, learning. He then proposed briefly to explain his own faith without coaxing anyone to accept it. He read from Ephesians 4 and I Corinthians 12.[113] But he quickly departed from the text and mixed together a great deal from the Old Testament and the New, without telling the first thing about his faith or the grounds for it. I observed at once that his speech had the same effect on the few other people who heard it as it had on me; I therefore made only a few remarks then, but I did point out that such a disjointed talk must have come from a confused spirit.

While the Mormons were here, they came to see me a couple of times. I did not give them the slightest excuse to ride the hobby-horse they always use to prove the truth of their teachings—the fact that they are ridiculed, hated, and persecuted by everyone. I showed them common human kindness and good will as far as I could, and urged members of the congregation to do likewise. When they prepared to leave, they said they had been treated so well that they would return soon. Gudmund did not attempt to speak in tongues at Koskonong, and so I cannot say that I have witnessed this gift, but other Norwegians have been present at meetings where the spirit came over Gudmund. They told me that he resorted to awful grimaces and trembling lips, and that he gave out sounds from which his listeners could make out only two words, repeated over and over: "Schavi! Schava!" When Gudmund had finished, a prayer was offered to heaven for an interpreter, who usually explained that the spirit, through Gudmund, had proclaimed the Mormons to be the true church, and so on.

Two other young Norwegians,[114] who were also pastors, later came to Koskonong to try fishing in troubled waters. Although they might have had reason to hope that they could catch a couple of big fish among the many not already in our congregation's net, their trip was not successful.

In Muskego, whence they came to us and where they already had some followers, a couple of Norwegians accepted Mormon baptism in a frozen stream. One of them was Gitle Danielsen (?) from Stavanger County who, in spite of a solemn warning from

Pastor Clausen, permitted himself to be deceived by this false doctrine.[115]

During my stay in the settlement at Fox River, I attended a Mormon meeting that I especially want to describe as a contribution to Norwegian-Mormon history. On a Sunday morning in spring, the weather clear and warm, a large audience gathered on the banks of Fox River, where big oak trees grow. After a hymn had been sung from the Mormon hymnbook, written in part by Joe Smith and in part by his wife and others, a talented young American—one of the seventy apostles—who had recently come from the Mormon headquarters at Nauvoo, stepped forward. He climbed into a big wagon already crowded with people, placed his arms with great care in an imposing position, and thereupon, eyes closed and in a loud voice, began a long prayer. He repeated over and over the words "Oh Holy Ghost, come down upon us!" He then took a text from St. John's Revelation and, interpreting it in the Mormon manner, maintained that baptism was invalid unless a person is completely immersed in water, and that one who has sinned must be baptized "again and again for the remission of sins."[116]

After him, another preacher took the same pulpit, crying woe upon all other sects. He attempted to prove that the Mormonism was Jesus Christ's true church, and that only for its members could grace be expected as affirmed "in the seventh and last Revelation of Grace," which the Lord in these last days had given to all mankind through his prophet Joseph Smith.

After this, another act began when the pastors, together with the entire audience, went down to the riverside, where the first preacher removed his neckerchief, jacket and vest, watch and chain, and handed everything over to a gray-haired Norwegian Mormon. The preacher then waded into the river to his knees. He talked about the significance of baptism for everyone who wanted to enter the church, as well as for all who had already joined. As they had sinned in one way or another, he encouraged and exhorted the people on the bank not to neglect, this beautiful day, the opportunity the Lord in his mercy had given them to receive grace and forgiveness and the gift of the Holy Ghost in "the living fountain opened by the Lord for the remission of sins."

Thereupon an American approached first, laid aside his jacket and vest, and waded into the water, led by the pastor. The latter placed one hand upon his neck, raised the other to the sky, spoke the name of the participant, and then pushed him backwards into the water (backwards because, in the act of baptism, one is to "see the heavens open"). He then spoke the words altogether too holy for this kind of charade, "I baptize you in the name of the Father, Son and Holy Ghost." The ceremony ended, the convert was led out of the water. This American was married to a Norwegian girl who had earlier accepted Mormonism. After a long resistance, he was joining the church.

After him came a little Norwegian girl six or seven years old. The pastor took her by the hand and led her into the river, turned, and addressed the audience somewhat as follows: "We do not baptize children because the Lord's apostles did not do so, but following the example of Christ, we embrace them and bless them with the laying on of hands. When these children have reached the age of discretion, we baptize them; come therefore, my child." He then repeated the same scene with her as with the man.

Next came two more Norwegians, who were baptized. One had been immersed three times before and was now again being baptized "for the remission of sins."

This action concluded the baptisms for that day, although surely, as a Mormon remarked the previous day, both the high priest Gudmund Haugaas and Bishop Ole Heier—in fact, the entire Mormon group among the Norwegians—ought to have been rebaptized that day "for the remission of sins." Their opponents in the settlement claimed that a member of "the holy ones" had fallen into disagreement over some pigs; therefore the Holy Spirit, who naturally could have no part of a disagreement over pigs, had left them. They should have been baptized anew that day, in order to attain forgiveness of this sin and to regain the gift of the Holy Spirit. The omission perhaps resulted from ridicule heaped on the madness of the baptismal rite by members of the audience who were not Mormons. One of the latter— improperly enough—grabbed a large dog and threw it into the middle of the river when a fourth person was being baptized. His act may have influenced the decision to postpone further baptizing to a more convenient time.

While the first preacher was in the pulpit, a sick man arrived in a one-horse buggy driven by his wife. He had been suffering from palsy for six years and had come to be healed. The healing scene was postponed to an evening meeting held in Gudmund's house, where the miracle, through prayer and the laying on of hands, was to take place. The miracle-workers were unsuccessful, because the gift of the Holy Spirit had temporarily departed them. I was not present at this last meeting, as I had had enough of what I regarded as unholy spectacles. I therefore never saw any miracle attempted, but Gudmund Haugaas assured me at Koskonong that he had seen clear proof of miraculous power in his own daughter when she was healed by Ole Heier, who possessed this gift.

The same Sunday afternoon, in response to requests from a few Norwegians who had remained loyal to the Lutheran church, I held services in a schoolhouse. Its fairly large room was entirely filled and a great many persons stood outside. All the Norwegian Mormons and members of other sects were also present. The text for that day, the fourth Sunday after Easter, gave me the Lord's words in John 16:13–14, to wit: "Howbeit when he, the Spirit of Truth, is come, he will guide you into all truth: for he shall not speak of himself . . . for he shall receive of mine, and shall show it unto you."

This text gave me an opportunity extemporaneously to discuss the false and twisted sects—among them the Mormons—all of which claimed to have the real spirit of truth. I showed them how the mark of the spirit of truth necessarily ought to be a guide to truth and not to lies. Speaking to their hearts, I sought to show them how impossible it would be for the spirit of truth to lead people to blaspheme and mock their own baptism, and how the spirit of truth does not speak by the devices of man or by madness, but takes that which belongs to Christ and proclaims and explains it to each who is willing to be led.

In the beginning, the Mormons laughed. In the course of my sermon, I dropped words like this: "Unfortunately I can see how you poor blinded countrymen of mine are unmoved by the preaching of the truth. The frivolous smiles upon your lips reveal that all too well. Still, I must proclaim the truth of God's Word and his true church. Whether you accept it or not is your choice." Upon hearing this, they became serious. When the service ended, Gudmund the high priest got up and said, "I want to say a few words in regard to what the pastor has said, if people will stay a moment; at least I assume the pastor will stay."

I took no notice of this remark but left, as I felt I had no right to get into a useless argument with a man whom, during his stay in Koskonong and on my visit to his place the previous day, I had already tried in vain to convince of the truth.[117] I heard later that Gudmund, pale and shaking, had raved against me and what I had said. I was also told that the Mormons had yelled after me as I pushed my way through the crowd: "He is like a wolf, who kills and runs away." Whereupon one of the others, naively enough, is said to have replied: "Then he did make a kill." I also heard that some of the Mormons were so angry with me that other persons were afraid for my safety. Next morning I decided to leave the settlement, crossed the Fox River at the spot where the day before I had witnessed the baptismal scene, let the horse drink of water that was entirely too fresh and clear for baptistmania, and returned hale and hearty to my cabin at Koskonong.

I have thought fit to report in some detail what I have seen of the Mormons, both because quite a few of our immigrant countrymen, as already noted, have been converted to their beliefs and because it is known to me that they are sending missionaries to various countries in Europe, including Norway.

The road between Koskonong and the Fox River settlement, about 120 or 130 miles, for the most part crosses an endless prairie, where in many places the eye meets nothing but the sky and waving grass. As I made this trip in springtime, ahead of me lay the fresh, green grass carpet which had been laid newly over a vast stretch of land—a beautiful sight, one especially delightful after the prairie fires that each year are started, partly by the Indians to make their hunting easier and partly by the settlers to speed the growth of the new grass. The burnt-over areas left by Indians and settlers are black and unsightly.

I stopped overnight with a pious Methodist who, upon my asking how much I owed him, replied, "Go and preach to your brethren!"

CHAPTER XI

Return to Norway

It should be possible to judge from conditions in the Fox River settlement—the oldest among the Norwegians—whether or not it is true that immigration has made of the settlers who have remained for twenty years a powerful and wealthy class of landlords, as described by the alluring and glittering reports one has heard. It is by no means true. Anyone who loves the truth would see and admit this fact. One would hope that the letter writers in America—whose accounts, it is true, are not as appealing now as before—would conscientiously describe conditions as they really are, painting not only the bright but also the dark side which America, like all countries, has. Then their letters, even if they advise emigration, would be the surest means of stemming the tide which, to the detriment of so many emigrants, has got such a hold upon our countrymen in the last years.

In no sense is the aim of this little book to describe the economic status of our countrymen; rather, it is to picture their church situation and related matters. Under no circumstances do I consider myself called upon to dissuade anyone from emigrating, beyond what I have written in the daily press and in private letters. I do not wish to extend this book, already grown longer than I expected, with additional details concerning the economic success of Norwegian immigrants. Even among those who have been in America for several years, it is generally only moderate. My mission in America was to investigate spiritual conditions and to give support to church organization among the settlers. As noted in these pages, I had done all I could to carry out that mission.

On my return trip to Norway, I left Koskonong via Muskego and Milwaukee and from Milwaukee went by steamship to Buffalo, where I remained for a few days. From there I did not take the train, but chose a somewhat slower but also much more pleasant and slightly cheaper trip by barge on the Erie Canal. This waterway, which links Lake Erie with the Hudson River, is certainly a gigantic work of construction. It stretches 363 miles from Buffalo to Albany, and in many places the terrain is such that the builders had to cut through forest and dig through cliffs. At Lockport, a small town named after the four important locks located there, one especially senses the great things that human intelligence and industry can achieve over nature. I was told that the Erie Canal cost more than eight million dollars.[118]

From Albany I took a steamship down the Hudson River to New York. While in New York, I made a trip to Philadelphia, where there are penitentiaries I wanted to see. Philadelphia, which in the 1840 census had a population of 258,832, is a lovely city, well developed and adorned with splendid public buildings of white marble. Among these, "the United States Bank" and the unfinished Girard College just outside the city are outstanding.

Philadelphia has a character different from busy and noisy New York. It has a clean, Sunday-like appearance, as most of the business and noise of the city is confined to the docks and streets along the river. The dam across the Schuylkill River provides both vast power and water for every house.

The first excursion I made in Philadelphia was to the penitentiaries, of which there are two—"the county prison" and "the state prison"—both of which are planned after the Pennsylvania, or Philadelphia, prison system.[119] As is well known, the principal feature of this plan is solitary confinement, in contrast to the Auburn system, in which the prisoners work together in the strictest silence. At the county prison, which I visited first, I made the acquaintance of a German Lutheran pastor, Professor Dr. Demme.[120] He met me with great friendliness and introduced me to the superintendent of the "state prison"—a real American "gentleman," who was wholly enthusiastic about the system, whose virtues he could not praise enough.

He told me that not so long ago a Norwegian convicted of a certain crime had been set free. He had been a seaman on a large American vessel that was wrecked; the passengers had had to abandon ship in lifeboats. The Norwegian had escaped, together with some others, in a small boat that was overloaded and in danger of sinking in the heavy seas. To save themselves and a few of the others, two of the strongest in the boat, including the

Norwegian, agreed to throw overboard as many as the boat could not safely hold. This plan was carried out. Among those who were spared was a girl who had been aboard the wrecked vessel. Four persons went overboard, although one of them voluntarily jumped out of the boat. The passengers were rescued a few days later by a passing ship that brought them in to Philadelphia, where the girl accused the Norwegian of originating the plan to lighten the boat. He was arrested and sentenced to prison—for how many years I do not recall—but, after serving one year, he was pardoned because of the special nature of his crime.

I visited many cells and talked to the prisoners. Among them was a Prussian from Halle who had been sentenced to three years on a forgery count. The prisoner had studied law at Halle University and was a highly cultured man. He expressed himself strongly in favor of the Philadelphia system. He emphasized that, among other things, solitary confinement had the moral advantage that the prisoner was left alone with God and his own thoughts. Also, in this system, unlike the Auburn system, the prisoner was not, after his release, exposed to recognition by former fellow prisoners. The latter might, for profit or desire, ruin the good reputation built up by a reformed convict, who possibly could make a place for himself if people did not know he had been imprisoned. He also thought it clear that punishment under the Auburn system, which enforces complete silence in the company of others, was both more unnatural and harder to endure than isolation. The German had been in prison for a year and a half and had learned to be a weaver. He assured me that the time in prison had not seemed long.

Another prisoner, who had served ten years, looked pale, but he said that he felt well and was in good spirits, and that his work went briskly. None of the middle-aged or older prisoners I visited looked as if they had suffered either in body or in mind from solitude. On the other hand, I visited a few young people, both men and women, who looked suspicious and queer, even though their speech did not suggest that they were mentally disturbed. The superintendent believed that the reason for this condition lay in secret sins which tempted the young people in their isolation.

The prison is built in a rotunda, so that each "block" or cell passageway radiates out from the center, where the guards keep watch. Outside each cell, the prisoner has a "yard" (a little garden) under the open sky, where he can go during the day. At least this is true in the cells occupied by the men. The women's quarters, which lie above them, although they have no such gardens, are arranged to give each prisoner two adjoining cells—one in which to work and one in which to sleep—a poor substitute no doubt for the loss of God's open sky.

Besides the four inspectors who head up the institution, there are a "warden" and, under him, other "overseers" and "officers," a doctor, and a "moral instructor" whose duty it is frequently to visit the prisoners. In addition, those who request it can have a clergyman of their own faith visit them. But there is something missing, it seems to me, in that no regular worship is held for the prisoners. This is no doubt a consequence of the system, although it seems to me it could be provided with proper cell arrangements. But probably because prisoners in America belong to so many denominations, it is impossible to hold a common service for them.

In the 16th annual report of the penitentiary, which was read to "the Senate and House of Representatives" in March, 1845, it is stated that 138 prisoners were held in the state prison from January 1, 1844, to January 1, 1845. In the same period, 157 were released; 98 had served their time, 46 had been pardoned, and 13 had died. The total number of prisoners accepted into the prison from October 25, 1829, when it opened, until January 1, 1845, was 1916. On January 1, 1845, there were 340 prisoners.

The 15th annual report makes a comparison of three prisons maintained under the Pennsylvania and five under the Auburn system. Two of the latter are located in places more favorable to the health of the prisoners than those in Philadelphia, yet the death rate of the prisoners under the Pennsylvania system has been lower than under the Auburn, where the mortality rate is 2.41 annually as compared to 1.96 under the Pennsylvania system.

After this trip to Philadelphia, I left New York on June 7 [1845], aboard the Swedish ship *Thore Petre* under Captain Anderson from Gefle, bound for Stettin with a cargo of oil and dyewood. With strong westerly winds, we sailed quickly and safely across the Atlantic, through the English Channel and the Sound, and anchored, after 28 days at sea, at Helsingør Roads, whence I hurried home by steamer to my beloved fatherland.

CHAPTER XII

An Assessment

So, dear reader, in this little book I have tried to give you an insight into "my journey among the Norwegian emigrants in the United States of North America." My plea that I have tried to present the record to the best of my ability naturally can be of little comfort either to you or to me. No one is more willing than I to admit the volume's shortcomings. I beg your indulgence. It is my hope that the booklet will help to awaken our people to the religious needs of our emigrated countrymen, and, simply by describing what has been accomplished, to enable interested persons to judge how best to build upon the foundation that has been laid.

Help must still come from the Norwegian church if there is to be hope for permanence and stability in the mission begun by one lonely, weak messenger. A single member of the Church of Norway, out of Christian charity toward the emigrants and by disinterested sacrifice, enabled me by his challenge and support to go over to that distant land. Our church has an important responsibility to help our scattered compatriots and fellow believers in their religious needs. True, the Norwegians who left for America were lured by the hope of temporal gain in a land they dreamed was flowing with milk and honey. They willingly gave up the great, indispensable blessing of the church order they had enjoyed at home, but no thinking Christian in Norway would dare to condemn them. Material want was great among many of them, and the lure of a better life suggested by exaggerated accounts was strong. No wonder if a desire for worldly riches blinded them to concern for the church. I know from experience that it never occurred to a great many of them that in America they would enjoy no ordered church.

A genuine feeling of necessity and longing, sometimes unconscious, has been stirring the immigrants to seek pastoral help. This is revealed even by the heretical sectarianism that has affected many and brought them openly to join sects or to follow self-made pastors. It is also shown by the call to Clausen, in whom they have a regularly examined and ordained servant of the Lord, and by the attempt made in the southwestern settlements on the boundary of Illinois and Wisconsin to secure a clergyman from Norway. I saw much evidence of how sincere this desire is after my arrival in America. Many earnest prayers and lovely Christian thank-you letters were sent with me by the founding congregations to Mr. Sørensen, whose sacrifice was a start toward helping them. The efforts that the immigrants themselves made, especially at Koskonong and in the southwestern prairies, have demonstrated that the people are willing to make sacrifices beyond their means, even though their economic circumstances are far from affluent. Their longing for a church counts for more than money. All this points to a tangible urge to regain what they left behind. A longer or shorter time without spiritual blessing has taught them to treasure the church both for themselves and for their children.

It seems clear to me that the time has come for the Norwegian church to aid the immigrants in their religious need. The obligation to help where there is need rests upon all Christians. I need not labor that point to anyone who remembers the admonition of God's word: "Let us do good to all men, and especially to those of the household of faith." The cry comes also from our brothers-in-the-faith living across the sea: "Come over [into Macedonia] and help us."

What is required now, above all else, if the new church is to develop, is naturally the emigration of regularly examined and ordained servants of the Lord. In Clausen we have one such, and I am ready to fulfill the obligation I have to the Koskonong congregation and to return there if no one else can be found to take my place. Through the newspapers (see *Morgenbladet* for 1845, no. 228), I have taken the liberty to challenge theologians and younger clergymen to consider whether one or another might not feel called to go in my place. Up to now, so far as I know, no one has indicated his willingness to do so.[121]

It may be necessary for me to accept a call other than the one

I had thought of for myself before I went to America the first time. Both in my application for ordination and in the newspapers before I left, I clearly stated that it was my role to investigate religious conditions among the immigrants and to lay the groundwork for a church among them. But now I have received a call from Koskonong to serve as resident pastor and shepherd in a congregation already established—a call which I had hoped someone better suited than I would have accepted once the ice was broken. If no one else will serve the congregation, I will find it necessary to accept the call, despite other claims upon me and my fear that I am quite inadequate in that theological clarity and firmness required to lead a congregation in sect-splintered America. The immigrant's religious need is certainly not solved by refusal to accept his call.

It is absolutely impossible for two pastors to serve the widely scattered settlements, even if they restrict themselves to those congregations which are already organized or where such organization hopefully will take place. Therefore, as one who is acquainted with conditions, I will make bold to state both the number of clergymen needed and how to distribute them if initial church organization is to achieve stability and permanence.

There should be one pastor based at Muskego as his main congregation, with Chicago and Scoponong as annexes. At Koskonong, there should be another major congregation, with Rock River as an annex. The settlement at Hamilton Diggings should be a main congregation, with Rock Ground as an annex; and, finally, Rock Prairie should be a major congregation, with Jefferson Prairie and Long Prairie as annexes. This program will require four parish pastors who, I can promise, will find more than enough to do if they conscientiously and benevolently carry out the duties of their office and seek to further Christian schools in the congregations.

In addition, there should be one pastor with a general call to work as an evangelist, traveling around to the various places where Norwegians live—in this way assisting the four parish ministers. The itinerant pastor should be a bachelor.[122]

My plan, which may seem grandiose to many, will require money; some of it must come from the fatherland, as it is impossible for the immigrants to support the entire program by themselves, even with the best of intentions. But the financial support would be less than many might expect. An annual contribution of 150 specie dollars for each of the four parish pastors, and 200 specie dollars for the evangelist or itinerant minister, would be augmented by what the congregations can contribute.

True, as mentioned earlier, Koskonong congregation, as well as the congregations on the southwestern prairies—where it was Knudsen of Wiota who wrote to the bishop for a minister—have established a salary of 300 dollars per annum for the pastor. With good management, he should be able to get along on this sum. But one must point out, as I have already suggested, that longing for a church has made the hearts of the immigrants promise more in this respect than they can afford. Ministers in a distant land ought not to suffer need if they are to carry out their mission with joy. On the other hand, neither should they be forced to extort the salary agreed upon from the less fortunate to the detriment of the congregation.

In addition to the sum required for the five pastors—multiplying four by 150 and adding 200 means 800 specie dollars annually —400 specie dollars would be needed to support parochial schools. This makes a total of 1,200 specie dollars. Much could be done with this amount of money. If it were forthcoming for the first five years, I would assume that ecclesiastical order among the immigrants would be so well established by that time that, with the increased economic well-being of the members, they would be able to support themselves for the most part.

In addition, travel expenses should be 200 specie dollars for each of the three resident pastors, assuming they are married men, and 100 specie dollars for the itinerant one, who, as mentioned, should be single. This would make for a total of 700 specie dollars.[123]

No doubt many will say, "That is a lot of money. Where is it coming from in our poor Norway?" But "silver and gold are mine," says the Lord, and if he will first bend the hearts of the people to bring help to the "brothers in exile" in their spiritual needs, then "many small creeks make a big river" and many shillings and *orter* from the less well-to-do—plus a few dollars from those who have more—would soon bring in the required amount from among the devout members of the home church.[124]

One person, who could by no means be called rich, and who had no more than what he earned by the labor of his hands, was able to give 500 specie dollars to assist in establishing a church among the immigrants. What could not the many do if they would take an interest in this project?[125]

There can be no purpose in this book other than to show what can be done by the fatherland and to express the hope that men with greater authority than I in the church will take up the cause and challenge the Norwegian church to a missionary effort performed by its members on a voluntary basis. I know that if this cause, for which I have the deepest feeling, is also the Lord's, it will no doubt overcome all obstacles to a victorious conclusion.

Finally, in the publication of this book I have been attempting to give an appraisal of my religious activities among our countrymen in America. I beg the Christian reader to judge with charity

RECORD OF MY MINISTERIAL ACTS AMONG THE NORWEGIAN IMMIGRANTS

Settlement	Worship Services	Bap- tisms	Con- firmed	Commu- nicants	Married*	Fu- nerals
Koskonong	36	48	22	·512	7	19
Rock River	2	2	—	35	—	—
Hamilton Diggings.	5	7	—	33	—	3
Rock Ground	4	14	—	50	—	—
Rock Prairie	7	14	1	85	2	2
Jefferson Prairie ...	5	13	4	84	1	—
Long Prairie	2	8	1	50	—	—
Scoponong	2	3	—	37	—	—
Milwaukee	2	1	—	3	—	—
Chicago	2	1	—	15	—	—
TOTAL	67	111	28	904	10	24

* Footnote by Dietrichson: "With regard to marriages, civil law permits a justice of the peace in his district, others in authority, or an ordained minister to perform the ceremony. Marriages may be performed by a pastor of whatever church denomination only after he has registered his certificate of ordination at the county seat in which the marriage is to be performed. But before a couple can be married, they must have a license from the justice of the peace or another authorized person. After the wedding, a certificate must be sent to the county clerk; otherwise the marriage is invalid. In the American situation it is impossible to prevent a person from claiming falsely to be a clergyman and registering forged ordination papers. I simply sent in an English copy of my Norwegian ordination certificate, paid the required sum to the secretary, and without further ado got it back stamped with the permission to perform marriages."

and to consider that it is no small task to serve as an instrument of order in the confused churchly circumstances which confronted me. I confess that a man with greater talents and strength could have accomplished the mission more successfully, but I have tried to fulfill what I thought was my calling. For what may have been accomplished, the honor goes to him who gives the power, while the failures are mine alone. I am including here a list of the ministerial acts I performed among the immigrants in the various settlements. I thought this might be of interest to the reader.

CHAPTER XIII

Postscript

After most of my manuscript was printed, I received a letter from Clausen advising me that the appeal in "the District Court" at Madison has been dismissed because it was not lodged within the time required by law. Clausen writes that, from what he was told in Madison, the appeal should have been filed the same day on which the original verdict was handed down. Because judgment was pronounced at 11:30 P.M., the appeal should have been filed not later than midnight the same day. The twenty-four hours which we were told was the time allotted to file an appeal should have been used to make out the necessary documents in connection with the case. The law was wrongly interpreted to us—perhaps a trick to hinder us from appealing. Even though Clausen writes that he did everything within his power to bring the case before the court, this did not help. There is nothing to do but to accept the legal injustice and comfort ourselves with the fact that any impartial and enlightened tribunal would know that the verdict was unjust.

Remarkably enough, Clausen says, neither the fines nor the court costs have been demanded. The heart of the matter is this: even if we do have to pay, there is no objective authority, only the specific judgment, that brands a churchly act as a crime in a nation hailed for its religious freedom.

Clausen also reports in his letter that another violent controversy has erupted in the newly founded congregation at Muskego, where one of the officers of the church refused to follow the discipline laid down in the *Ritual* and wanted to change it so as to nullify all power to ban the openly ungodly from the congregation. Everyone in the congregation supported his position. Clausen, who naturally is bound by his ordination vow, neither can nor will change the *Ritual*, because he knows that the church cannot surrender its discipline. He therefore had to tell them that he could have nothing further to do with a congregation that refuses to honor the churchly rules on which it is founded.

It is deplorable that these blessed notions about freedom, even in churchly affairs, shall be applied in such a manner that the church is not even to have the right held, not only by a nation, but by any private club, to exclude open offenders. Clausen states that he is consequently free to accept the call from the southwestern prairies. But, when he weighs the difficulties associated with the widely scattered settlements against his strength, and especially when he takes into account the poor health of which he complains now as before, he is not sure that he dares to accept it. He says he would prefer that a new man from Norway take over these settlements. For the rest, everything is as before in the congregations.

As soon as I had received Clausen's letter, I wrote to him and told him that, as no one had indicated his willingness to go to Koskonong in my place, I was therefore obliged to return unless the congregation should wish to call him in my place, now that Clausen is freed of his duties in Muskego. I asked him to consider this call, both for his sake (because he himself says that he is reluctant to accept the call to the southwestern prairies) and for mine, as he knows that I would rather not return if Koskonong obtains able leadership. I have no doubt that the congregation would just as soon, perhaps rather, have Clausen as their pastor. Because of his frequent visits, they have learned to know him much better, and, I am sure, to respect and love him as well.

Should Clausen not stay in Muskego and should he not accept the call to the southwestern prairies before he receives my letter, it is reasonable to assume that the Koskonong congregation will call him. I would hope that he would then accept the call, in which case I will be free of my obligations to that congregation. I cannot persuade myself to take over any other congregation in the event of my return to America. In all probability, Pastor Clausen, independently of my last letter, has already promised to accept the call to the southwest, in which case I shall have to go back again. Thus, the situation with regard to my return trip is now more uncertain than before. I will have to wait for a reply from Clausen before I know what my lot will be: whether again to sail the Atlantic waves to that foreign land or to remain at home in this beloved fatherland. God's will be done!

I also wish in this postscript to report to those who are interested in the religious life of the Norwegian immigrants, that in the past few days I have received donations amounting to sixty specie dollars for Norwegian immigrant schools through Provost Magelssen of the deanery at Foss; fifty specie dollars from Pastor Emeritus Brodtkorb of Hitra parish, Sør-Trøndelag, and ten specie dollars from Johannes Jørgensen, who lives on the Haavik farm of the same parish.[126] These unexpected gifts are a source of great joy and a sure sign that the Lord will not disappoint a sincere trust in Him. Trusting that I would get the necessary aid from the fatherland, as mentioned before, on my own initiative I had hired the precentor at Koskonong to start a parochial school there, at a salary of ten specie dollars a month, for three months in 1845. I agreed to pay him on condition that he wait for his money until sometime this year. The contributions received from the two donors for the parochial school not only covered this amount, but doubled it, and so we have enough money for three months of school this year too. So the Lord helps. In his name, heartfelt thanks to the donors on behalf of the Koskonong congregation. An accounting of expenditures will be made eventually. These unsolicited and therefore unexpected donations are, I hope, a testimony that here and there in Norway's church there are many who wish to contribute a little something to aid the Norwegian immigrants in their spiritual needs—when they are called upon by some of the church's esteemed men who are also interested in the cause.

Stavanger
February, 1846   J. W. C. DIETRICHSON

The Koshkonong Parish Journal

Original title: *Kirkebog for Den Norsk*
Lutherske Menighed paa Koskonongs Prairier i
Dane og Jefferson Countier i Wisconsin
i Nordamerika

Translated by
HARRIS E. KAASA

CHAPTER I

The Founding of the Congregation

On Friday, August 30, 1844, I, Johannes Wilhelm Christian Dietrichson, regularly ordained pastor in the Lutheran church in my
fatherland Norway, conducted a service of worship for the settlers
at Koskonong Prairie.[1] This was the first service which I conducted here. It was held in the afternoon in Amund Andersen's
barn (*love*), and I preached on the words in Rev. 3:11: "I am
coming soon; hold fast what you have, so that no one may seize
your crown." As God gave me grace, I sought earnestly to lay
upon the hearts of my countrymen here, where there are so many
erring (*vilfarende*) sects,[2] their obligation to hold fast to the true
saving doctrine of the church of our fatherland and its edifying
church order.[3]

On Sunday forenoon, September 1, the thirteenth Sunday after
Trinity, I conducted divine service for a large congregation at the
same place and administered the Lord's Supper. This was in the
eastern part of the settlement. On Monday, September 2, I conducted the service and administered the Lord's Supper out of
doors under an oak tree on the farm of Knud Aslaksen Juve, in
the western part of the settlement.[4]

On this, my first, visit I was asked by a large number of the
Norwegian settlers to locate here, which request was later repeated in writing. I therefore decided to choose this settlement as
the focal point for my temporary ministry. At present it is the
largest Norwegian colony in America and it is also very near the
middle of the Norwegian settlements in Wisconsin. Consequently,
when I came here again in October, 1844, I held a meeting on
October 10 at the home of Amund Andersen, in which I first told
the people the purpose for and the manner of my coming to
America. I told them how an earnest Christian man, Mr. [Peter]
Sørensen, a dyer in Christiania, Norway, who had long been

deeply concerned about the religious circumstances of the Norwegian emigrants, asked me to undertake a journey to America,
to investigate the church situation among them, and to try to arrange something for them in this regard. I told them how I had
pondered this proposal for a long time, and how, after consultation with several able Christian men in Christiania, I had come to
see in this request a call from God that demanded obedience, provided the Church of Norway would grant me ordination. I
pointed out how the Norwegian government had been ready and
willing to grant my request on this occasion. Finally, I assured
them that I had not come seeking their money. Due to the fine
Christian sacrifice Sørensen had made, I would need no support
from them while I labored to set their ecclesiastical affairs in
order. As stated above, I proved to the people the truth of my
statements by reading the papers I had brought from home. From
these, I now quote my *vita,* as it was read from the pulpit on my
ordination day in Opsloe[5] Church in Christiania, and also the
certificate of ordination given me by the bishop of Christiania.

Johannes Wilhelm Christian Dietrichson's Vita

Johannes Wilhelm Christian Dietrichson was born at Fredrikstad on April 4, 1815. His parents were former Captain of the
Guard, now Military and Naval Commissary Fredrik Dietrichson,
and Karen Sophie Henriette Dietrichson, nee Radich. In his childhood and youth, he attended Fredrikstad's middle school, principal
of which was the distinguished educator, the Right Reverend Mr.
Riddervold,[6] bishop of Trondhjem, who was then pastor in Fredrikstad and headmaster of the school. When he [Dietrichson] was
seventeen years old, he was privately certified to the university
and took the examination in arts (*artium*) in 1832,[7] receiving the
grade *haud illaudabilis.*[8] The following year he took the philo-
logico-philosophical examination and received the same grade.

The truths of Christianity had been brought nearer to his mind
and heart through confirmation instruction. His teacher was that
zealous and reverend servant of the Lord, the present pastor of
Modum, Provost [J.] Tandberg, who was then pastor in Fredriks-
hald. It was with real enthusiasm, therefore, that he chose theology as his field of study. He began this study at once, after

passing his "second"[9] (*anden*) examination, and in February, 1837, he passed his theological degree examination (*embedsexamen*), receiving the grade of *laudabilis*. In 1838 he took the homiletical and catechetical examinations and again received the grade of *laudabilis*. Upon completion of his examinations, he accepted a position as private teacher at the Vallø salt works near Tønsberg, where he remained for·one year. Early in 1838, he returned to Christiania, primarily to attend lectures and participate in study groups at the university's practical theological seminary. Besides taking this instruction, he joined two others in opening a private school and a preparatory school for confirmands, and was retained by the Board of Penal Institutions to catechize the prisoners at Christiania Reformatory on every Sunday and holy day.

In November, 1839, he was married to Jørgine Laurentze Broch. The memory of this beloved and understanding woman is his life's most precious treasure. Their union was a most happy one, until God in his inscrutable wisdom called her home to himself, though not before she had given him a son as a pledge of her love and faithfulness. In his severe sorrow he was directed the more to the loving Lord who wounds in order to heal, who chastens because he loves and wishes to draw us closer to himself. With renewed zeal he learned to embrace the life of Christ in his church. Despite financial handicap, he undertook in the spring of 1842 a trip to Denmark, Germany, and Switzerland, to study practical theology and to prepare himself for the ministerial calling. To this end he now strove with all his might. His weak faith strengthened through contact with humble believers, he returned in the spring of 1843. In June, 1843, when Garrison Chaplain Fangen was installed as prison chaplain in Christiania, he was appointed by the Right Reverend Bishop Sørenssen to assist the chaplain in those matters wherein he, as an unordained man, could function. He continued in this position [until departure for America].

From a Christian man lovingly concerned for the religious needs of the Norwegian emigrants to America, there came to him in the summer of 1843, along with an offer of support, an appeal to undertake a voyage to North America to investigate the church situation among the Norwegians there, and possibly to do something toward establishing a permanent church order among them. This appeal stirred the recipient the more because it was prompted by Christian love and because it came from one who gave of the widow's mite rather than of the rich man's abundance. The recipient had often and anxiously thought of the needs of his emigrated countrymen, now subjected to every wind of doctrine, but it had never occurred to him that he would be called upon to act so immediately in their behalf.[10]

This appeal served to increase his concern for the condition of the emigrants. He fully understood the importance and the difficult nature of this call.[11] He considered it and consulted with several Christian men whose judgment he placed far above his own. Encouraged by them, and trusting in the Lord whose power is made perfect in weakness, he decided to accept the call, if ordination to the ministerial office were granted him by the Church of Norway. It was clear both to him and to those with whom he counseled that, if he were to accomplish anything, he would need to possess the authority that only ordination can give. In ordination, he would receive the Lord's testimony that he was called to be a servant of the church. Then and only then could he see in the appeal a definite call from God, and make bold to accept it. It has pleased His Majesty, under date of October 12, 1843, to grant his humble request for ordination to the ministerial office.[12] To this holy office he is to be ordained today, and he prays for the blessing of God and the intercession of Christian people for him.

Read in Opsloe Church, February 23, 1844.

The Certificate of Ordination

I, the undersigned, bishop of Christiania, do hereby declare that, in accord with royal decree, I have on the 23rd day of February,[13] in Opsloe Church, ordained and placed under oath Candidate Johannes Wilhelm Christian Dietrichson, so that, according to his wish and desire, he may proceed with authority to perform ministerial acts to our emigrated countrymen in North America. I therefore declare him to be a legally commissioned servant of the Word, ordained in conformity with the rites of our church; and I congratulate the community that gets him as a teacher, for he possesses a thorough knowledge of that which belongs to the teaching office, combined with a constant zeal for its performance and a most exemplary life. May the God who paternally has followed him from his earliest years continue to follow him! May he open not only the ears but also the hearts of his hearers, so that the Word of Life which he proposes to preach may thrive and flower among them unto joyous fruits in a God-pleasing life, to the comfort and blessing of both young and old. Amen, for Jesus' sake! Amen!

Opsloe bishop's residence, March 30, 1844.

SØRENSSEN
(L. S.)[14]

*   *   *   *   *

I next asked the congregation whether they earnestly desired to hold fast to the church into which they had been grafted by baptism, and whether they wanted me to try to set their church affairs in order. Their reply was a unanimous yes. I therefore read to them the terms I considered essential. Everyone desiring to belong to the congregation agreed voluntarily to these conditions. The conditions I presented after the most earnest deliberation and according to the best of my understanding were the following:

(1) Do you desire to belong to the Norwegian Lutheran congregation here?

(2) To that end, are you willing to submit to the church order which the Church of Norway prescribes?

(3) Do you promise that hereafter you will not accept or acknowledge anyone as your minister and pastor unless he can prove that he is a rightly called and regularly ordained Lutheran pastor according to the order of the Church of Norway? And will you render the pastor, thus called to be your clerical authority, the deference and obedience that a church member owes his pastor, in everything he may require in conformity with the church *Ritual*[15] of your fatherland Norway?

(4) Will you, by signing your name or by permitting your name to be signed, avow that you join this church on the basis of the foregoing conditions?

About forty families and a number of single persons signed that day. This took place in the eastern part of the settlement. I proceeded in precisely the same manner in the western part on Saturday, October 19, at which time about thirty families and a number of single persons signed. This, then, was the beginning of the congregation to which more members were added daily. Never did I in any way try to persuade anyone to join. On the contrary, whenever anyone has come and asked to enroll, I have rather asked him not to join. If he still persists, however, I have of course had to accept him on the basis of his verbal confession.[16] All the same, the congregation thus became a net which gathered in all sorts of fish. This soon became obvious in the person of an ungodly drunkard named Halvor Christian Pedersen Funkelien, who to this day has hardened himself against every admonition from pastor and deacons, and who therefore, unless he repents, will be publicly excommunicated and expelled from the congregation.

Up to now there has been the greatest confusion among the Norwegian settlers in everything pertaining to the church. A certain person calling himself John G. Smith[17] passed himself off as a clergyman from Sweden, and persuaded some Norwegians to follow him. He administered the Lord's holy sacraments and performed all ministerial acts among them, until finally they had their eyes opened to his many lies and deceits. They left him when they learned that he had openly scorned and blasphemed his holy infant baptism by permitting himself to be rebaptized and joining the Baptist sect, in which he did have a sort of consecration. Pastor [C. L.] Clausen [Muskego] had been here a couple of times, had preached, and had administered the sacraments before I came, but there was no organized congregation. I certainly needed grace and wisdom from God in order to establish some order in all this confusion.

To those who joined the church I preached the Word of God and administered the most holy sacraments according to the *Ritual* of our church. At my request, the congregation decided to erect as soon as possible two simple structures to be dedicated and used as churches. Both congregation and pastor found it unsatisfactory to meet in the small and wretched huts these people call homes.

In the western part of the settlement especially, the people worked diligently and with some sacrifice. God blessed the work with weather unusually mild for that time of year, and to the mutual joy of the congregation and myself, we were able with prayer and meditation on the Word of God gratefully to dedicate a simple log house as the church for the western part of the congregation. The dedication took place on Thursday, December 19, 1844,[18] and it was carried out according to the established ritual of the Church of Norway. My fellow servant of the Word, Pastor Clausen, assisted in the dedication ceremony. He offered the opening prayer and delivered the preparatory address. I acted as liturgist and preached on Heb. 10:19–25. My theme was: "How our boldness to enter into the invisible heavenly sanctuary is preserved, nourished, and strengthened by our presence in the visible and earthly."

From that time on, services of worship were conducted in this church until the church in the eastern part of the settlement was completed. Work there progressed more slowly, but we were able on January 31, 1845, to dedicate that church also. This time Pastor Clausen was unable to be present, and so I conducted the entire service alone. At this dedication I preached on Genesis 35:2–3, on the theme "How we should prepare ourselves worthily to go up to Bethel (the house of God); 1) What we must put off, 2) What we must put on, 3) What we there must build up."

Since then, divine service has been conducted alternately in the two churches. Immediately after the church was established, a *klokker*[19] was elected. Ole Knudsen Trovatten[20] was the unanimous choice for this position. As yet, no fixed salary has been voted for him. Likewise, eight deacons[21] were elected, four for the west and four for the east half of the settlement, where each was assigned an area of responsibility. The four deacons for the east half are Lars Johannesen Hollo, Gulbrand Gulbransen Holtene, Gunstein Rolfsen Omdal, and Gunder Jørgensen Fladland. The four for the west half are Ole Knudsen Trovatten, Knud Aslaksen Juve, Knud Olsen Holtene, and Tron Kittilsen Svimbill. On Sunday, December 8, the 2nd Sunday in Advent, following the service in the west church, the congregation gathered at the home of widow Tone Aslaksen Lien. Here the deacons were charged with their duties as prescribed in the laws of the Church of Norway and as summarized in Pontoppidan's *Collegium Pastorale*, pp. 587–590, with the modifications made necessary by conditions here.[22] Each man gave me his word and hand that he would perform the duties incumbent upon him in this office.

After this had been done, the deacons met and formulated certain proposals to govern the future election of a permanent pastor. The pastor did not, of course, interfere in this matter. The deacons laid the proposals before the congregation, and some disagreement arose. When it became apparent that the discussion might come to naught, the congregation requested that I involve myself in it. Not attempting to dictate in regard to the conditions themselves, I did try to get the different groups to reach a common mind. It was generally agreed to hold a joint congregational meeting at the home of Jens Pedersen Vedhuus in the east part of the settlement. On Sunday, February 2, the members of the church met there after the service. Three different factions proposed stipulations of the call: The first favored the deacons' proposal; the second favored Amund Andersen's view, which agreed generally with the first except that the pastor's salary was to be fixed at $200; the third proposal from a Swede, Reuterskjöld, was based entirely upon voluntary contributions.

The deacons' motion received a majority of the votes and, after some nonsense, all except a few individuals accepted it. As adopted by the congregation, it reads as follows: "Motivated by a heartfelt longing to hold fast to the true, saving doctrine of our Evangelical Lutheran Church and the edifying church order of our fatherland, we Norwegian settlers in Dane and Jefferson counties have resolved to found a Norwegian Lutheran congregation. Accordingly, in the month of October last year we did entrust to the Norwegian Lutheran pastor, J. W. C. Dietrichson, who arrived from our fatherland last year, the task of ordering our ecclesiastical affairs. Of our own free will we have all by hand and mouth made known our desire to be members of the Norwegian Lutheran congregation here, and that we to that end will submit to that church order prescribed in the *Ritual* of our Norwegian church. We also agree that in future we will call and accept as our minister only such as can prove and clearly substantiate that he is a regularly ordained pastor according to the order of the Norwegian Lutheran church.[23] We further promise that, in everything which a properly called pastor should require of us in accordance with the *Ritual* of the Church of Norway, we are willing to render to him, as our ecclesiastical authority, that deference and obedience which a church member owes his pastor.

"As the said Pastor Dietrichson has completed the task temporarily entrusted to him, we may now proceed to determine the conditions under which we will choose a permanent pastor in the future. As Christians, we acknowledge the Lord's command in I Cor. 9:14, "that those who proclaim the gospel should get their living by the gospel," and we are heartily willing to obey this Word of the Lord in so far as we are able.

"The conditions upon which we have agreed and under which we propose to call a pastor are the following: 1) That the congregation shall purchase 40 (forty) acres of land as nearly as possible halfway between the two church buildings erected by the Norwegian Lutheran congregation here; that on this land there shall be built a simple dwelling containing a living room, two other rooms, and a kitchen; and that 10 (ten) acres of the land be plowed and fenced in.[24] 2) That for a period of at least 5 (five) years from April 1, 1845, the sum of 300 (three hundred) dollars annually be the pastor's regular salary. This sum shall be paid in three installments of 100 (one hundred) dollars each during the course of the year, by March 1, July 1, and October 1 respectively. 3) That for ministerial acts such as the churching of mothers, infant baptisms, confirmation, weddings, and funerals payment shall be made by the persons concerned as they wish. 4) That on each of the three great festivals—Christmas, Easter, and Pentecost—the pastor shall receive a free-will offering. Responsibility for whatever steps may be necessary in order to carry out these stipulations we leave in the hands of eight men,[25] to be chosen by us for a term of three years. They are empowered to assess each member in such manner as can be justified before God, their consciences, and us. With reference to the carrying out of these conditions the pastor depends on these men. We hereby acknowledge this to be our will and our decision by signing our names or having them signed. The Norwegian Lutheran congregation at Koskonong Prairie, Dane and Jefferson counties, Wisconsin Territory, North America, February 2, 1845."

There follow the signatures of all the heads of families and the adult members of the congregation. When the terms of the call had been agreed on, the members voted by written ballot on their choice for permanent pastor. As previously stated, the congregation had entrusted to me only the temporary task of setting its church affairs in order. Since this was now considered accomplished as far as possible under present conditions, it was necessary to call a permanent pastor. Under date of March 3 this year, the congregation issued me the following letter of call:

Reverend Mr. Dietrichson!

Following your reverence's visit to us in September of last year, we were able to prevail upon you to make our settlement the focal point of your temporary ministry here. We therefore authorized you in October last year to set in order our then highly confused church affairs. To our great joy you accepted our call to attempt to establish a Norwegian Lutheran congregation among us according to the church order of our fatherland. You have now fulfilled the terms of this call, as far as possible under present circumstances, by setting everything in proper order and in the best manner. Your work in this connection is at an end, and we feel it both necessary and obligatory to proceed to call a permanent pastor who can continue the work in the same spirit and order, so that what has been built up may not be torn down or scattered.

Your reverence's work has been richly blessed by the Lord, and we have learned to know you as a man who possesses those qualities we believe every ordained minister of the Lord in this land and in our circumstances should have. We have found in you upright zeal for the glory of God and for the true welfare of the congregation, combined with wisdom, meekness, and love. We have found in you firmness and constancy in your work, coupled with a wise insistence on respect from the laity, which is so necessary for a pastor. This respect you have retained and increased by your clean, Christian manner of life. All these are qualities which, by the Lord's gracious help, enable you to work in the holy office in a most worthy and blessed manner. This is not meant as vain flattery, but as the chief reason why we hereby respectfully extend to your reverence this call to assume the office of pastor in the Norwegian Lutheran church established by you here at Koskonong Prairie, Dane and Jefferson counties, Wisconsin Territory.

The following is what we as Christians must require of our pastor: 1) That the Word of God be preached in its truth and purity, that the most precious sacraments be administered, and, on the whole, that all churchly acts be performed in complete agreement with the church order of our fatherland Norway, just as every pastor in that church is bound by his ordination oath. 2) Because we have already learned by experience how necessary church discipline is for the maintenance of church order, we require that the pastor strictly maintain the same in accordance with the church *Ritual*. 3) That our pastor lead a pure and blameless life according to the exhortation of the Apostle Paul in I Timothy, chapter 3.

Cordially hoping that you, Pastor Dietrichson, will accept this call, we repeat what we in essence have promised already by hand and mouth when we joined the congregation: that we will render to our pastor the deference and obedience that are proper for a church member, in everything he requires and does in accordance with the church *Ritual* of our fatherland Norway. Likewise, we pledge ourselves to comply with the conditions previously drawn up and agreed to regarding the permanent pastor's salary punctually and without fail.

With a heartfelt prayer to God that he, our Father in Jesus Christ, will grant to our minister the Holy Spirit's power and gracious assistance to strive and suffer as a true and worthy soldier of God, we hereby inform you of your unanimous election as our permanent pastor. We enclose the terms governing the election of a minister for this church.

We hereby confirm that this is our will and firm resolve by our signatures.

Koskonong Prairie, Dane and Jefferson counties, Wisconsin Territory, the Norwegian Lutheran congregation here, March 3, 1845.

Then follow the signatures of all heads of families and adult members.

This is the letter of call issued to me. A rough draft had been made by the deacons of the congregation. It was then written in proper style by Pastor Clausen, to whom it had been sent for that purpose.[26] Together with this came the terms, previously referred to, governing the election of a permanent pastor. At the bottom were the signatures of the eight deacons of the church.

That all the preceding—both the election, conditions, and signatures—are in every respect in complete accord with the decision of the congregation, we the eight deacons elected by the congregation do confirm by our signatures.

O. Knudsen, Lars Johannesen Hollo, Knud Aslaksen, Gulbrand Gulbransen Holtene, Gunstein Rolfsen Omdal, Gunder J. Fladeland, Thor Kittelsen.

I replied as follows:

To the Norwegian Lutheran congregation at Koskonong Prairie, Dane and Jefferson counties: May grace and peace from God our father be richly granted you all in Jesus Christ, by the good and worthy Holy Spirit!

I have received the letter sent me by you, dear members of the Norwegian Lutheran congregation here, calling me to be your permanent pastor and spiritual counselor. From the heart [The phrase "from the heart" was a part of the "religious" language of Norway. It was used, for example, in the confessional service at Holy Communion and in the ordination rite.] I thank you, first for the evidence of your love for and confidence in me which I cannot help seeing in this unanimous call. For whatever I, an insignificant and weak instrument whom the Lord has willed to use in setting your church affairs in order, have been able to accomplish by his power, the honor is due to him, the good and wise and mighty one, to whom be praise through all eternity! With earnest prayer to God, I tried, with the ability and power which he graciously granted me to labor in the call you extended to me in October last year, to put your church affairs in order. You yourselves know what problems I faced in this respect. You yourselves know with what suspicion and discontent I had to deal in my most sincere efforts. You yourselves know how several persons, even among those who willingly joined the congregation, not to mention the antagonists from without, have tried to break down and scatter what was my most earnest purpose to build up and gather on the foundation of truth. God be merciful to them! Yet the Lord has been mighty in that which was weak, and I am sure that the congregation will receive blessing even from this opposition, if only it gives heed to the voice of God speaking through opposition.

But the church here is now so well established that, apart from God, it will depend on the church members themselves whether the church is to weather the storm both from without and from within, and whether or not the church order established here is to endure.

Through the letter of call you have now made known your request and desire that I become your pastor. I can only reply in the words which I wrote to my fatherland anticipating your call: "Should the congregation elect me," I wrote, "and should the congregation's conditions be such that I can justifiably accept, I could only see in this congregational election a call from God which I would have to accept if I were to be found faithful to him. Otherwise, what would I say when the Lord calls me to account on judgment day? True, my answer would still be weak; yet for conscience's sake I would not dare flee from and give up the work that has been begun here and for which there is hope of continuation. And so, if there should be no one in the fatherland whom intelligent, able, and Christian men consider to be far more capable than I to continue the work already begun here, and who would be willing to take my place, then I would once again traverse the Atlantic and the highways of a foreign land to work and to battle!"

Thus I wrote to my fatherland even before you had clearly expressed your wishes. And since the conditions governing the election of the permanent pastor are such that, provided they are fulfilled according to your promise, I believe it possible for me to make ends meet, my answer to you is: If it is the Lord's will that I return here—and he will surely reveal his will in the upcoming developments—then I will return to you when I have made a trip to Norway. There are certain matters to attend to if I am to stay in America for an extended period.[27]

Should there be in Norway a pastor whom earnest and able Christian men consider competent for this work, and who, out of Christian love for you, dear countrymen, and true zeal for the advancement of the Kingdom of God among you, is willing to go in my place, then I am sure you can understand that it would be most wrong of me to try to put myself forward in his stead. This would be to interfere in a clear instance of a divine call, and would certainly not be the right way for me to look after the best interests of the congregation.

God is my witness that this congregation, established by me with the help of God in this land so torn asunder by sects and parties, is dear to my heart. It has always been and will ever be my prayer and endeavor that God will preserve it on the sure foundation of the true church. God is my witness that I will always care for it in the best manner possible, so far as I am able. But would I be doing that if I did not wish to see the congregation supplied with the best and ablest minister obtainable? And if the Lord should call someone else, it would be a glorious testimony to me that he wished you well. You, dear members, should interpret this in like manner. You, too, should seek the highest gifts, and the ablest pastor that you could get is, spiritually speaking, one of the best gifts.

There is also another reason why I must tell you frankly that I cannot unconditionally accept your call. You yourselves know, as mentioned above, how much suspicion I have had to put up with from various quarters as I worked among you. If now I should reply that I accept your call unconditionally, then my opponents would have a wonderful excuse to say something like this: "Aha! Now we've got Pastor Dietrichson figured out; he knows what he's about, working and striving to set everything up, so he can take over the parish. And now he has everything just the way he wants it, etc. etc." "Avoid all appearance of evil," the apostle commands; and in order that you may see clearly what shameful liars the backbiters are also in this matter, I hereby frankly and publicly declare to you that my only purpose is to see this congregation under the leadership of the ablest possible pastor. I would therefore gladly step aside for a better man.

In order that you may understand me perfectly, I acknowledge receipt of the call to become your permanent pastor in the name of the Lord Jesus, and I promise you that, if I see it is the Lord's will, I shall return to you when I have made a trip to Norway to make the necessary arrangements. And if, in accord with God's will, I do come back, I promise that I, keeping close to him, my blessed Saviour, who is strong in those who are weak, will try to fulfill the requirements that you rightfully ask of your pastor: 1) to preach to you the Word of God in its truth and purity; to administer the most precious sacraments, and on the whole to perform all churchly matters in complete agreement with the church *Ritual* of our fatherland Norway; 2) strictly but impartially to see to it there is churchly order in accord with the church *Ritual;* 3) to strive to lead a pure and blameless life, according to St. Paul's exhortation in I Tim. 3. All of this I am in duty bound to do by my vow at ordination. Should I fail to live up to it, then you not only have the privilege and the right to dismiss me at once, but I demand that you do so. Otherwise, I would be entirely unworthy of the holy office. If, on the other hand, the Lord should clearly demonstrate that he prefers another man in my place, then you are the better served. In that case, you would not need me.

With prayer to God for you, my dear congregation, that the Lord will look in mercy upon you and order and lead and guide in everything for your best, I shall, during my stay in the fatherland, if indeed the Lord delivers me safely there, do all I can for your true welfare.

Koskonong, March 21, 1845.

J. W. C. Dietrichson
Pastor

This answer was read to the congregation on the first Sunday after Easter, confirmation Sunday, March 30, 1845, in the East Church. It was repeated on the fifth Sunday after Easter in the West Church. The congregation was well satisfied with this, and in accordance with what had been previously agreed upon by the congregation and by me regarding the best manner of arranging the affairs of the congregation during my absence, the temporary call was sent on behalf of the congregation and me to Pastor C. L. Clausen to take charge of the congregation in the interim. This temporary call, sent by me to him, was also read in both churches. [Dietrichson's lengthy letter (below), repeating much of the above and adding nothing essentially new, has been condensed.]

Reverend Pastor Clausen:[28]

Beloved brother in the holy office of the ministry! . . . The Norwegian Lutheran congregation established here has reached agreement regarding the conditions under which it will accept a permanent pastor as of April 1, and has sent me the call to accept the holy office of pastor here. Since I cannot but see a call from the Lord in this action, I must consider it, if I am to be true to him. I have replied that I acknowledge receipt of this call, and have promised to return to this church following a voyage to Norway, if no one is found in the fatherland who is judged far more able than I to continue the work that has been begun and who is willing to go in my place.

It will be necessary in any case for me to make a journey to Norway, as quickly as possible, in order to make the necessary arrangements for a prolonged stay in America if the Lord wills. Therefore, after having discussed with the congregation the best way of arranging things during my absence, we have resolved to call you, Pastor Clausen, to assume the pastoral office in the Norwegian Lutheran congregation at Koskonong during the absence of the regular pastor. . . .

If you accept this temporary call, you have, naturally, as long as you serve this congregation as your main congregation, the same right as I to demand that the congregation fulfill the obligations it has assumed in the calling of a permanent pastor.

This letter of call I hereby send to you in the blessed name of our Lord, the Triune God, in behalf of the congregation and of myself with my own signature and seal.

> J. W. C. DIETRICHSON
> Norwegian Lutheran pastor
> (L.S.)[29]

Pastor Clausen replied as follows in a letter dated March 31:

Your call to me to come to Koskonong Prairie and, during the absence of the regular pastor, to take charge of the Norwegian Lutheran congregation established there by you, I accept as a call from the Lord and do promise to fulfill as well as I am able by

God's grace, though with certain reservations. Although I am prepared to make my home at Koskonong Prairie temporarily, I cannot for the present consider Koskonong as the main congregation, except in the sense that I shall divide the time not spent among the other congregations about equally between Koskonong and Musquigo [Muskego]. Since my activity will be about the same in both places, both will in fact have to be considered "main" congregations.

This answer from Pastor Clausen was read in both churches. The congregation thereupon voted to pay Pastor Clausen a salary for the interim. This arrangement was satisfactory in every respect. I suggested that for the year from April 1, 1845, to April 1, 1846, he be paid two hundred dollars in three installments, in addition to the offerings on festival days and remuneration for ministerial acts as each saw fit. The congregation agreed to this. When Pastor Clausen arrives, he will have to work out any further details.

Since Pastor Clausen, by his own decision, either cannot or will not consider Koskonong as his main congregation, but plans to minister to Musquigo in addition to Koskonong as such, it goes without saying that this church cannot offer the salary agreed upon for a permanent pastor who would minister solely to Koskonong as his main congregation.

On March 23, 1845, Gunnul Olsen Vindeg was elected sexton for the East Church. The same day Knud Aslaksen Juve was elected for the West Church.

On April 1, 1845, arrangements were made for a parish school. Hoping to secure support from Norway for this school, I made an agreement with the *klokker* of the church, Ole Knudsen, whereby he was to hold three months of school during this calendar year for the children of the parish only. His salary was fixed at $10 per month. This school is to teach religion in accordance with the pure doctrine of the Lutheran church. It is assumed that the other subjects will be taught in the American school organized for this settlement. The parish school is under the pastor's control, and he also selects the teacher. The purchase of a school record book has been authorized, and everything pertaining to the school is entered there.

On the 1st Sunday after Easter, March 30, 1845, that most godless and hardened drunkard, Halvor Christian Pedersen Funkelien,
was publicly excommunicated according to the *Ritual*, chapter 7,
article 1.[30] Nevertheless, on Pentecost Sunday he came to church.
He was advised that he was either to sit in the place reserved for
the excommunicate or to leave the church. He refused to do
either. He was therefore ejected from the church by the *klokker*
and two of the deacons. He has accused the pastor and the three
men who ejected him of assault and battery, and we have been
found guilty, contrary to American law, by a most ignorant and
prejudiced jury. We have appealed the case to the district court in
Maddison [*sic*], where the verdict will undoubtedly be reversed.
I make mention of this matter here because it is of *ecclesiastical*
significance. It involves the question of our right to maintain our
church order. The next pastor will record the final decision in
the case.[31]

On Monday, May 12, 1845, the 2nd day of Pentecost, after the
service, Ole Knudsen Trovatten was installed as *klokker* according
to the *Ritual*. On the same day, I departed from the congregation.
Upon arrival at Musquigo on Monday, May 19, I delivered the
church book and the other things pertaining to the congregation
to Pastor Clausen.[32] From that moment he became the *temporary*
pastor of the congregation. May the Lord in his grace grant him
wisdom and power in this charge! Amen.

I hereby testify that all the preceding has occurred exactly as
recorded here.

Musquigo, May 19, 1845.[33]

J. W. C. DIETRICHSON
Norwegian Lutheran pastor

[At this point Pastor Clausen took over the recording of events
in the Koshkonong parish register. Dietrichson resumed the record upon his return from Norway in September, 1846.]

CHAPTER II

The Clausen Interim

On Friday, May 23, 1845, I, Claus Lauritz Clausen, a pastor of the Lutheran church, regularly called and ordained in accordance with the order of the Church of Norway, arrived in the Norwegian Lutheran congregation at Koskonong Prairie, Dane and Jefferson counties, Wisconsin Territory, North America. I came to take charge of this congregation in accord with the call issued to me, recorded herein on pages 222–223,[34] as temporary pastor during the permanent pastor's absence.

On May 25, the 1st Sunday after Trinity, I conducted my first public worship in the East Church, and on this occasion I read first to the congregation my certificate of ordination (translated into Norwegian)[35] and the aforementioned call to become its temporary pastor. I repeated this on the following Sunday in the West Church. Following this service on the second Sunday after Trinity, I summoned three church members—Henrich Olsen Hæve, Gaute Ingebrechtsen Gulliksrud, and Ole Larsen Strømi—to a meeting at the home of Deacon Knud Aslaken Juve. They arrived at the proper time. Already prior to the permanent pastor's departure, these men had been elected to serve as deacons in place of Ole Knudsen Trovatten, Thor Kittilsen Svimbill, and Knud Olsen Holtene. The latter two had been elected to the assessment and collection committee for the congregation and were therefore to be relieved of their offices as deacons.[36]

At this meeting the new deacons were charged with their duties according to the laws of the Church of Norway as they are outlined in Pontoppidan's *Collegium Pastorale* (pp. 587–590),[37] with the modifications necessary in our situation. Each gave me his promise and his hand that he would comply with the duties incumbent upon him in this office.

The court case between the excommunicated Halvor Chr. Ped. Funkelien and Herr Pastor Dietrichson *et al.*, referred to on p.

224, has been decided. The appeal to the district court in Maddison [sic] was not made within the time prescribed by law, and so the case could not be taken up by that court in Maddison. Consequently, the judgment of the lower court stands. It was, however, made clear on this occasion that we might retain and carry out our church order in every respect freely and without hindrance, except where it involves involuntary corporal punishment. Such punishment can only be carried out in accordance with and with the help of the civil authorities.

Some time ago, Bjørn Olsen Rom, formerly one of the parish assessors and treasurer in Deacon Gunder J. Fladland's district, moved to Texas. At a meeting of deacons and pastor, Niels Olsen Smitbakken was appointed in his place. He was at once installed and charged with the duties pertaining to this office.

According to the reply of the permanent pastor, the Rev. J. W. C. Dietrichson, to the call extended to him (recorded on pp. 219–222),[38] he pledged that, following a necessary trip to Norway, he would either return himself or secure another man in his stead whom earnest, Christian, and able men considered to be much more capable than he. Accordingly, the temporary call was issued to me. Both the congregation and I believed for sure that Pastor Dietrichson or some other pastor in his place would come back here in the course of the summer of 1846. I, therefore, saw nothing to prevent my accepting a call which came to me in the latter part of December, 1845, from the Norwegian Lutheran church in Rock Prairie[39] to be their permanent pastor. I promised Rock Prairie I would assume the sacred office of pastor among them about St. John's Day,[40] or at the latest before the end of July, 1846. I assumed that by that time Pastor Dietrichson would be back again. His first letter to us after his arrival in Norway seemed to confirm this. Later, however, a second letter has come, according to which it must be considered doubtful whether his promise to this congregation will be kept this year. I now have waited until the very limit of my time, without receiving the slightest additional information about when I may expect to be relieved of my temporary call by the permanent pastor, and I write these lines so that it may be seen that it was only for valid reasons and because of my promise to Rock Prairie that I left this congregation before the return of its permanent pastor.

Last Sunday, the 26th of this month, I preached my farewell sermon in the West Church, and on Monday, the 27th, in the East Church. God grant that this congregation which has become so dear to me may not long be without a rightly called and ordained, faithful and honest, shepherd who will preach the pure Word and rightly administer the precious sacraments and will feed the flock in green pastures and beside the still waters. God grant this by his grace.

Koskonong, July 29, 1846.

C. L. Clausen
Evangelical Lutheran pastor

CHAPTER III

My Return to Koskonong

In accordance with the promise which I, J. W. C. Dietrichson, pastor in the Norwegian Lutheran church, gave to the Koskonong congregation to return to it if God so willed and if no other capable pastor from the fatherland was willing to come in my place, I determined in Jesus' name to come back to this congregation, which is so dear to me. I made this decision as soon as it became apparent that, despite all my efforts, there was no hope for the present of getting any other able man to take charge in my stead. And so, in spite of the inner struggle it cost me to leave my fatherland again, to which so many precious bonds bind me, I sailed with my beloved wife from Norway on July 11, 1846, and came by way of Copenhagen, Hamburg, Hull, and Liverpool to New York. From New York I hurried as fast as possible to this congregation, arriving here on Sept. 23. On Sunday, Sept. 28, the 16th Sunday after Trinity, I conducted divine worship in the East Church for the first time after my return. I thus returned to the ministry to which this congregation called me on March 3, 1845; that is, to be its permanent[41] pastor for a term of five years beginning April 1, 1845. With God's gracious help, I shall try as well as I can to fulfill the requirements of this call, and shall not leave this congregation (unless the Lord should call before that time) before my term is finished, provided, of course, that the church fulfills the conditions to which it voluntarily agreed in calling a permanent pastor. It goes without saying that without the promised salary, which is certainly none too large, I cannot serve as pastor of this church. I so informed the members in a meeting held after services on the same Sunday. On the following Sunday, October 4, the 17th Sunday after Trinity, I conducted the first services in the West Church after my return. At both churches,

170

speaking from the chancel at the close of the service, I brought greetings from the fatherland and read a letter from Dyer Sørensen in Christiania (cf. p. 112) in answer to the letter of thanks the congregation sent by me to this man, for whose Christian sacrifice the congregation is so indebted. The letter is appended to this Parish Journal.[42]

I also presented to the parish a gift from the estate of the late Bishop Sørenssen of Akershus Diocese, a beautiful silver chalice which shall be its property so long as the church remains faithful to the pure doctrine and the edifying order of the church of our fatherland.[43] The cup bears the following inscription in Latin:

> Episcopo Agershusiensi
> VIRO SUMME VENERANDO
> Christiano Sørensen
> hocce poculum in pignus
> intimae Amicitiae
> et Venerationis
> deditissimus consecrat
> MATTHIAS SIGVARDT
> Episcopus Christiansandensis[44]

This cup which, according to the express desire of the giver, shall serve the congregation as an altar chalice, was given to me shortly before my departure from Christiania by Prof. Kaurin, professor of theology at the university in Christiania, as a gift to this congregation from the children of the late bishop.

During my first stay here I began a parish library with some books donated by Publisher Grøndahl in Christiania and by the Society for the Publication of Devotional Books. To these I now added two copies of my book published in Stavanger, Norway, in 1846, *Reise blandt de norske Emigranter i "De forenede nordamerikanske Fristater."*[45] I refer to this book for a record of my efforts to fulfill the promise which I gave the congregation here before my departure, namely, to do what I could for the good of the congregation while I was in the fatherland (cf. end of my answer to the letter of call from this congregation to me, pp. 219–222). In this regard, I reminded the congregation that it is again obliged to thank the fatherland that I was able to keep my promise to return, for my travel expenses were covered by voluntary cash gifts from Norway. I also informed them that a gift of sixty dollars to the parish school had been received in Norway (see my book *Reise blandt de norske Emigranter i "De forenede nord-amerikanske Fristater,"* pp. 127–128). Out of this gift plus one dollar in interest and one dollar, six shillings, as a gift to the parish school from Dyer Sørensen (the remainder of the 168 specie dollars he gave me to help defray my travel expenses), thirty dollars were paid on Dec. 12, 1846, to *Klokker* Ole Knudsen for conducting three months' school last year. His receipt for this sum was received. At the close of the church year, the congregation has in its school fund thirty-two dollars and six shillings (see p. 224 [Vol. 1 of Parish Journal]).[46]

Shortly before my departure, Gunnul Olsen Vindeg had been selected as sexton[47] in the East Church (see p. 224). As this man died on October 13, 1846, a meeting of the deacons in the east half of the parish was held on Saturday, October 24, to elect a successor. The three deacons present and the pastor chose Ole Syvertsen in his place. He accepted the office. Following the service on Sunday, November 8, the 22nd Sunday after Trinity, in the presence of the congregation in the East Church, he was charged with the duties of sexton. These include responsibility for the care of church building and cemetery, that nothing belonging to the church be lost or damaged. It is also his duty to collect and, when required, to give account of the income received by the church. This income is not only from voluntary contributions but also from (1) fees charged each new member upon his acceptance, in accordance with a resolution adopted by the congregation that every family father and every bachelor shall pay one dollar when he is enrolled as a member, and every confirmed girl shall pay fifty cents (though it is stipulated that due consideration should be given the financial status of the individual); and (2) thirty-seven and a half cents for the burial of every nonmember in the parish cemetery. The sexton is also to provide the necessary bread and wine and the candles for Holy Communion. To cover this latter expense, he is to receive two cents from each communion guest. It is also his duty to keep the church neat and clean. He shall keep his accounts in a book authorized by the pastor.

In place of Deacon Gunder Jørgensen Fladland, who has been

ill for a long time and often neglectful of his duties and whose
assigned territory is too close to that of Gunstein Rolfsen Omdahl
anyway, the pastor and the other three deacons, on October 24,
1846, elected Gisle Helliksen Venaas. He accepted the office. On
Sunday, November 8, the 22nd Sunday after Trinity, in the presence of the congregation following the service, he was charged
with his duties and gave his promise and his hand to uphold them
(cf. p. 216).

Knud Aslaksen Juve was elected sexton for the West Church
shortly before my departure from the congregation (see p. 224).
As this man wished to resign, the pastor and the deacons present
on November 15, 1846, the 23rd Sunday after Trinity, elected in
his place Halvor Laurantsen Fosheim. He accepted the office, and
on the same Sunday, at the close of the service in the West
Church, was charged with his duties as sexton (see pp. 228–229).

CHAPTER IV

The Church Year 1846–47 [48]

On December 21, 1846, the Monday before Christmas, I moved into the dwelling erected for the pastor of this congregation. It was then sufficiently finished so that it could be occupied. Besides the house, there are twenty acres of land, purchased for $47.50 from Knud Olsen Aaretuen and located on the east side of the northeast quarter of the southwest quarter of section no. 20, township no. 6, range no. 12, in Dane County, Wisconsin. For the present the house consists of three rooms with kitchen and pantry and is built of oak. The sitting room is furnished with a little stove and seven lengths of stovepipe, each about eighteen inches long. A simple outbuilding has been erected a short distance from the house to the southwest. The congregation has fenced in about fourteen acres of the parsonage land. Each member was assessed ten fence posts for every forty acres of land he owned. The fenced-in area lies between the projected road to Maddison on the north side and the projected road to Catfish[49] on the south side. On the east and west sides the fence follows the boundary lines of the twenty acres. The rest of the land (not fenced in) is situated on the north side of the Maddison road, which cuts through the land. Nine or ten acres have been plowed for the pastor's use.

A meeting of the *klokker* and the deacons was called for Friday, February 12, 1847, at the parsonage. The following were present: the *klokker* and seven deacons, Gunstein Rolfsen Omdahl, Lars Johannesen Hollo, Gisle Helliksen Venaas, Gulbrand Gulbrandsen Holtene from the east half of the parish, and Ole Larson Strøm, Henrik Olsen Hæve, and Gaute Ingebretsen Gulliksrud from the west half. They met here with the pastor. Knud Aslaksen was absent. Following is a report of this meeting:

(1) The membership roll was examined. Because the membership of the West Church is so scattered, it was divided into five

174

districts. The East Church was divided into four as before. A list of the members in each district was given to the deacons present. All deacons promised to continue in office until fall, when new men were to be installed.

(2) A discussion about the most discreet and best manner of collecting the pastor's salary was held. The pastor suggested that, since the settlement had been visited with much sickness during the past year, he might await payment of his salary for the October term last year and for the March term this year until May 1st next. He further proposed that announcement be made in the churches that instead of having his salary collected by assessors, the members could pay their voluntary contributions for the past two terms directly to the pastor some time before May 1. He recommended that obstinate members, who were unwilling to bear the burdens of the church, be deprived of sharing in its benefits. However, instead of using the civil arm to compel them to live up to the terms of the agreement—which action lies within our power[50]—he suggested dropping such persons from the church membership. This proposal was unanimously adopted.

(3) Agreement was reached regarding the form in which the deed to the parsonage land should be written. It was, of course, early perceived that the deed could not be made out in the names of all the individual members of the church, whose numbers increased or decreased according to circumstances. In such a situation a new deed would have to be drawn up every time someone joined the church or withdrew from it. Furthermore, we realized that the deed could not be made out to the whole assembled congregation as a body. In the first place, according to the law here, no religious group can have joint right of ownership unless it is incorporated as a body in the United States, and this is impossible until Wisconsin Territory has been received as an independent state in the Union.[51] In the second place, even if such a deed could be drawn up, it would in all likelihood occasion much division and disagreement in the congregation every time a member of the church wished to withdraw or was dropped from membership because of perversity or excommunicated on account of ungodliness. Such an individual might demand his share in the parsonage land and buildings, and increase his demand each year and thereby engender hate and strife. It was therefore agreed

that the most correct form for the deed would be to make it out to the pastor and his successors in the pastoral office for the Norwegian Lutheran congregation. In this way, we would ensure that land and buildings would be used as intended, and all the aforementioned problems would be avoided. This form of deed would obviously not give the present pastor or his successors in the office any right of ownership except that which he has as pastor, i.e., to use the property while in office.[52]

For the same reason, the deed to the half acre of the southeast corner of the northwest quarter of the southwest quarter of section 26, township 6, range 12, Dane County, on which the East Church is erected was drafted in the same form. And so the deed to the parsonage land was drawn up and signed by Knud Olsen Aaretuen, in whose hands was the deed to that forty of which the twenty acres are a part. In the presence of witnesses, he received from the pastor the forty-seven dollars and fifty cents for the land. His wife, however, whose signature was also required by law, and who is a stubborn and godless woman, at first refused to sign. She gave as her reason that she wanted to cause trouble for her husband, with whom she often disagrees. She has since maintained that it was because some ungodly and perverse disturbers of the peace within and without the congregation had convinced her that the deed was incorrectly drawn up. A few days before the meeting she had indeed promised Schoolmaster Iver Ingebretsen, whom I sent to her regarding this matter, that she would sign the deed if the deacons would personally assure her that they thought it proper. Yet, when she was called to the meeting she refused to come. What trickery and intrigue she and the other godless troublemakers really intend by this perverseness time will tell. It is to be hoped that truth and right will prevail in this matter also.

(4) The deacons were questioned concerning the best way of getting around the pastor's shortage of timber for fuel. Up to now, he has had to buy fuel at a cost of one dollar a week. It was decided that each deacon should require the members in his district to furnish one load of fuel per family. It was thought that, if this was done, there would be sufficient wood for at least two years.

(5) The pastor questioned the deacons concerning the Chris-

tian and moral conditions in the parish, and was told that, on the whole, conditions were good.

(6) As the pastor had heard that there was some grumbling about him here and there among some of the members, the deacons were asked whether they had anything to complain about on their part regarding his practices or about his general conduct as pastor. Their unanimous reply was that, far from having anything to complain about, they had, as usual, every reason to give him the best commendation. They also declared that they had not run across any complaint against the pastor, except from the usual enemies outside the church and from a few perverse and godless individuals within it.

(7) It was decided that the west half of the parish, which is too large for one school district, should be divided into two: the southern and the northern. In the northern, the *klokker* is retained as teacher; in the southern, Ole Laurantsen, who taught during Pastor Clausen's stay here. Iver Ingebretsen was retained as schoolteacher for the east half of the parish.

For a long time both pastor and congregation had recognized the importance of incorporating the congregation in the United States, for only such incorporation can insure the church a completely valid right of ownership according to the law here. We therefore received with joy a law passed by the legislature in Maddison in February, 1847, entitled: "An Act to provide for the incorporation of the Protestant Episcopal Church and other religious denominations in the Territory of Wisconsin." In conformity with this law of incorporation, announcement was made on two successive holy days in both churches that a meeting would be held in the West Church to which all voting members (all males of age 21 or over) were invited, in order, in agreement with the law, (1) to elect two persons to preside over the election of trustees for the congregation, and (2) to vote for such persons as they considered able to act in this capacity.

This meeting was held [one] Sunday,[53] following services in the West Church. *Klokker* Ole Knudsen and Deacon Henrik Olsen Hæve were chosen as the two who should direct the election of trustees, decide who was entitled to vote, and record the names of those elected by a majority of those present. (In the law these two persons are called "returning officers.") The following three persons were then elected trustees: Gabriel Bjørnsen, Aslak Olsen Olsnæs, and Tron Kittilsen Svimbill. Their term of office was set at one year from the day of election.[54]

Under the provisions of the law, the two men elected as "returning officers" shall under their hand and seal draw up a certificate stating that such election of trustees has taken place according to the conditions stipulated in the law. According to the law, this certificate, to be a valid legal document, must be recorded with the register of deeds of this county. This was done. Ole Knudsen and Henrik Olsen Hæve, the "returning officers," met with the newly elected trustees in the parsonage, where the certificate was filled out. It was later recorded.

According to the law referred to, the duties of the trustees consist in making contracts with pastor and other functionaries in the church regarding their salaries, in administration of all the financial affairs of the congregation, and in exercising general supervision over and giving account to the congregation regarding all its temporal affairs. They are not to involve themselves in the spiritual and purely churchly matters of the congregation.[55]

The trustees have taken charge of the accounts of the church, and they have drafted documents containing the salary terms under which the pastor ("the rector of the congregation") and the *klokker* are called. In the certificate the trustees are called "Trustees for the Norwegian Lutheran Church at Koskonong Prairie, Dane and Jefferson Counties, W. T." The congregation is to be called by this name "forever," and, under it, the trustees are to be considered "a body corporate and politic."[56]

Although the location chosen by the congregation for the parsonage is very convenient for members of the congregation (halfway between the two churches), and although it may be well chosen in other respects, still, for the present pastor, it has truly proved to be the most unfortunate place that could have been chosen in the entire Norwegian settlement. For if what Luther says in his explanation of the Fourth Petition is true, that to daily bread belong also "peace and good neighbors," then it has become apparent here that the pastor lacks that part of his "daily bread." The fact is that the parsonage is surrounded by the meanest people in the whole congregation and by the worst neighbors that a man could have to put up with. I am robbed of outward peace by the most tiresome quarreling and carrying on. How much strife and unpleasantness that unchristian woman Anne Knudsd[atter] Aaretuen has sought to stir up has been shown already in this book, pp. 230–231.[57] Her husband is probably more stable and outwardly more refined, but he is surely as hostile. They have now moved away, but her unchristian parents, both of whom are fighters and drinkers, of whom the mother is the worse, are our nearest neighbors on the north.

Lars Gjellum, a weak wretch who lets himself be misled and used as a tool by others, is our nearest neighbor on the south. Near Gjellum lives the worst of them all, Thomas Johnsen Braaten, from the neighborhood of Kongsberg [Norway]. This man, who carries the reputation from Norway of a profane drunkard and brawler, has of late certainly shown that he intends to live up to his reputation. Since shortly after Christmas there has hardly been a week that this man has not either by day or by night used abusive language about the pastor, cursed and shouted, and sung the vilest and lewdest songs about the pastor, sometimes just outside and sometimes inside the fence at the parsonage. He has attempted to disturb my wife's peace and mine, and has been somewhat successful, I must admit. Both my wife and I have been deeply offended at such treatment from a church member to whom I had never spoken a harsh word until after he began these ungodly sprees. Shameful abuse of my honor both as a man and as a pastor, coupled with threats against my life, have poured from the mouth of this man, drunk or sober. And it has been easy for him to get drunk, since one of his friends and companions, Mr. Ole Ingebretson Homstad from Overhalden in the Trondhjem Diocese, also one of our neighbors, has for some time supplied Thomas and his kind with liquor. (See also the remarks about these people in the congregational rolls, pp. 197, 199, 201.)[58]

There has thus been continual strife and disagreement, alarm, and disturbance ever since shortly after Christmas. This has offended and disturbed not only the pastor's household, but to a greater or lesser degree the whole congregation. The effect on the weak members has been that they have sided more or less with these manifest enemies of the church, who, in their hatred for and persecution of pastor and church order, seem to have provided a rallying point that commends itself to some.

(It may perhaps seem to many that I have used too harsh and sharp words here and elsewhere in this Parish Journal. But it must be remembered that I am a servant of God's Word. It is my duty to speak the truth, however sharp it may seem, and to call persons and things by their right names, no matter how ugly they may sound. What I have written here and elsewhere about these persons is the truth, and I comfort myself with the knowledge that every truly upright and Christian member of this congregation who has followed the course of events with reasonable attention will bear me out.)

As long as these disturbances were confined to my own residence, I thought it best, no matter how much I might deplore it, to endure them. But when, as happened on Sunday, September 19, the 10th Sunday after Trinity, it became apparent that we were not even to have peace in our house of worship, I was convinced that as pastor of this congregation I could no longer stand for this. On that Sunday Thomas Johnsen Braaten came to the East Church. He first proceeded to stir up all the trouble he could outside the church by calling the people together and reading to them from no. 6 of a paper published in the Musquigo settlement called *Nordlyset*.[59] Someone has submitted an article in which he accused me of fraud and deceit in the disposition of a sum of $1100 (800 Norwegian specie dollars) which he asserts I have received from Norway "for the benefit of Norwegians in Wisconsin." (Compare this accusation with the accounting I made to the church here immediately upon my return from Norway. This statement, together with my answer to the accusation, is briefly outlined in no. [original illegible] of the same paper.)

After reading the article, Thomas proceeded to comment with profanity and slanders against me, calling me a thief, a scoundrel, etc., etc. I arrived at church later than usual that day. I soon noticed an unusual stir and commotion among the people. I knew the reason for it, because the day before Thomas and his friend Lars Gunderson Gjellum and another fellow (not a church member) had come to my house and intruded upon my study. When I saw that Thomas had only come to rant and rave as usual, in the presence of witnesses I chased him out. He continued to rave out-of-doors, and swore that on the next day the people in church would hear more from him than from the pastor.

I therefore thought it best before officiating as pastor that Sunday to address the congregation from the chancel regarding the accusation against me in the paper. I related how the godless Thomas Johnsen and other like-minded individuals now sought to use this as evidence against me. I reminded the congregation that I had spoken to them previously about this, and that I had made an accounting to them for the money received from Norway and expended, as was my duty. While I spoke, Mr. Thomas stormed into the church and with an insolent air stationed himself with his friends by the door. There he stood, laughing and whispering, and even began to talk out loud in opposition to what I said about him. I demanded that he be quiet, and said that if he would not, I would feel compelled to leave. He was quiet for a while, but then he began again, and so I declared that either he or I would have to leave. There was a tumult and a commotion, but Thomas stayed where he was. He swore that he would not leave and that he would see whether anyone dared lay hands on him. Meanwhile, I left the church and prepared to drive home.

Shortly after I arrived home, the parsonage was filled with the most faithful and upright members of the east half of the parish. They asked me sorrowfully what they should do. I then demanded, as evidence that they did not share the opinion of Thomas and his companions and as a testimony that they loved and honored me as pastor, that the whole congregation should bring suit against Thomas Johnsen [Braaten] for his godless conduct. I asked that they accuse him (1) of disturbing our worship, and (2) of repeatedly threatening the life of the pastor and disturbing my wife's peace and mine. I further stated that if the congregation did not do this, and thus assure me of peace in church and in my home, I would feel compelled to resign from the pastoral office and to leave a place where I could not have what I considered necessary to the carrying out of my office. In this situation a large part of the congregation showed an energy and a determination which really brought me comfort and joy in my sorrow at such ungodliness. Messengers were out all that night arranging a meeting for the following day at the home of

one of the trustees, Gabriel Bjørnsen. Here 112 of the family
fathers of the church voted to bring suit against Thomas, as I had
asked, and pledged to share the expense connected with the case.
I, of course, took no part in this meeting or its decisions.

Accordingly, Thomas was charged with having disturbed the
congregation on that Sunday. But in the meantime, he became
suspicious and was therefore nowhere to be found when a "con-
stable" (a kind of policeman) came to arrest him on the following
day. He was not actually apprehended until the end of the week.
He was arraigned before the justice of the peace but, at the request of his lawyer, the coarse and somewhat notorious Mr.
Botkin,[60] the hearing was postponed until Tuesday, September
28, so as to cause the congregation so much more bother by having its members appear in vain. In the meantime, Thomas's friend
Ole Ingebretsen Homstad put up bail for him. The day came for
the trial, and Thomas was acquitted, despite the clear and specific
wording of the law, which on this point reads as follows: "That
every person who on the Lord's day, or at any other time, shall
willfully interrupt or disturb any assembly of people met for
the worship of God, within the place of such meeting or out of
it, shall be punished by fine not exceeding twenty dollars, not less
than five dollars."[61] This law was clearly intended to ensure peace
and quiet for every religious assembly, and to protect not only
the actual hour of worship, but also its purpose in gathering. Yet
the jury found the accused innocent because of the foul language
that Mr. Botkin used against both pastor and congregation, and
against the Lutheran church in general, whose order and rules he
tried to present as being dangerous for the blessed freedom here.

The reasons for such a verdict, directly contrary to law and
justice, can only be these: First, that the members of the jury, who
were under oath, forgot both oath and duty because Mr. Botkin,
due to the ill will which this politician has for our congregation,
wanted it that way (this man, who was elected to the legislature
this year [1847?] by the Whigs[62] of Dane County, is the unchal-
lenged leader of a political clique here in the county); secondly,
because according to the judgment of the Americans themselves,
Dane County is one of the worst in Wisconsin with regard to
public officials, most of whom are base fellows who are not at all
concerned about the truth; and, finally, because contempt for

Norwegians in general, and hatred for our congregation in particular, determined the outcome. This contempt and this hatred
were clearly manifested every time a witness for the congregation
was called to testify against the accused, and in the joy and satis-
faction among most of the Americans present when Braaten, with
whom they sympathized, was acquitted.

(I have so thoroughly reported on these events in this journal
because it seems likely that in the history of the Norwegian
Lutheran church here in Wisconsin, long after my time, they will
be of importance. It is precisely the details in a case that make it
possible for an outsider to gain a somewhat clear insight into
conditions of the past.)

These tiresome and involved conditions prompted me to call a
meeting of the congregation for Sunday, October 3, 1847, at the
parsonage. (This place was chosen instead of one of the churches
both because of convenience and because it is reported that Mr.
Thomas Johnsen has threatened to be present at next Sunday's
meeting in the church and to create another disturbance.)

At this meeting, I intend to read a letter presenting my reasons
for asking the congregation to release me from my promise and
obligation to continue as its pastor until April 1, 1850, unless the
congregation can take such steps as will ensure me peace in
church and at home from Mr. Thomas Johnsen and others like
him. Should the congregation be amenable to this, I shall ask
that it give me a testimony concerning the discharge of my duties
here, so that I may resign and leave. The letter to the congregation on this occasion reads as follows:

To the Norwegian Lutheran congregation at Koskonong
Prairie, Dane and Jefferson counties, Wisconsin Territory:

Grace be unto you and peace from God our Father and
the Lord Jesus Christ by the Holy Spirit!

Dear church members:

The reason I have called you together today in my residence,
and the reason I have written this letter to you, instead of our
worshiping together as usual in one of our consecrated churches,

are to be found in the disturbances which have occurred lately in the congregation, at the instigation of the unchristian Thomas Johnsen Braaten (whose name has been stricken from the church rolls) and others. Their purpose has obviously been to make me as pastor of this church so sick and tired of my stay here that the church order established among you shall be brought to naught, and a new one formed according to the evil wishes of the unbelieving, the fleshly minded, and the godless.

It is sufficiently well known by those among you who have followed with some attention the course of events in our congregation, that ever since shortly after the parsonage was built, and continuing until this very day, there has been turmoil and strife which has disturbed and offended the peace of my home and the members of the congregation. It is generally known that the person who has been the meanest and most godless among the pastor's neighbors is the aforementioned Thomas Johnsen Braaten. He especially has been the evil instrument through whom the troubles to which I refer have been brought about. You know how this man seems to be saturated with hatred for the pastor, because I, as my duty as a minister of God's Word bids me, have spoken "evil of the evil" that is in him and in others like him. He is full of ill will toward the congregation of which he once was a member. He has been excommunicated, and no longer has nor can have a part in the congregation's blessings, unless he experience a true and radical conversion and shows that a complete change has taken place in him—which may God graciously grant! You know how he, drunk and sober, almost every week since New Year's Day, has sought to disturb the peace of our home day and night by shouting, swearing, cursing and bellowing the vilest, filthiest songs about the pastor, songs which he probably composed himself. You know that he has not even hesitated to threaten my life.

I must confess that my mind and heart have strongly rebelled against such treatment from one who has been a member of my congregation. As all of you have done, upon joining the congregation, he gave me his promise and his hand to esteem, honor, and obey his pastor. Still, I thought it right to endure all this as long as the trouble he made did not go beyond my residence. But now that he has also disturbed the peace in and around our church with his cursing and swearing, and since it appears that I am to be denied respite from the persecution of this tool of the evil spirit even during the few hours that we gather together to hear the Word of God, the struggle has become too much for me. I do not consider it proper for a pastor, because of his sacred office, to endure such treatment.

If a man had dared thus to curse, slander, and threaten his minister back home in the fatherland, we know that the law would ensure the minister protection and would severely punish the guilty one. But we have seen with our own eyes how those that are responsible for upholding the law here make their decisions contrary to all that is just and true. The result is that such evil persons are allowed to go free.

You all know how this man behaved, both outside and inside our church, on the 16th Sunday after Trinity, and you know also how the congregation's most just charge against him was treated, contrary to the clear wording of the law. To the faithful members of the congregation, who showed an earnest zeal to defend and maintain order and peace in their church by bringing suit against Thomas Johnsen, I owe my warm acknowledgment and thanks for the love and respect for church discipline and the ministerial office they displayed. Not because I hate the man, but because from the heart I hate the evil which he loves and therefore speaks and does, it was comfort and joy to me in the midst of my sorrow to see the speed and determination with which the church members adopted, and, as far as they were able, carried out the resolution to oppose this evil. I only regret that you thus incurred expenses without attaining our objective, which surely would have been the case before enlightened and just magistrates.

But, my friends, permit me to get to the real purpose for which I have written this letter to you. I consider it right to make a request of you in view of the aforementioned offenses, unless in some way or other I can be assured of peace, first in church and also at home. I am, dear church members, a weak and sinful man who cannot but grow tired and weary of all the troubles and strife which I have had to struggle against here, particularly of late; I am also tired of the lack of appreciation and the evil suspicion which have been my lot in spite of earnest and honest endeavors among you.

Well do I know that we all, and especially a minister of the church, must "pass through much tribulation." It is my daily prayer and endeavor to receive and utilize that power which God for Jesus' sake by his Holy Spirit would give us all, and especially to the servants of the church. I pray that I may be able to endure the difficult and evil times with patience and to practice humility in better and happier days. But I also know that there are conditions and circumstances which, while they may not justify, yet may excuse a poor, weak, and wretched person before God and man for desiring to leave a place where he believes he can accomplish nothing. So much the more ought a pastor to have the right to resign from a place where experience teaches him that conditions are such that he cannot administer his office in the manner his oath and duty demand.

You, my friends, know that in response to the call of March 3, 1845, sent to me by the congregation which had just then been established here, I gave the promise that, after a trip to Norway, I would return to you if no other pastor from Norway would come in my place. You know that I kept my promise regardless of what it might have cost me. It is now something over a year since I returned to become your permanent pastor. It is still my intention to keep my word to you, if you will live up to your promises, so that I can live among you. In that case, I will remain and work with you during the full term for which you called me. I am a servant called by this congregation and consecrated by the church, and I will not break my promise. But my heartfelt prayer and request of you, presented herewith to the assembled congregation, is that the congregation itself will release me from my obligation so that I may resign my office here and leave. I make this petition and hope it will be fulfilled. Moreover, I hope the church can adopt such measures, Christian and legal, which will ensure me peace, first and foremost in the churches and also in my home, from Thomas Johnsen and others like him.

As I say, it is by no means my intention to break my promise to you, no more than it is my intention to run away from my parish without your consent. On the contrary, it is my intention, if in one way or another I can be assured of peace and if your promises to me are fulfilled, to continue among you to the end of my term. True, I often miss and long for and always will remember my beloved fatherland, where I hope that God has a happier and better position for me. Nevertheless, I shall be content to work with confidence among you if only outward peace, one of the greatest temporal blessings, is not denied me, and conditions become such that I am not hindered in the performance of my duties.

It may indeed seem harsh that so many people should suffer because of the wickedness and ungodliness of certain individuals. Indeed, there is no one among you who finds this harder or more sorrowful than I. I regret that the church order here begun will be disturbed in this way, or at least be interrupted for a time. But, my friends, we must remember that this is the way of the world, the necessary result of sin and wickedness which brings punishment upon those who do not seem to have any share in it. The wickedness of one single man often brings misery to thousands, and almost every home in a society sooner or later comes to grief because of the sin of one or another who at some time has come under its roof. We must also acknowledge the sad truth that, even though there are many honest and upright members in this congregation who really have made great sacrifices and have borne all the burdens of the church, there is yet much spiritual sloth and apathy. Christians and members of the true church ought to practice zealous prayer against evil and severity in its punishment.

O my friends! If our whole congregation, both in church and at home, would more earnestly and fervently pray our holy Lord's Prayer, and especially the second and the last petitions, "Thy Kingdom come" and "deliver us from evil"; if every church member had worked more earnestly and more zealously that this might come to pass; if the members of the church in general had complied with the earnest exhortation of the Lord's Word and my oft-repeated warning to shun and scorn all evil wherever it meets us, and especially in the present situation; if the clear and express admonition of the Apostle Paul in I Cor. 5:11 & 13: "But rather I wrote to you not to associate with anyone who bears the name of brother if he is guilty of immorality or greed or is an idolator, reviler, drunkard, or robber—not even to eat with such a one. . . . Drive out the wicked person from you" had been heeded; if

only there had been sufficient Christian strength in the congregation to demonstrate a proper contempt and disgust for the ungodliness of this evil man, instead of consorting with him in one way
or another, either from fear of men or from misguided politeness
—then this wickedness and effrontery would not have made such
inroads.

God's Holy Word and the admonition of Paul to every member
of the Lord's church, II Cor. 6:14, 15, 17 is: "Do not be mis-
mated with unbelievers. For what partnership have righteousness
and iniquity? Or what fellowship has light with darkness? What
accord has Christ with Belial? Or what has a believer in common
with an unbeliever? Therefore come out from them, and be
separate from them, says the Lord. . . ." These solemn words of
the Lord have been rendered powerless or have been completely
forgotten among a large part of this congregation. Evil has gained
the upper hand among us to an extent that otherwise would not
have been the case. And unless the Lord's Spirit succeeds in dis-
ciplining the people and in opening their eyes to a more earnest
and a higher endeavor and in giving them the Christian courage
and strength to oppose evil, the Lord will surely remove the light
of his church from this place, either for a long time or forever.
My friends, the cause of the strife and disturbance which seem
now to have reached a climax here is, to be sure, most manifest
in the consciously impenitent and ungodly people among us. But
even if more hidden and secret, it is also to be sought in the many
who are outwardly more respectable but who are inwardly spiritually dead and lukewarm, who are not, as Christians should be,
zealous and earnest (albeit in love) against the evil ones.

I say this, dear members, not because I wish to find fault with
you, but because I must speak the truth to you and help you to
see that mention of the injustice of the many suffering for the
few is not altogether correct. I must also frankly tell you, my
friends, that I am certain that even if I should terminate my
ministry among you, and there consequently should be little
prospect of church order among you (at least for some time), the
more upright and faithful among you would surely be grieved.
But the greater part, even though they today shed momentary
tears, would soon forget not only me and what I have tried so
hard to do for you, but also the church to which they have

belonged. They would wind up either joining some sect or living their lives in complete disregard for things spiritual and eternal.

This spiritual lukewarmness among the great majority of the congregation is also the cause of the sluggishness and reluctance which so many display when called upon to sacrifice for the common good of the church. The living spirit of God has, by the blessings of the church, the preaching of God's Word and the administration of the sacraments, been able to awaken only a part of the congregation from its spiritual slumber. This lukewarmness, which the Word of God depicts as the worst trait in a member of the church, cannot but contribute its share toward making a pastor weary.

Understand me aright then! Since I realize that I am the called servant of this congregation and that I am bound to it by sacred word and promise, I also know that the congregation alone, and not I myself, can release me from my obligation. If the church cannot take such steps or find such means in accordance with the requirements of Christianity and the law of the land which can secure peace, first in our church (so necessary in order that I may carry out my duties as pastor) and next in my home (so necessary for every man if his life is not to be miserable and bitter), then it is my heartfelt prayer and request to the congregation that it release me from my promise to be its minister. Should the congregation agree, and should it further recognize that I can no longer hold out under the present circumstances, I request a testimony concerning my manner of life and my conduct in office during the time I have been the pastor of this church.

If, however, the congregation is able to find such means and adopt such measures as can assure me of peace, then I am willing for the sake of the congregation, whose churchly affairs and spiritual well-being will always be upon my heart, to continue to function as its pastor to the end of my term.

I shall permit the congregation to consider this matter until next Sunday, and I hereby request that by that time a proper written answer to this letter be given me, clearly and definitely informing me whether it proposes to release me from my promise or whether it has been able to take such steps as will permit a pastor to carry on his work here.

May God by his spirit and grace be with you all.

The parsonage of Koskonong Norwegian Lutheran
Church, Oct. 3, 1847

J. W. C. DIETRICHSON
Pastor[63]

To this letter the congregation replied that it would do everything possible from its side to ensure the peace for church and
parsonage, and asked that I remain here. On the following Sunday
I promised to try to continue in office until spring, and that if
things are quiet during that time I shall endeavor to remain until
the expiration of my term of call.

CHAPTER V

The Church Year 1847–48

For the new church year the following persons were elected deacons: Hellik Gundersen Vashøvd, Amund Andersen, Kittil Kittilsen Strømmen, and Even Stenersen Bilstad for the eastern half of the parish, and Neri Hauge, Anver Groven, Ole Qualen, Ole Gilderhuus, and Lars Røthe for the western half. They were installed in the customary manner following services in the churches. As of the New Year, Anders Johannesen Tømmerstig was retained as sexton in the East Church and Endre Endresen Rudi in the West Church.

At the pastor's request, a singing school was begun by Ole Knudsen in the East Church and by Aslak Olsen Olsnæs in the West.

At the close of the service on Ascension Day, June 1, 1848, announcement having been made on three preceding holy days, three new trustees were elected: Iver Knudsen Seim, Anders Sandersen Bondalsgaard, and Richard Bjørnsen Rotkjøn.

Report on the Parish School for the Last Church Year

Three months of school were held in the east half of the parish last winter by *klokker* Ole Knudsen. In the west half, which is divided into northern and southern districts, Aslak Olsen Olsnæs conducted the school one month in the north, and Lars Knudsen Aaker three months in the south. This was accomplished despite obstacles of various kinds: the distance between church members, the unwillingness of several to contribute as needed to pay the expenses, and the lack of capable teachers. These three men proved to be capable teachers. Their salaries have been paid partly by voluntary contributions, augmented by the money that was donated from Norway for the school fund.

Following are the accounts of the parish school:

INCOME

Gifts from Norway:
(1) from Pastor Brodtkorb $50.00
(2) Johannes Jørgensen, Inner
    Haavig of Hiltenes   10.00
(3) Remainder of Pastor Diet-
    richson's travel money,
    donated by Dyer Sørensen   1.75
(4) Interest on money rec'd
    from Norway (from Jørgen-
    sen and Brodtkorb)   1.30
Gift from Torbjørn Gundersen
    Fladland   0.25
Gift from Ole Colbart   1.50
Gift from Ole Larsen   1.00

Total, from October,
1846, to end of church
year, 1848, INCOME $65.80
Balance in treasury $15.48

EXPENSE

Ole Knudsen's salary, for
    three months school,
    church year 1845–6 $30.00
Ole Knudsen, for ½ month
    of school   5.00
Lars Knudsen Aaker, for
    teaching in west half of
    parish, south district   5.80
Paid to Ole Knudsen for
    school in east half   8.52
To Aslak Olsen Olsnæs for
    teaching in north district of
    west half of parish   1.00

EXPENSE $50.32

During this church year there has been a blessed peace and quiet in the congregation, for which we cannot be thankful enough to the Lord. Our church order, which throughout the previous year was threatened by so many enemies, now seems to be built on a solid foundation. Regarding moral conditions in the congregation, there is not generally any grounds for complaint, except that, alas, drunkenness is prevalent among some of the members.

May God help us in Christ, and grant us the assistance of his Spirit in order that this evil and every other grievous thing among the members of his church may more and more vanish, and may the Kingdom of God in righteousness, peace, and joy in the Holy Spirit increase more and more in us all. Amen, for Jesus' sake!

The parsonage of Koskonong Norwegian Lutheran
congregation, December 2, 1848

J. W. C. DIETRICHSON
Pastor

[This ends volume I of the original Parish Journal. The chronicle, which reappears on p. 200 of volume II becomes the content of our chapter VI and chapter VII.]

CHAPTER VI

Toward the Founding of a Synod [64]

During this year the same persons as last year have served as deacons, with the exception that in the east half of the parish Amund Andersen has been replaced by Johannes Johnsen Berge and Even Stenersen Bilstad by Tollef Johannesen Backhuus. In the west half, Anver Groven resigned and Johannes Menæs took his place. As of the New Year, Halvor Larsen Kravig was retained as sexton for the East Church and Endre Endresen Rudi continued to serve as sexton of the West Church.

Since the membership of the west half of the congregation has increased considerably, it was decided, in order to take better care of the graves in the cemetery there, to appoint a cemetery custodian. It shall be his duty to see that no grave is less than six feet deep, and that it is dug in the place he indicates. For every nonmember burial, he is to collect thirty-seven cents if the deceased is an adult, and eighteen cents if the deceased is under fourteen years of age. He is responsible to the trustees for this part of the church's income, but is entitled to a fee of six cents for each grave he assigns. Ole Knudsen Dyrland was elected to this position. In his keeping are a spade and a pickaxe which were purchased for that purpose by the church.

Because there has been so much sickness this year—cholera, tuberculosis,[65] and other kinds, especially in the east half of the parish—graveyard regulations have repeatedly been strongly enforced. Application must be made to the sexton for assignment of graves, and they must be dug under his supervision to a depth of at least six feet. Since the east half of the parish is not as large as the west, it was thought unnecessary to appoint a special person as graveyard custodian, but rather to have the sexton assume these duties. The same rule regarding burial fees for nonmembers applies alike in both churches.

As trustees for this year, the following persons were elected on Ascension Day, 1849 (see volume I, pp. 232–233): Ole Laurantsen Hopedalen, Gaute Ingebretsen Gulliksrud, Iver Knudsen Gilderhuus. Prior to the election, however, it was agreed that the outgoing trustees should continue in office until the work connected with the well at the parsonage, begun under their supervision, is completed. The following persons were chosen to audit the accounts of the outgoing trustees before they turn them over to the new ones: Ole Knudsen, Tjortolt Skaatøe, Christen Hole, Knud Gilderhuus, Knud Aaker.

With regard to the parish school, it may be said that perennial hindrances made it difficult this year, too, to accomplish anything beneficial. These hindrances include the distance between church members, which forces us to hold school alternately in the various homes; a lack of capable teachers; and an unwillingness on the part of members to contribute the necessary funds. It should be appreciatively acknowledged that a great many of the church members, among others especially those immediately surrounding the West Church, are notable exceptions to this last statement. In the east half of the parish, both of the teachers are ineffective, but in the west half Amund Bjørnsen is an especially capable man. The persons who taught last year were not willing to continue this year.

In order to improve the faltering school situation a little, the pastor suggested the establishment of Sunday schools. For this purpose some Christian-minded men were appointed. They kindly agreed, without pay, to gather the children in the neighborhood every Sunday afternoon and instruct them. In the east half of the parish, the following persons accepted this task: Iver Seim, Kittil Stenersen, Ole Scheng, Ole Teigen, and Michael Strømme; in the west half, Knud Juve, Johannes Melaas, Knud Aaker, Halvor Dahl, Jens Tærum, Anfind Hansen.

On those Sundays this summer when the Lord's Supper has not been celebrated, the children have met for catechization in the churches.[66] The pastor has visited some of the Sunday schools in the west half of the parish and has had the greatest cause to rejoice at the diligence displayed by the teachers. We have every reason to believe that these schools have had a good effect.

It is greatly to be regretted that the singing schools begun in the churches by Ole Knudsen and Aslak Olsen lasted but a short time, due to lack of interest on the part of the members.

Accounts of the Parish School
from October, 1846, when the school fund was
established, to the end of this church year

EXPENSES		INCOME	
To Ole Knudsen, for three months school during church year 1845–1846	$30.00	Rec'd in 1846 as gifts from Norway: (1) from Pastor Brodtkorb	$50.00
To Ole Knudsen, for ½ mo. school	5.00	(2) from Johannes Jørgensen Haavig	10.00
To Lars Aaker, for teaching school in the south district of the west half of the parish	5.80	Interest on this money Remainder of Dietrichson's travel money, donated	1.30
To Ole Knudsen, for teaching in the east half of the parish	8.52	by Dyer Sørensen	1.75
To Aslak Olsen, for teaching in the north district of the West Church	1.00	Gift from Torbjørn Fladland	0.25
		Gift from Ole Colbart	1.50
		Gift from Ole Larsen	1.00
Total expenses from October, 1846, to end of church year, 1848	$50.32	Total income from October, 1846, to end of church year, 1848	$65.80
Amund Bjørnsen, for teaching in the west half of the parish	1.41	Total income from October, 1846, to end of church year, 1849	$65.80
Total expenses from October, 1846, to end of church year, 1849	$51.73		
Balance in treasury			$14.07

Up to now [1849], the Koskonong congregation and the other congregations organized in this country existed alone and independent of one another. Pastor Clausen of Luther Valley (Rock Prairie) and I have long felt this to be a drawback and have discussed it. If the church order among the different Norwegian Lutheran congregations here is to win strength and stability, they must not stand isolated, but an organic union of all congregations having the same doctrine and order must be brought about.[67] This can only take place through a *joint meeting* of pastors and elected lay representatives of the various congregations. Together with Pastors Clausen and Stub,[68] I issued an invitation to such a meeting to the various congregations. This invitation, which we had printed at Musquigo, is appended to this book.[69]

It should have been obvious to every church member that the purpose of such a synod [*kirkemøde*] could only be to bring about a union which, if established on the proper basis, would of necessity serve to strengthen the congregations, both inwardly and outwardly. Nevertheless, this effort, like so much else that has been done to safeguard the church order, was misunderstood by some, both in this congregation and in others.[70] Some here at Koskonong joined forces with the open opponents of the church and the bitter enemies outside the church on this matter. The latter tried to convince the church members that the purpose of the proposed meeting was to levy heavy financial burdens on them. There were even accusations that if this synod were held, a new doctrine and a papistic church order would be forced on the congregations. There were some, especially in the east half of the parish, who believed this, although the invitation to the meeting was repeatedly explained in both churches by the pastor. He also declared that he was prepared to explain the purpose of the meeting to anyone who came to him privately. However, as often happens, the lie was believed more than the truth. Opposition went so far in the case of some that, when they saw they could accomplish nothing, they withdrew from the congregation—which was the best thing both for the congregation and for themselves. Yet despite all this opposition, representatives to the synod were elected both in the East and in the West Churches on June 24. The five annex congregations then being served by the pastor of this church did the same.[71]

The synod planned for July 15 and following days at Koskonong was not held, but not because of opposition to it in this settlement. Rather, it was caused by unforeseen hindrances in the other places. What happened is related in the following document, written here at Koskonong at the time. The original is appended to this book.[72] It reads as follows:

In accord with the invitation issued in April this year by Pastors Stub, Clausen, and Dietrichson of the Church of Norway in America to the congregations of the Church of Norway in America to meet with them through representatives elected for that purpose in a joint church meeting to be held at Koskonong on July 15 and following days this year, the following persons, having been elected by their respective congregations to be accredited, authorized delegates, were present:

I. For the east half of Koskonong Norwegian Lutheran Church:
    1. Lars Johannesen Hollo
    2. Kittil Hansen Strømmen
    3. Ole Knudsen Trovatten
       (Gulbrand Gulbrandsen Holtene was elected as the third representative, but before the meeting he moved to the west half of the parish. He therefore could not be seated as a delegate from the East Church, and was replaced by Ole Trovatten, who was runner-up in the voting.)

II. For the west half of Koskonong Norwegian Lutheran congregation:
    4. Gaute Ingebretsen Gulliksrud
    5. Knud Saavesen Aaker
    6. Neri Tarjesen Hauge, substituting for the ailing Henrik Olsen Hæve

III. For the annex congregation at Heart Prairie:
    7. Ole Nielsen

IV. For the annex congregation at Pine Lake:
    8. Christopher Olsen Satre

V. For the annex congregation at Rock River:
    9. Ole Olsen

VI. For the annex congregation at Norway Grove:
    10. Erik Johnsen Engesæther

VII. For the annex congregation at Bonnet Prairie:
    11. Peder Halvorsen

The credentials of all these are appended.

In accordance with the aforementioned invitation from the Norwegian church's pastors in America, these representatives were present at the opening service in the East Church of Koskonong Norwegian Lutheran parish, where Pastor Dietrichson preached on Acts 2:42. At the close of the service, Pastor Dietrichson reported that he had received the unfortunate information from Pastor Stub that he would be unable to take part in the meeting because of illness. He also had received a letter by express[73] from Pastor Clausen, dated July 8 this year, stating that representatives from his congregations had been elected, but that Pastor Clausen thought it would be best, if it could possibly be done, to postpone the synod until a more convenient time. To this Dietrichson had answered that although he might agree to the desirability of postponement under different circumstances, he believed it would cause still more offense and inconvenience if the church meeting were not held at the appointed time. He was also of the opinion that it would be almost impossible, between the 9th and the 14th of July, to send letters by express to five different annex congregations, from which he had information that delegates had been elected, and he thought it would be wrong to have these men come long distances in vain. Therefore, Dietrichson had most urgently requested Clausen to come.

In his answer he also called attention to the fact that, although it was most unfortunate that Pastor Stub was unable to come, he still thought that, under the circumstances, this first meeting, which in reality was only a preparatory meeting for annual synods, could be held with two pastors and could adopt resolutions which could later be referred to Pastor Stub for his ratification. If there should be certain matters that Pastor Stub wished to have changed, this could, upon his motion, be done at the next meeting. Dietrichson had also requested Clausen to preach that day. He had therefore waited expectantly for the arrival of Pastor Clausen and the delegates from his churches. Unfortunately, they did not come, probably due to unforeseen circumstances. Dietrichson declared that he would consider it wrong to convene a church meeting in which he was the only pastor present. He deplored the fact that delegates from afar would be unable to realize the purpose of their journey, but he could not help it. He requested the representatives from his congregations to meet at the parsonage on Monday morning, July 16, not for the purpose of taking any action, but merely to discuss in a friendly manner what they thought best for the future existence of the Church of Norway in America. The aforementioned eleven delegates responded to this invitation.

At the request of Knud Aaker, Pastor Dietrichson was unanimously chosen chairman for the discussion. Knud Aaker was elected secretary, and the papers pertaining to this discussion were entrusted to Ole Knudsen for safekeeping.

All were agreed that it was absolutely necessary, if the church order begun under God's protection among the Norwegians in America, is to gain such permanence that it can continue in the pure, evangelical spirit of the Norwegian church, that synods be held as proposed by the pastors in their invitation to consider matters of mutual interest to the various congregations. There was unanimous agreement that the first objective of such a meeting would have to be the writing of a constitution and the drafting of regulations for the Norwegian church here, but that these should in no wise encroach upon the decisions made within the congregations themselves.

Pastor Dietrichson presented a "Proposed Constitution for the Church of Norway in America," and also "Proposed Regulations for the Internal Government of the Church," which he read and explained. In our opinion, it would be most beneficial and desirable to have these proposals read at a subsequent synod and put up for adoption. The secretary was requested to make a number of copies so that they might be sent around to the various churches in preparation for the meeting.

It was further agreed that a synod should study the question of what changes should be made in the church ritual of our fatherland because of conditions existing in this country, though the delegates opposed any change whatever in the external customs of worship which can be performed here. In this connection, Pastor Dietrichson called attention to certain changes that he considered appropriate.

Furthermore, all were agreed that the opposition that has appeared in some quarters to the proposed synod was due to a misunderstanding of its purpose. It is our confident hope that when the proposals offered here are made known in the various congregations and are understood by them, it will be seen that the clergy do not wish us ill, but good.

These were the results of our discussion, and we desire that they may be presented to the congregations preparatory to the synod. Pastor Dietrichson was requested to reissue the invitation to the other pastors and [to urge] that the synod be held as soon as possible. This he promised to do. As we could do no more in this matter, the meeting was adjourned.

The parsonage of Koskonong Norwegian Lutheran Church, July 16, 1849.

J. W. C. Dietrichson	Knud L. Aaker	Ole Knudsen
Chairman	*Secretary*	Gaute Ingebretson
		Erik Johnsen
		Kittil Hansen
		Neri Tarjesen
		Peter Halvorsen
		Lars Johannesen
		O. Olsen
		Christopher Olsen
		Ole Nielsen

Dietrichson's proposed "Constitution for the Church of Norway in America" reads as follows:

ARTICLE I

The name of the church shall be "The Church of Norway in America."

ARTICLE II

The doctrine of the church is that which is revealed through God's Holy Word in our baptismal covenant, and also in the canonical books of the Old and New Testaments, interpreted in agreement with the symbolical books or confessional writings of the Norwegian Church, which are:
1. The Apostles' Creed.
2. The Nicene Creed.
3. The Athanasian Creed.
4. The Articles of the correct, unaltered Augsburg Confession, as presented to Emperor Charles V at Augsburg, 1530.
5. Luther's Small or Lesser Catechism.

ARTICLE III

The ceremonies or external rites of worship shall be performed in accordance with the Dano-Norwegian *Ritual* of 1685 and the *Altar Book* in use in those kingdoms, modified, however, as the church in synod may decide.

ARTICLE IV

For the present, the church's form of government[74] shall be synodical-presbyterian, so that a synod or general convention[75] shall be held annually, which shall be the highest ecclesiastical authority of the church. From among the members of the synod a *presbyterium* or church council shall be elected which shall govern the joint ecclesiastical affairs of the church from one synod to the next.

ARTICLE V

Sec. 1. The general synod shall consist of the clergy of the church and the elected representatives or authorized delegates of each individual congregation.

Sec. 2. Every clergyman acknowledged by this church as a clergyman, and who is associated with the Norwegian Church in America, shall be entitled to a seat in the general convention.

Sec. 3. Delegates to the general synod shall be members of a congregation in union with the church, and they must be elected by a majority vote in the congregation which they represent. Credentials for each delegate shall be presented to the convention, and their validity shall be determined by it before the delegate is seated and awarded the right to vote. The convention shall have power by a majority vote to refuse to seat any delegate regarding whose Christian life or relation to the church there is reason for censure.

ARTICLE VI

So long as the church has no bishop, the convention shall elect a superintendent[76] from among the clergy.

ARTICLE VII

Sec. 1. The superintendent of the church and the pastors and elected lay delegates, whenever rightly assembled in synod, shall have power to adopt resolutions in all ecclesiastical matters.

Sec. 2. As a rule, every question shall be decided and receive validity by a majority vote in the convention.

Sec. 3. If a majority of the clergy should consider it necessary in certain cases, a majority vote of the clergy present in the convention on the one hand, and a majority vote of the lay delegates on the other, shall be necessary to decide a question and make the decision valid.

Sec. 4. The superintendent shall preside over the convention. He shall be entitled to one vote only, but in case of a tie vote, his vote shall be decisive.

ARTICLE VIII

At every annual synod, a secretary shall be elected by majority vote from among the members of the convention. He may be either a pastor or a layman. His duty shall be to record the minutes of the convention and to enter same in a book authorized for that purpose by the superintendent; to have charge of all journals and other documents belonging to the convention; in company with the superintendent to attest to the official resolutions of the convention, and upon request of the superintendent promptly to turn over to him all books and documents belonging to the convention. The secretary shall continue in office until his successor is legally elected. If the secretary requests it, a member of the convention shall be designated to assist him.

ARTICLE IX

Sec. 1. The convention shall annually elect a *presbyterium* or church council which shall consist of the superintendent, at least two other clergymen, and two laymen for each three clergymen.

Sec. 2. These clergymen must be acknowledged clergymen of the church, and must be associated with the church.

Sec. 3. The laymen who shall be elected as members of the

church council must be members of congregations belonging to the church.

Sec. 4. The superintendent shall preside at meetings of the church council. At the first meeting a secretary shall be elected, either clergy or lay, who shall record all the minutes of the *presbyterium's* meetings and enter them in a book authorized for that purpose by the superintendent, which book and all documents pertaining to the *presbyterium* shall be presented by the secretary to each annual convention.

Sec. 5. The superintendent shall be empowered to fill vacancies that may occur in the *presbyterium* between synods [conventions].

Sec. 6. Between synods it shall be in the power of the *presbyterium* to manage all ecclesiastical affairs of the church, to watch over the doctrine and life of the clergy, to exercise church discipline, and to adopt temporary resolutions which shall be valid until the next convention.

Sec. 7. The *presbyterium* shall meet semiannually at a place chosen by majority vote.

Sec. 8. Every matter that comes before the *presbyterium* shall be decided by a majority vote of the clergy, on the one hand, and of the lay members on the other.

Sec. 9. The superintendent shall be entitled to only one vote in the *presbyterium*. In case of ties his vote shall, however, decide the issue.

ARTICLE X

Sec. 1. The superintendent shall be empowered to call extraordinary synods.

Sec. 2. In an extraordinary synod, the members of the previous synod shall constitute the synod.

Sec. 3. In such cases, at least six weeks' notice shall be given to the various congregations, stating where and when this special synod is to be held.

Sec. 4. Such special synods shall be held at the place designated by the ecclesiastical authority calling the convention. As a rule, no other business shall come before an extraordinary convention except the matter which occasions it, unless the convention by a majority vote deems it absolutely necessary to consider other matters.

ARTICLE XI

Every congregation wishing to unite with the Church of Norway in America must submit to the church's constitution and its other resolutions. The congregation shall, however, retain its own regulations, insofar as these do not conflict with the constitution and other rules of the church. When a congregation desires to unite with the church, it shall present through the *presbyterium* a petition to that effect, signed by the pastor and deacons or other members of the congregation elected by the congregation to do so. Such a petition shall be addressed to the superintendent of the church and directed to the synod of the church. In this petition it must be expressly stated that the congregation desiring to join the church accepts the constitution, rules, and regulations of the Church of Norway in America.

ARTICLE XII

Every congregation sending delegates to the synod shall be obliged to submit to the decisions of the convention. However, any member of the congregation who is unwilling to do so shall be free to withdraw from the congregation, in which case he ceases to be a member of the Church of Norway in America.

ARTICLE XIII

With the exception of Articles I and II, which shall remain forever unaltered, this constitution or any part of it may be altered in the following manner: The proposed amendment or change shall be presented at the annual convention, and if its members by a majority vote of the clergy, on the one hand, and of the lay delegates on the other, approve the change, it shall lie over until the next convention. If it is then accepted by a majority vote in the same way, the change shall become valid.

Dietrichson's proposed "Regulations for the Internal Government of the Church of Norway in America," which he presented at the same time, read as follows:

1st Canon.[77] It shall be the duty of the superintendent, on or before the first day of the synod, to present to the convention, through its secretary, a list under his hand and seal of the pastors who are associated with the church and entitled to a seat and a vote in the convention.

2nd Canon. Every congregation belonging to this church shall secure a proper "church" register; it shall be authorized by the superintendent. The parish pastor shall enter in that book all ministerial acts performed in the congregation, and all parish business. This register shall be presented at every meeting of the *presbyterium.* From it the parish pastor shall, at the beginning of every church year and at other times as often as the superintendent (for whose inspection the church book always shall be open) requests it, give the superintendent a written summary of the number of his church members and of all acts and business involving the congregation.

3rd Canon. Whenever a pastor denies a parishioner the Lord's Supper, he must notify the convention. If the convention finds that his action was justified, no pastor associated with the church shall admit that member to absolution and Holy Communion; neither shall any other pastor receive him into membership until he is accepted by his own pastor and acknowledged by the convention as one who may receive the sacrament.

4th Canon. Any person thus denied the sacrament has the right to appeal to the *presbyterium,* and thence to the synod, the judgment of which is final.

5th Canon. No pastor associated with the church shall administer the Lord's Supper to, or receive into membership, anyone unless he presents satisfactory testimonies regarding his status from his former pastor. In the case of a person who has emigrated from Norway but who does not seek membership in one of the congregations until several years afterward, testimonials from Christian church members shall be required, and in general he is to be thoroughly examined before being accepted into membership.

6th Canon. Sec. 1. If any pastor in this church offends against the church, its constitution, or its regulations, in doctrine or in conduct, charges may be brought against him before the synod of the church. Such charges shall be signed by at least two persons who can be considered Christian members of one of the congregations of the church (and also by one clergyman in the same church?).[78] Anonymous accusations shall not be considered.

Sec. 2. If in the judgment of the church council the accusation is well founded, the church council shall suspend the accused minister until the next synod, if the offense or error he has committed is of that nature. The council shall then bring the matter before the convention for further investigation.

Sec. 3. In a case of this kind, the superintendent shall appoint a tribunal (a jury) consisting of not more than three pastors and not less than two, plus one of the most worthy lay delegates in the convention. This jury shall pass on both the facts in the case and its outcome, and shall determine the punishment if the accused is found guilty. None of the accusers may be a member of the jury.

Sec. 4. The *presbyterium* shall prosecute the case, and it shall name a prosecutor, who must be a pastor in the church. The *presbyterium* shall also be in duty bound to give the accused a copy of the accusation, and 60 days' notice of the time and place of trial.

Sec. 5. If the accused does not appear, and does not give sufficient reason for his absence, he shall be adjudged guilty of contempt of the ecclesiastical authority under which he stands and whose *presbyterium* previously has suspended him. This judgment shall stand until the next synod. If he then fails to appear or give an acceptable reason for his absence, he shall be dismissed from his office.

Sec. 6. The accused shall in every case be informed in writing of the court's decision, and it shall likewise be made known to the deacons and trustees or church council in his congregation. In this communication both the charge brought against him and the evidence presented against him in the trial shall be cited.

Sec. 7. Within 30 days after sentencing, the superintendent shall execute the sentence in the manner decided upon by the synod.

Sec. 8. If the superintendent himself should be accused, he shall be dealt with in precisely the same manner. In this event, the convention shall select another person to act as superintendent until the verdict is announced. If he is acquitted, he shall again assume his office as superintendent.

Sec. 9. Should a pastor thus be convicted and sentenced to suspension, such suspension shall be for a definite period of time or until the transgressor gives the convention satisfactory evidence of admission of guilt and improvement.

Sec. 10. In case the accused is adjudged unworthy of his office and is deposed therefrom, he shall not be reinstated in any other manner than the one decided upon by the convention.

Sec. 11. Suspension or dismissal shall *ipso facto* immediately abrogate the connection existing between the pastor concerned and his congregation. Ecclesiastical acts performed by a pastor under suspension or dismissal shall be considered ecclesiastically invalid.[79] Likewise, the congregation or church member that knowingly employs such a person as minister thereby excludes itself from the church.

Sec. 12. In all cases where accusation is brought against a minister, he shall have the right to demand an investigation. This request must be in writing to the *presbyterium*. Should the *presbyterium* find that the accusation is of such a nature that it does not merit investigation, this fact shall be made known to the accused within three months after receiving his request, and the accusation shall be considered null and void.

7th Canon. No one can be recognized as a pastor in this church unless he be rightly examined, regularly called, and ordained by the church to the ministerial office. The church in synod shall determine in each individual case whether these requirements have been met, and whether the individual in question can be admitted to the ministerium.

8th Canon. Each individual congregation is to retain both its right to call its own pastor and the right to manage its own church affairs in the manner that the congregation, in harmony with the constitution of the church and with its other rules, may determine. It shall, however, be the duty of every main congregation that finds itself without a pastor, and also of every annex congregation desiring to become a main congregation, to apply to the church council for its opinion regarding both their choice of pastor and the arrangement of the congregation's ecclesiastical affairs.

9th Canon. When a minister wishes to resign from a parish, it shall be his duty to inform the church council of the time of his departure, and also of his reason for leaving.

10th Canon. The superintendent should visit each congregation at least once every other year. Every annual convention shall determine the object of the visitations. The superintendent shall report to the convention the result of the visitation.

11th Canon. The expense of procuring the necessary record books and other writing materials for the convention shall be paid by the pastors until the convention decides otherwise, in order that this may not prove a stumbling block for the congregations.

12th Canon. These regulations may be altered by a majority vote of the clergy and the lay delegates in convention assembled.

According to information received later, Pastor Clausen was not present at the proposed synod because he did not believe there could be any meeting when Pastor Stub and his delegates could not come. Pastors Clausen and Stub said later that they thought it best to schedule the synod planned for last July 15 for January or February next year. Because of the fact that there would then be only a rather short time remaining before I would resign and return to Norway, I stated that for my part I thought it best to let the matter rest until my successor at Koskonong could participate in it.

On Tuesday,[80] August 21, 1849, a meeting of the deacons, trustees, and all voting members of the congregation was held at the parsonage. At this meeting, I informed the congregation of my decision to terminate my ministry here when my term expires next year. I also informed them that some time previously I had had a letter from the Rev. A. C. Preus, assistant pastor of Gjerpen Parish,[81] dated June 20, 1849, in which he offered his services to Koskonong congregation, in case I intended to resign next year. He enclosed with his letter the most satisfactory testimonials from various pastors in Norway. Therefore, with peace and the hope that the church work begun here would be continued, I announced my decision to follow the desire of my heart and return to my fatherland, thus declining the congregation's request that I remain here as its pastor.

The letter from Pastor Preus and the accompanying testimonials were read to the congregation. They gave us every reason to hope that, if the congregation would call him to be its pastor, the spiritual interests of the church would be assured. I therefore requested the congregation to adopt (1) a resolution containing the basic constitution of the congregation, and (2) a decision as to whether they would call the Rev. A. C. Preus to be their pastor, beginning next year.

With regard to the first point, the following resolutions were unanimously adopted and subscribed to by all the members present.

With thanksgiving to God, we acknowledge the great benefit we have received from the church order established among us since October, 1844, by the Rev. J. W. C. Dietrichson, who responded to our call to set our church affairs in order. Despite our heartfelt desire to retain him, he feels compelled out of consideration for his family to leave the congregation when his term expires next year. We, the undersigned members of the Norwegian Lutheran congregation, in an earnest desire to hold fast to the true, saving doctrine and the edifying church order of our fatherland, do adopt the following resolutions regarding our church order:

(1) The name of the congregation shall continue to be "The Norwegian Lutheran Congregation at Koskonong Prairie."

(2) The doctrine of this church shall always be that which is revealed in God's Holy Word through our baptismal covenant and in the canonical Scriptures of the Old and New Testaments, interpreted according to the symbolical books or confessional writings of the Church of Norway.

(3) The ceremonies or outward rites of worship, as well as the church order in the congregation, shall be carried out in accordance with the *Ritual* of 1685 of the Church of Norway and Denmark and the *Altar Book* prescribed for use in the same kingdoms, modified by the pastor as he thinks necessary because of conditions existing in this country.

(4) The churchly affairs of the congregation shall be conducted by a parish council, consisting of the pastor as chairman and the deacons[82] of the church. Deacons shall be elected as often as the pastor considers necessary, by a majority vote of the church members. They shall be installed by the pastor in the manner pre-

scribed for deacons in the Church of Norway, modified as the pastor may determine.

(5) The temporal affairs of the congregation shall be managed by the trustees, elected by the congregation in accordance with the law of February, 1847.

(6) This congregation may not call or utilize anyone as pastor who is not rightly examined and ordained by the church, in accordance with the requirements of the Church of Norway.

(7) The congregation is pledged to show to any pastor thus called respect and obedience in everything that the pastor demands and does in accord with the Word of God and our church order, and the respect and deference which is due a servant of the Lord, all according to the admonition of the Apostle Paul: "Obey those that are over you in the Lord. . . ."

(8) Since we as Christians know the Lord's command that they that preach the gospel shall get their living by the gospel, we are also from the heart willing to obey this Word of the Lord. We therefore propose the following regarding the pastor's salary:

(a) The minister shall receive from his predecessor in office the parsonage property and shall enjoy the use of it as his property so long as he continues to serve this congregation as its pastor.

(b) The pastor's regular salary shall be set at not less than 300 dollars per year, figured from the date he assumes the office. It is to be raised by voluntary contributions from every confirmed member of the church and is to be paid to the pastor in two installments, to be more definitely determined by him. These stipulations shall be valid for a period of at least five years, from June 1, 1850, to June 1, 1855.

(c) For ministerial acts such as the churching of mothers, infant baptisms, confirmation, weddings, and funerals, payment shall be made at the pleasure of those concerned.

(d) On the great festival days—Christmas, Easter, and Pentecost—the pastor is to receive a free-will offering.

(e) If the pastor so requests, the trustees of the church shall see that his salary is raised by collectors appointed for that purpose.

That we the undersigned, members of the Norwegian Lutheran Congregation at Koskonong Prairie, do submit in every particular to the above conditions and do pledge ourselves to fulfill them, we hereby acknowledge by signing our names or having them signed.

The Norwegian Lutheran congregation at Koskonong Prairie, August 21, 1849.

With regard to the other point, the congregation unanimously resolved to accept with thanks and joy Pastor Preus's offer to become their pastor, and through its *klokker*, deacons, and trustees to extend a letter of call to him. It was also decided that in the district of each deacon a list should be circulated, on which the members should indicate (1) how large an annual contribution each would make toward paying the pastor's salary, and (2) how much each would contribute toward Pastor Preus's travel expenses from Norway. (Pastor Preus stated in his letter of June 20 this year that, since he was without means, he would have to "request the congregation to help him to the extent of half of his expenses" in coming here.)

Following adoption of these resolutions, the meeting was adjourned.

In accordance with resolutions adopted on Aug. 21 this year, a meeting of the *klokker*, deacons, and trustees was held in the parsonage on Thursday, September 6, 1849. The following letter of call was drafted:

To the Rev. Mr. A. C. Preus, assistant pastor of Gjerpen Parish
in Christiania Diocese in the Kingdom of Norway:

Our present pastor, the Rev. J. W. C. Dietrichson, has announced that, because of family considerations in Norway, he has decided to leave us when his term expires next spring. As it is our earnest desire to have the blessings of the church continually among us, administered by a rightly examined and ordained servant of the Lord, we consider, Rev. Mr. A. C. Preus, your offer to become our pastor (per your letter to Pastor Dietrichson dated Gjerpen, June 20, 1849) as coming from God. We the undersigned, deacons and trustees of the Norwegian Lutheran congregation at Koskonong Prairie, Dane and Jefferson counties, in the state of Wisconsin, North America, do therefore, in the name of the Lord and on behalf of the congregation and of ourselves, respectfully issue to you the call to become the pastor of this congregation from June 1, 1850, until June 1, 1855.

From the testimonials accompanying your letter, we can see

what able Christian guidance we may expect to receive from you. We rejoice in this our steadfast hope that you will accept our call so that next year we may welcome you as our pastor.

Following is what we as Christians must needs require of our pastor:

(1) That the Word of God be preached in its truth and purity and that the most precious sacraments be administered and in general all churchly acts be performed according to the ordination vow of every pastor in the church of our fatherland, and in accordance with the resolutions adopted by this congregation on August 21 this year. To these resolutions both pastor and congregation are bound. As for minor changes in the church ritual of our fatherland which may be necessary to meet conditions in this country, the congregation desires that the church order be carried out by you in the manner hitherto practiced here.

(2) Since we have often experienced the necessity of church discipline, if order is to be maintained in the church, we require that the pastor strictly observe the same in accordance with our church order.

(3) Our pastor must lead a pure and blameless life according to the exhortation of the Apostle Paul in I Tim. 3.

With the heartfelt prayer that God by his Holy Spirit in Christ may equip you with his power worthily to attend to your calling as a servant of the Lord, that he will bring you to us sound and strong in soul and body, we do now on behalf of the congregation send you this call to assume the holy office of pastor. We enclose a copy of the constitution adopted by our church, to which the call to become pastor of this congregation is bound, and we promise that we will fulfill in every particular the obligations entered into.

The parsonage of Koskonong Norwegian Lutheran Church, town of Christiana, Dane County, Wisconsin, North America, Sept. 6, 1849.

Ole Knudsen, *klokker*
Ole Knudsen Gilderhuus, deacon
Lars Torgersen Røthe, deacon
Neri Tarjessen Hauge, deacon
Johannes Johannesen Menses, deacon

Ole Vetlesen Qvalen, deacon
Kittil Hansen Strømmen, deacon
Hellik Gundersen Vashøvd, deacon
Johannes Johnsen Berge, deacon
Tollef Johannesen Bækhus, deacon
Iver Knudsen Gilderhuus, trustee
Ole Laurantsen, trustee
Gaute Ingebretsen Gulliksrud, trustee

At the meeting of Sept. 6, the lists circulated in each deacon's district for subscriptions to Pastor Preus's salary and travel expenses were returned. They showed that members in the nine districts had pledged $223.67 toward Pastor Preus's annual salary and $90.82 toward his travel expenses. These lists were again examined at the close of the church year, and they then showed a sum of [the ms. has a blank here]. I promised to write to Pastor Preus as soon as possible. The meeting then adjourned.

I wrote to Pastor Preus shortly thereafter and enclosed a copy of the constitution of the congregation and a copy of the letter of call. The originals are appended to the church register.[83] Pastor Preus has thus been called to become pastor of this church beginning June 1 next year.[84]

On Monday, November 19, 1849, a meeting of deacons and trustees was held in the parsonage. At this meeting, the pastor submitted an accounting for the books donated from Norway during my ministry here. Some of these have been sold, others given away. The statement is as follows:

(1) Received in 1847 through Candidate of Theology J. P. Broch, Christiania, a box of books, including 28 copies of Guldberg's Hymnal.[85] These were given to the congregation by Bookseller Dybwad in Christiania. Of these 28 hymnbooks

25 were sold @ 50¢ each	$12.50
3 were given away	
Total income from these books	12.50
Expense of transporting the books from New York to Koskonong	3.50
Balance	9.00

(2) Received in 1848, from Merchant A. Helland in Bergen, a box containing the following books:

533 copies of Pontoppidan's simple Explanation[86]
392 copies of the Catechism[87]
12 copies of the ABC's
10 copies of *Devotional Book for the Common Man* by Wexels[88]
10 three-volume sets of *Edifying Meditations*
5 copies of Wexels's *Exposition of Corinthians*
5 copies of Wexels's *Exposition of Galatians*
71 Bergen Tracts
(100 Bergen Tracts received later)
10 copies of *Survey of Luther's Life*
Of these were sold (up to Nov. 19, 1849):

140 Catechisms @ 6¢	$ 8.40
136 Explanations @ 10¢	13.60
10 ABC's @ 4¢	.40
4 Devotional books @ 37½ ¢	1.50

The following were given away:
94 Catechisms
96 Explanations
2 ABC's
6 Devotional books
5 sets of *Edifying Meditations*
5 *Survey of Luther's Life*
1 *Exposition of Corinthians*
1 *Exposition of Galatians*
81 Bergen Tracts

Total income from these books	23.40
Expense of transporting them from Chicago to Koskonong	1.50
Balance	21.90

(3) In 1849 a gift of books was received from Norway, brought by Pastor Stub. Of these the following have been sold:

1 Wexels's hymnbook @ $1.00	1.00
3 " " given away	
5 Guldberg's hymnals @ 50¢	2.50
13 Wexels's Bible History @ 15¢	1.95

1 Postil on the Gospels @ $1.50	1.50
2 Postils on the Epistles @ $1.00	2.00
Total income from these books, up to Nov. 19, this year .	8.95
Total income from all books received from Norway, up to Nov. 19, 1849	$39.85

On a motion from the pastor, the deacons and trustees decided to make the following disposition of this money: The school fund is to receive $25.00, and the remaining $14.85 shall be given to the library being established in the parish.

At the Nov. 19 meeting I also reported on the box of books sent to Koskonong congregation as a gift from the American Bible Society, New York, in 1847. This box contained 40 Bibles and 75 New Testaments in the Norwegian language. My report is as follows:

38 Bibles sold @ $1.18	$44.84
30 New Testaments sold @ 60¢	18.00
15 New Testaments sold @ 50¢	7.50
2 Bibles given away	
17 New Testaments given away	
Total Income	70.34
Expense of transporting the books from New York to Milwaukee	13.48
and from Milwaukee to Koskonong	1.00
Balance	55.86
Of this money the trustees received of me in 1848, as their records show	38.00
Balance	17.86

This sum is earmarked by the trustees for upkeep of the two churches.

In the fall of 1848 I sent a letter of thanks signed by the trustees to the American Bible Society, addressed to the Society's corresponding secretary, Dr. D. C. Brigham, New York, with a statement of the income received from sale of the Bibles up to that time. It was decided at this meeting that a similar letter of thanks with an accounting of the New Testaments sold should be sent this year. This was done in May, 1850.

The November 19 meeting also decided that the following letter of thanks should be sent to Norway for the books received from there:

Our church has on several occasions received evidence of the fatherland's readiness to help us in our spiritual need. Our present pastor has decided to resign when his term expires next spring, and so this is the last year Pastor Dietrichson will be with us. Our church has benefited from several gifts sent from Norway through him. We therefore consider it our duty, on behalf of our congregation and ourselves, to acknowledge with thanks the receipt of a number of books which have been sent to us at various times. Our church owes most heartfelt thanks to the Society for the Publication of Christian Books of Instruction and Devotion, to Pastor Wexels, and to several of the booksellers in Christiania, especially to Bookseller Dybwad, for these gifts. With equal gratitude the congregation acknowledges receipt of a shipment from Merchant A. Helland in Bergen containing a large number of Explanations and Catechisms, several tracts, and some other books.

Pastor Dietrichson has distributed some of these books *gratis* and has sold some. Part of the income has been divided between the parish school fund and a reading society which has been started in the parish. When Pastor Dietrichson leaves, he will turn over the balance to Pastor Clausen, who will keep it until the arrival of our new pastor, the Rev. A. C. Preus, next year. The rest of the books will also be placed at the disposal of Pastor Preus.

We have been informed that two more boxes of books have been sent by ship from Norway by Candidate of Theology J. P. Broch of Christiania. His untiring efforts to provide our congregation with books has earned our grateful appreciation. For this gift, although it has not yet arrived despite all our inquiries about it, we nevertheless owe a vote of thanks. May God reward these noble givers with his richest blessings.

Koskonong Norwegian Lutheran congregation, Dane and Jeferson counties, state of Wisconsin, North America, November 19, 1849.

Ole Knudsen, *klokker*
Aslak Olsen Olsnæs, schoolteacher
Ole Knudsen Gilderhuus, deacon

I sent this letter of thanks to Norway, and requested that it be printed in Norwegian newspapers.

At the November 19 meeting, it was also decided that, when I left, a letter of thanks should be sent with me to the relatives of the late Bishop Sørenssen, who through Professor Kaurin gave the congregation the silver cup which is now being used as a communion chalice. The cover for the cup serves as a paten.

It was also decided that the church should send a letter with me to Dyer Sørensen's widow, in which should be expressed the congregation's sympathy in the loss of her noble husband, to whom this congregation owes so much.

The pastor then questioned each deacon individually about Christian and churchly conditions in his district. The deacons replied that with a few exceptions they must be considered good. Drunkenness, which has unfortunately been all too prevalent in the congregation, seems to have diminished somewhat during the past church year. I asked whether the deacons had heard any complaint about the pastor or the management of the congregation. They replied that, with the exception of those persons who had opposed the church meeting [synod], of whom the worst ones are now no longer members of the congregation, the congregation was very well satisfied. Indeed, it was said that even some of those who had opposed the church meeting now had come to see how right and necessary it was, and to regret that they had not realized before that in this matter, too, the pastor had had their best interests at heart.

The deacons were asked whether they were willing to remain in office during the remainder of my term and for at least one month after Pastor Preus arrives. They declared themselves willing to do so, if they might retire next year, since most of them have served as deacons for two years. The meeting was then adjourned.

Endre Rudi, sexton of the West Church, has, without the knowledge of the pastor and without making any accounting of his office, moved away from the congregation. Gulbrand Gulbrandsen Holtene has been elected in his place.

The pastor had thought it good and profitable to set up a parish library, and thus to awaken in the congregation an interest in reading. He therefore suggested last year the establishment of a reading society. A number of members were enrolled. Circumstances, however, made it impossible to collect the books for the parish library before this last summer. Through the efforts of Candidate of Theology J. P. Broch, we have received a shipment of some books donated by various men in Christiania, as well as some purchased on my account in Christiania. The library was finally opened on September 17 this year, with a total of 133 volumes, valued at $62.45. Every library member is required to pay 25¢ when he joins, and 12½¢ annual dues. This entitles him to borrow books. He is responsible for them, and must return them within the proper time. Every member must submit to the library rules. The pastor is chairman of the society, and the *klokker* is treasurer and librarian. A letter of thanks for the gifts of books, signed by the chairman and the librarian, is being sent to Norway.

Things have been quiet and peaceful this year except for disturbances caused by troublemakers outside the church. They have been supported by certain individuals within it, especially in the east half of the parish. But this was of very little significance. The Lord be thanked and praised for this peace and quiet! Yet I pray that God, by his Holy Spirit in Christ, may awaken more life and fervor for sanctification in the church's narrow way, to the blessing of every member of the congregation. Amen, for Jesus' sake! Amen!

The parsonage of Koskonong Norwegian Lutheran congregation,
Dec. 1, 1849

J. W. C. DIETRICHSON
Pastor

CHAPTER VII

The Church Year 1849–50
(Sixth year from the founding of the congregation)

Now that a parish library has been established, the books that belonged to the congregations of the parish have been turned over to this library.[89] They are thus assembled in one place, making it easier to keep track of them than would be the case if they were left in the churches.

On Pentecost, 1850, at the close of the service in the West Church, I thought it necessary to read to the congregation the following announcement (the same was also read in the East Church the next day):

Since I shall only be with you a few more days, I think it best to report today on the amount of cash belonging to the congregation. I have turned it over to the trustees. As the whole congregation knows, I have not handled any of the money paid in by church members for the parsonage and church buildings since 1847, when the first trustees for the temporal affairs of the congregation were elected as required by Wisconsin law. When they assumed office, I submitted an accounting in writing (appended to the trustees' books) of the church funds received and expended by me. The balance was turned over to the trustees. For this I received their written receipt, which is appended to the Parish Journal.

The trustees have thus received from me the following sums:

1. For the parsonage and the well	30.88
2. For the West Church	15.00
3. For the East Church	10.98
Later in 1848 I turned over to the trustees, from the sale of 38 Bibles, for the benefit of the church	38.00
Total paid by me to the trustees	$94.86

It is suggested that the auditors chosen by the congregation last year now examine the accounts of the trustees, so that the congregation may know what sums were received and paid out, and how much there is in the treasury now. Also, in my opinion, the trustees should be enjoined not to use the money for anything except the stated purpose, so that the money of each may be used only for it, and the parsonage money for the parsonage only. The need for this is now acute because of the expected arrival of your new pastor. I am sure the congregation is aware that, as I have sought to impress upon you before, the parsonage needs some repairs. The exterior should be sided, the interior should be plastered, and a number of minor repairs are needed. For these the parsonage needs the money that properly belongs to it. As I have previously suggested to the congregation, this work should be started immediately after I leave, so that it may be completed by the time Pastor Preus arrives.

So that the congregation may get an overview of the accounts of the parish school prior to my departure, I submit the following summarized statement:

INCOME OF PARISH SCHOOL

Gifts from Norway, 1846	
(1) From Pastor Brodtkorb	$50.00
(2) From J. Jørgensen Haavig, Trondhjem Diocese	10.00
Interest on this money	1.30
Remainder of Dietrichson's travel money, donated by Dyer Sørensen	1.75
Gift from Torbjørn Fladland	0.25
Gift from Ole Colbart	1.50
Gift from Ole Larsen	1.00
Income from sale of books donated from Norway	25.00
(Do.)	8.00
(Do.)	10.95
Total from October, 1846, to May 19, 1850	$109.75
Balance in school fund (This sum will be paid by me to Pastor A. C. Preus)	$ 48.02

EXPENSES OF PARISH SCHOOL

To Ole Knudsen, for three months' school, 1845–6	$30.00
To Ole Knudsen for ½ mo. school	5.00
To Lars Aaker, for teaching in the west half of the parish	5.80
To Ole Knudsen	8.52
To Aslak Olsnæs	1.00
To Amund Bjørnsen	1.41
To Aslak Olsnæs for one month of school, 1849–50	8.00
To Lars Aaker for teaching school (1849–50)	2.00
	$61.73

Report on the Disposition of Books received from Norway
Income from sale of books up to Nov. 19, 1849 .... $ 39.85
Income from sale of books between Nov. 19, 1849, and May 19, 1850 $ 18.95
and sold since Nov. 19, 1849, follows:

1 Postil on Ephesians	$1.00
2 Postils on Gospels @ $1.50	3.00
10 Bible Histories @ 15¢	1.50
(The rest of these books were given away)	
Total	$5.50

Of the books donated by A. Helland of Bergen, the following have been disposed of since Nov. 19, 1849:

102 Explanations sold @ 10¢	$10.20
93 Explanations given away	
206 Explanations remaining in the box	
(These total 533, the number we received)	
52 Catechisms sold @ 6¢	3.25 [*sic!*]
24 Catechisms given away	
82 Catechisms remaining in the box	
(These total 392, the number we received)	

The rest of the books sent by Helland have been given away.
Total income from sale of books donated from Norway in the period Nov.
19, 1849–May 19, 1850 <u>$18.95</u>
Report on the disposition of Bibles and New Testaments received from New
York in 1847 (from American Bible Society):

Income from sale of Bibles and Testaments to Nov. 19, 1849	$55.86
Since then,	
2 New Testaments sold @ 50¢	1.00
7 New Testaments given away	
4 New Testaments remaining	
62 previously sold or given away	
(These total 75, the number we received)	
(All 40 Bibles had previously been sold or given away)	

TOTAL INCOME FROM SALE OF BOOKS DURING MY PASTORATE HERE	<u>$115.66</u>
Of this amount the trustees have received from me (in 1848)	$38.00
Balance on hand	77.66
Of this amount, the parish school is to receive	43.95
the parish library	14.85
the churches of the parish	18.86
All told, then, the congregation has coming from me:	
1) Balance in school fund	48.02
2) Belonging to the churches of the parish	18.86
Total	<u>$66.88</u>

(I have already paid $14.85 to the parish library)
This $66.88 will be paid by me to Pastor A. C. Preus.

Of this sum, Ole Knudsen Trovatten received from me on May 28, 1850, $43.34, for which amount I received his receipt and his promise that this money would be turned over to Pastor Preus upon his arrival here. The balance, $23.54, I shall pay to Pastor Preus, and he will be responsible to the congregation for it.

On Trinity Sunday, May 26, 1850, I preached my farewell sermon in the West Church. (Before the service I admonished the congregation not to be hasty about administering private baptism in the interim between my departure and Pastor Preus's arrival, except in the most extreme emergency. Even in case of emergency, I advised them not to let just anyone administer baptism, but to call upon the *klokker* or one of the deacons.)

On Tuesday, May 28, 1850, I held my last meeting with the *klokker*, the deacons, and trustees. We went through the membership rolls together, and I questioned the deacons about the moral conduct and relation of each member to the church. Our remarks are recorded in the register. We also went over the list of contributions toward Pastor Preus's travel expenses, and the $76.46 then paid in was turned over to me in accord with an arrangement between Pastor Preus and me. I gave my receipt for this. A letter of thanks was written to the family of the late Bishop Sørenssen for the silver cup given by them to the congregation.

The auditors elected by the congregation were also present, and they examined the accounts of the outgoing trustees. In closing, I bade farewell to the deacons and trustees.

In thus terminating my ministry here, I have nothing to add except the heartfelt wish that God the Father will bestow his grace and blessing in Christ Jesus by the Holy Spirit upon this congregation, which is so precious to me, and upon the man it has called to be its new pastor. May God add his amen for Christ's sake.

The parsonage of Koskonong Norwegian Lutheran congregation, town of Christiana, Dane County, Wisconsin, North America, May 29, 1850.

J. W. C. DIETRICHSON

Appendices

Appendix A

Agreement for Sale of Original Property, 1844

Recorded Jan 17th 1845
at 11½ oclock A M
G. T. Lang Register D. C.

Lien & Foshein [*Fosheim?*]
        to
Norwegian Lutheran Denomination
  The signers of this paper living in Town 6 Range 11 Dane County Wisconsin Territory acknowledge that we are willing to sell for government price to the Norwegian Lutheran Denomination on Koskonong (1) one acre of land on which they have built their church
Koskonong November 11th 1844
As witnesses
Knud Aslaksen   Thone & Aslaksdatter Lien
Ole Knudsen Trovatten
As witnesses
O. Knudzon   Halvor Laurandsen Foshein
O. Laurandzen   [*Laurandsen Fosheim*]

Appendix B

Dyer Peter Sørensen's Reply
to Koshkonong Congregation's Letter of
Thanks to Him

Dear Brethren:

It was with a happy heart and heartfelt thanks to God that I read the letter you sent to me last year via Pastor Dietrichson. For it showed me that one of my dearest wishes, to see you, my dear countrymen, enrolled in a proper church had now come true, and that God had [given his] "yea and amen" to my most fervent prayers in this matter. And [I return] every word of thanks which you sent to me [to the heavenly] Father, who works in us both to will and to do according to his pleasure, and who has added his rich blessing to the little I have tried to do. I send herewith my greetings and brotherly thanks for your letter and for all the good will and love you express for me therein. May God, who has begun the good work in and among you, perfect it until the day of Jesus Christ. This [is my] prayer and my joyful, confident hope for you, for [God] himself has promised to perfect it.

My heart is indeed troubled when I think of the many who have wormed their way into your flock, the many false, blind shepherds who take pains to lead you away from the way of truth and into the perilous sects, which according to your own statements are so prevalent among you. But I place my hope in the great and faithful Chief Shepherd in heaven, that he will surely be able to preserve his flock which he has but lately gathered, and that he will graciously watch over the many lambs scattered throughout that foreign land, who have had to go so long without care and without a shepherd. Praise and thanks be to him for setting apart as your leader and pastor a man whom God himself has equipped with his Spirit and grace and love, to preserve the order and to defend you powerfully against the wolves and the hirelings who would force their way into your flock.

I can see by your letter that you yourselves recognize this, and that you join me in thanks to God for his great grace, for you speak of your pastor with such love and respect. And certainly he deserves your love and honor for what he has done for you, for, next to God's blessing, you have his strength and endurance to thank for the order and church discipline that again exists among you. The Lord [grant] me therefore also that joy that comes from knowing that you follow the apostle's admonition [I Thess. 5:12–13] and respect those that labor among you and are over you in the Lord . . . and esteem them very highly in love, for they watch over your souls as those who must give an accounting thereof, that they may do this gladly, not with sighing, for such is not profitable for you.

Then, [although] your pastor can expect much trouble from those who are outside the church, he will be gladdened and strengthened by the devotion and love of the members of the congregation and, above all, by their faith and longing to follow in the steps of the crucified Lord. He could not have greater happiness or receive better thanks from you for all his faithfulness and love toward you.

I thank you sincerely for praying for me and mine and for your promise to continue to pray for us. My faithful wife and I will never forget to include the congregation in that far-off part of the world in our prayers. The congregation has become so precious to our hearts and its weal and woe will always be on our hearts as long as we live. And because we pray for one another here on earth, in faith to him in whom we all are one, our meeting in the heavenly mansions will be joyous and blessed when at last we go home to the Lord, freed from all the tribulation and temptation of this world. God help us to that end, for his mercy's sake, in Jesus' name!

P. Sørensen

Christiania, Norway
May 11, 1846

Appendix C

Deed to Parsonage Land

Knud Olsen to Norwegian L. C.

Know all men by these presents, that I Knud Olsen & Anne my wife of the town of Albion in the county of Dane and Territory of Wisconsin, in consideration of forty seven dollars and fifty cents paid by Rev. Mr. Dietrichson the receipt whereof we do hereby acknowledge, do hereby give, grant, bargain, sell and convey unto the said Rev. Mr. J. W. C. Dietrichson and his successors for the use of him and his successors in the ministry of the Norwegian Lutheran congregation forever, the following tract of land, twenty acres on the east side from the Northeast quarter of Southwest quarter of Section number twenty township number six North of Range number twelve according to survey. To have and to hold the foregranted premise to the said Rev. Mr. J. W. C. Dietrichson and to his successors in the ministry of the Norwegian Lutheran congregation, to their use and behoof forever: And we do for ourselves, our heirs, executors, and administrators, covenant with the said Rev. Mr. J. W. C. Dietrichson and to his successors that we are lawfully seized in fee of the aforegranted premises, that they are free from all incumbrances, that we have good right to sell and convey the same to the said Rev. Mr. J. W. C. Dietrichson and to his successors and that we will warrant and defend the said premises to the said Rev. Mr. J. W. C. Dietrichson and to his successors forever against the lawful claims and demands of all persons.

In witness whereof, we the said Knud Olsen and Anne Olsen have hereunto set our hands and seals this 14th day of January in the year of our Lord one thousand eight hundred and forty seven.

Signed Sealed and Delivered in
presence of

Ole Knudzon. Erik Johannesen [*his* X *mark*]   Knud Olsen [*his* X *mark*] (Seal)

Wisconsin Territory)
Dane County ss.   )

On the twenty-fifth day of May in the year one thousand eight hundred and forty seven, Ole Knudzon came before me and being duly by me sworn deposes and says he resides in the town of Cottage Grove in the county of Dane and Territory of Wisconsin, that he saw Knude Olsen execute the within conveyance and that he subscribed his name thereto as a witness that he knew the said Knude Olsen to be the same person described in and who executed the said conveyance, and that at the time of the execution thereof they were residents of the town of Albion in the Territory of Wisconsin at the same time appeared before me Eric Johnson residing in the town of Albion county of Dane who being also duly sworn by me desposed and said that he knew the said Ole Knudzon to be the same person who was a subscribing witness to the within conveyance which is to me satisfactory evidence thereof.

Wm. N N Coon, Justice of the peace

Recorded May 27th 1847)
at 3 o'clock P.M.   )
Register   )

Notes and References

Introduction

1. *Varselsord til de udvandringslystne bønder i Bergens stift: Et hyrdebrev fra stiftets biskop* (Bergen, 1837). For an English translation, see Gunnar J. Malmin, tr. and ed., "Bishop Jacob Neumann's Word of Admonition to the Peasants," in Norwegian-American Historical Association, *Studies and Records*, 1:95–109 (Minneapolis, 1926).

2. In connection with the two-hundredth anniversary of Hauge's birth, several new biographies were published. One of the ablest is Andreas Aarflot, *Hans Nielsen Hauge: Liv og budskap* (Oslo, 1971). An earlier standard work is A. S. Bang, *Hans Nielsen Hauge og hans samtid* (Kristiania, 1910).

3. The best known work on Wexels is D. Thrap, *Wilhelm Andreas Wexels: Livs- og tidsbillede* (Christiania, 1905). The definitive work on Norwegian Grundtvigianism is in two volumes by Anders Skrondal: *Grundtvig og Noreg: Kyrkje og skule 1812–1872* (Bergen, 1929) and *Grundtvigianismen i Noreg: Kyrkje og skule 1872–1890* (Bergen, 1936). The first volume is especially helpful in understanding the milieu out of which Dietrichson emerged.

4. The English translation ("Built on a rock the church doth stand") does not convey Grundtvig's basic idea.

5. The first group of immigrants had come to New York in 1825, arriving aboard the now famous sloop *Restauration*. The "Sloopers" settled for a time at Kendall in upstate New York, but many of them later moved on to Illinois. The best studies of Norwegian emigration written from the American side are Theodore C. Blegen, *Norwegian Migration to America, 1825–1860* (Northfield, Minnesota, 1931) and *Norwegian Migration to America: The American Transition* (Northfield, 1940). From the Norwegian side the outstanding work is Ingrid Semmingsen, *Veien mot vest*, 2 vols. (Oslo, 1941 and 1950).

6. Valeur was belatedly approved for ordination. See Gunnar J. Malmin, "Litt norsk-amerikansk kirkehistorie fra de norske arkiver," in *Lutheraneren* (Minneapolis), 8:75–79 (January 16, 1924). The au-

231

thorization for Valeur's ordination is to be found in the records of the Department of Ecclesiastical Affairs in the Norwegian State Archives in Oslo; see *Departements-Tidende*, 12:89–92 (1840).

7. Blegen, *Norwegian Migration to America: The American Transition*, 132.

8. Thus Dietrichson quotes Eielsen in his *Reise*, 31 (American edition).

9. E. Clifford Nelson and Eugene L. Fevold, *The Lutheran Church Among Norwegian-Americans*, 1:95 (Minneapolis, 1960).

10. The name "Koshkonong," an Ojibwa Indian word, can best be translated "Where there is a heavy fog." It was applied to a lake formed by a widening of the Rock River, to a creek flowing into the lake, and to an area of fertile farmland in southeastern Dane County and southwestern Jefferson County. The Norwegians spoke of the latter as "Koshkonong Prairie." See Frederic G. Cassidy, " 'Koshkonong,' a Misunderstood Place-Name," in *Wisconsin Magazine of History*, 31:429–40 (June, 1948).

11. C. A. Clausen and Andreas Elviken, trs. and eds., *A Chronicle of Old Muskego: The Diary of Søren Bache, 1839–1847*, 120 (Northfield, 1951).

12. Bache, *A Chronicle*, 121.

13. Erasmus Dietrichson's father was Diderik Rasmussen, a Copenhagen burgher. His son was, patronymically speaking, therefore "Dideriksen" or Dietrichson. The patronymic pattern apparently ended in the seventeenth century for the Dietrichson family, as henceforth all descendants bore the surname Dietrichson. See "Oversigtstavle over slegten Dietrichson," in *Norsk biografisk leksikon*, 3:317, n. 1 (Oslo, 1926).

14. Additional biographical data are to be found in J. B. Halvorsen, ed., *Norsk forfatter-lexikon, 1814–1880*, 2:152–54 (Kristiania, 1888), and *Dictionary of American Biography*, 5:307 (New York, 1943).

15. See "Examens Protocol" for 1837 in the Norsk Historisk Kjeldeskrift-Institutt, Oslo.

16. A. Brandrud, "Teologien," in *Festskrift, Det kongelige Frederiks universitet 1811–1911*, 2:19–21 (Kristiania, 1911).

17. Skrondal, *Grundtvig og Noreg*, 90.

18. Skrondal, *Grundtvig og Noreg*, 79–89, 296.

19. J. W. C. Dietrichson, *Katekismusprædiken over det første bud holden i tugthuuskirken i Christiania*, 5 (Christiania, 1845).

20. The son, Jørgen Laurentz Wilhelm, was reared by his mother's parents. He became a teacher and scientist. See Halvorsen, *Norsk forfatter-lexikon, 1814–1880*, 154. Dietrichson remarried in 1846. His second wife, Charlotte Müller, bore him two children, Jørgine Eleonore Louise (1851) and Johan Joachim Otto Fredrik (1855). The latter was trained in the Hanover (Germany) Technical High School

(Hochschule). For information on the Dietrichson family, see David Dietrichson, *Stamtavle over slægten Dietrichson*, 6–8 (Kristiania, 1882).

21. Halfdan Sommerfeldt, *Den norske Zulumission*, 51–54 (Christiania, 1865); A. S. Burgess, "Burning Zeal, Missionary Endeavor," in J. C. K. Preus, ed., *Norsemen Found a Church*, 336 (Minneapolis, 1953).

22. Thrap, *Wilhelm Andreas Wexels*, 95.

23. J. W. C. Dietrichson, *Reise blandt de norske Emigranter i "De forenede nordamerikanske Fristater,"* 3 (Stavanger, 1846; American edition, Madison, 1896). The *Reise* gives the date of ordination as February 26, 1844. This is apparently a mistake, for the certificate of ordination, quoted by Dietrichson in the Koshkonong Parish Journal, says February 23. See Gunnar J. Malmin, "Litt norsk-amerikansk kirkehistorie fra de norske arkiver," in *Lutheraneren*, 8:76 (January 16, 1924).

24. Bache, *A Chronicle*, 121.

25. For a discussion of Dietrichson's negotiations with the Norwegian government, see Blegen, *Norwegian Migration to America, 1825–1860*, 252, and Malmin, "Litt norsk-amerikansk kirkehistorie," in *Lutheraneren*, 8:77. The royal resolution covering the decision is found in *Departements-Tidende*, 18:744–46 (1846).

26. Dietrichson's negotiations with H. A. Preus are discussed in Linka Preus, *Linka's Diary on Land and Sea*, tr. and ed. by J. C. K. and Mrs. Preus, 67, 80, 104–108, 116 (Minneapolis, 1952).

27. Dietrichson, *Nogle ord fra prædikestolen i Amerika og Norge*, 33–35 (Stavanger, 1851). The Koshkonong congregations as well as others founded by or ministered to by Dietrichson have continued into the present. They, like so many other congregations, suffered dissension and schism during the election (predestination) controversy of the 1880s.

28. The royal permission for ordination is found in *Departements-Tidende* for 1843, 15:715 (Christiania).

29. "Johannes Wilhelm Christian Dietrichson," in *Gamla presta i Nedstrand—For "Stavangeren"* av B. Ø., August 5, 1927.

30. Skrondal, *Grundtvig og Noreg*, 295–97.

31. Skrondal, *Grundtvig og Noreg*, 152. It is interesting to note that Søren Kierkegaard, like the pietists, had been sharply critical of Grundtvig's views. The pietists criticized him for "religious" reasons; Kierkegaard, for historical, theological, and philosophical reasons. His episcopal brother, however, found Grundtvigianism quite congenial.

32. W. A. Wexels, "Den kirkelige anskuelse: Et foredrag," in *Theologisk Tidsskrift for den norske Kirke*, 2:545, cited in Skrondal, 153, n. 113.

33. Skrondal, *Grundtvig og Noreg*, 297. Oftedal was a brother of

Sven Oftedal, who a few years later with Georg Sverdrup became a professor at Augsburg Seminary in Minneapolis.

34. The point of dispute about which the trouble seemed to crystallize was his refusal to use the altar book's rendition of the third article of the creed in the baptismal rite. Whereas the altar book used the phrase "holy, *Christian* church," Dietrichson insisted on using what was a Grundtvigian trademark (and historically correct), namely, the phrase "the holy, catholic (*almindelig*) church" (Skrondal, 295). The extent to which the conflict was carried is illustrated by an incident cited by Skrondal (p. 300). One mother was prepared to use the baptism of her own child as an occasion "to demonstrate against the pastor" ("*at demonstrera mot presten*"). When the pastor asked, "Do you believe in the holy catholic church?" she answered in the local dialect, "*Nei, eg trur ikkje paa ei heilag aalmenn kyrkje*" ("No, I do not believe in a holy catholic church"), and she strode off with her unbaptized baby! Some pietists added that it was blasphemous to speak of believing "in" the church; rather one believed in God.

35. Adolf Carl Preus (1814–1878), a cousin of H. A. Preus, was Dietrichson's successor at Koshkonong in 1850. He had graduated from Christiania University in 1841 and served as a teacher and vicar prior to going to America. He was pastor at Koshkonong until 1860, served pastorates in Chicago (1860–1863) and Coon Prairie, Wisconsin (1863–1872). It was in 1872 that he became pastor of the Holt parish, where Dietrichson had been receiving communion. O. M. Norlie *et al.*, *Who's Who Among Pastors in All Norwegian Lutheran Synods of America, 1843–1927*, 463 (Minneapolis, 1928). Ironically, Dietrichson's daughter by his second marriage, Jørine Eleonore Louise Dietrichson, born in 1851 at Slidre in Valdres, was married in 1879 to Johan Nordahl Brun Preus, the son of Adolf Carl Preus and his first wife, Engel Brun. The young husband, a teacher in Porsgrund, was born (1855) in the Koshkonong parsonage previously occupied by the Dietrichson family. See David Dietrichson, *Stamtavle over slægten Dietrichson*, 7.

36. Skrondal, *Grundtvig og Noreg*, 316; Halvorsen, *Norsk forfatterlexikon 1814–1880*, 153.

37. J. W. C. Dietrichson, *Offentlige dokumenter udgivne til redegjørelse for min overgang fra præstestillingen til civilt embede* (Arendal, 1876); *Afskedsprædikener i Østre Molands annekskirke og i Tromø hovedkirke* (Arendal, 1877).

38. Einar Haugen, "Pastor Dietrichson of Old Koshkonong," in *Wisconsin Magazine of History*, 29:301 (March, 1946).

39. Theodore C. Blegen, ed., *Land of their Choice: The Immigrants Write Home*, 140 (Minneapolis, 1955).

40. See *The Parish Journal*, 170; Blegen, *Land of Their Choice*, 140–142.

41. *The Travel Narrative*, 67; *The Parish Journal*, 152.

42. *Dannemarkes og Norges kirke-ritual* (Copenhagen, 1685). The king ordered a revision of the *Ritual* later; this was done under the supervision of Bishop Bagger of the Copenhagen Diocese in 1688.

43. *The Travel Narrative*, 74; *The Parish Journal*, 195.

44. *The Travel Narrative*, 55.

45. *The Travel Narrative*, 107.

46. See E. Clifford Nelson, "The Making of a Constitution," in J. C. K. Preus, ed., *Norsemen Found a Church*, 191–221 (Minneapolis, 1953).

47. The constitution is consequently not included in the records of the Koshkonong parish. It may be found in H. Halvorsen, ed., *Festskrift til Den norske synodes jubilæum 1853–1903*, 37–39 (Decorah, Iowa, 1903). For comments, see Nelson and Fevold, *The Lutheran Church Among Norwegian-Americans*, 1:114–116.

48. See *Forslag til constitution for den ev. luth. menighed i America*, 5–7 (Chicago, 1857). This proposal for a constitution was no doubt recommended to Swedish and Norwegian congregations in the Northern Illinois Synod prior to the formation of the Scandinavian Augustana Synod (1860). The authors appear to be T. N. Hasselquist, a leader among the Swedish Lutherans, and Paul Andersen, pastor of the first Norwegian congregation in Chicago.

49. *The Parish Journal*, 178.

50. *The Parish Journal*, 202; Art. VII, Sec. 3.

51. *The Parish Journal*, 154.

52. J. H. A. Lacher, "Nashotah House, Wisconsin's Oldest School of Higher Learning," in *Wisconsin Magazine of History*, 16:137 (December, 1932). See also N. W. Olsson, ed., *A Pioneer in Northwest America 1841–1858: The Memoirs of Gustaf Unonius*, 252–60 (Minneapolis, 1950). Breck was a friend of Clausen in Muskego; he was present at the dedication of the Muskego Church (1845); Bache, *A Chronicle*, 149. The Muskego Church now stands on the campus of Luther Theological Seminary, St. Paul. Interestingly enough, the seminary campus was enlarged by the purchase (1955) of the contiguous campus of an Episcopal military academy, the Breck School; for some time the Lutherans referred to their new property as "the Breck Campus."

53. *The Travel Narrative*, 101–104; George M. Stephenson, tr. and ed., *Letters Relating to Gustaf Unonius*, 25–39 (Rock Island, Illinois, 1937).

54. *The Travel Narrative*, 120–32.

55. *Wisconsin Magazine of History*, 306–309 (March, 1946).

56. J. C. K. Preus, "The Widening Frontier," in *Norsemen Found a Church*, 97–99; Bjørn Holland, "Elev ved den første norske kirke-

skole i Amerika," in *Ungdommens Ven* (Minneapolis), 21:382 (June, 1910). One of Miss Dillon's pupils, Knute Nelson (1843–1923), later became United States senator from Minnesota. Dietrichson, incidentally, corresponded with Miss Dillon until the time of his death.

57. *The Parish Journal*, 194.

58. *The Parish Journal*, 218. In the spring of 1957, the writer discovered three volumes in the Koshkonong parish that seemed to date back to Dietrichson's era. One of the three was definitely identified as a part of the library; these volumes are now in the library of Luther Theological Seminary, St. Paul.

59. *The Parish Journal*, 183.

The Travel Narrative

1. All references in the text to Christiania refer to the capital city of Norway. Originally known as Oslo (Opsloe), the city became known as Christiania in 1624 (in honor of King Christian IV, who, following a devastating fire, rebuilt the city closer to the fortress of Akershus). In 1924 the parliament (Stortinget) voted to restore the old name Oslo as of January 1, 1925.

2. Footnote by Dietrichson: "From the above it may be seen how much truth there is in Mr. Reiersen's insinuations against me that have appeared in the press as well as in his brochure *Norway and America*. He seeks to make me suspect as 'a government-paid spy-priest in the ministry whose pastoral activities in America served as a vehicle for material interests and other hidden motives in order to discourage emigration.' Beyond this, it is quite unnecessary to make the slightest reference to his well-known attack upon me. Why he chose to make such rancorous attacks on me when I cannot always paint a picture of emigration as rosy as he, will be obvious to everyone." Editor's note: The reference here is to Johan Reinert Reiersen, who after a trip to America in 1843-1844 wrote a small book called *Veiviser for norske emigranter til de forenede nordamerikanske Stater og Texas* (Guide for Norwegian Emigrants to the United States and Texas, Christiania, 1844).

3. The certificate of ordination gives the date February 23. See *The Parish Journal*, 152.

4. Herman Roosen Smith (1812–1900) received his commission from the Sjøkadettinstituttet (Naval Academy) at Fredriksvern in 1832; *Norsk biografisk leksikon*, 14:77.

5. Probably an erroneous reference to Fair Isle, lying half way between the Orkney and Shetland islands.

CHAPTER II

6. John Jacob Astor (1763–1848), founder of the American Fur Company.

7. Footnote by Dietrichson: "One dollar is about 112 Norwegian shillings (*skilling*)."

8. The mission of the Bethel ships appears to have originated in England in 1814 with a Captain Wilkins and his wife, who also designed the first Bethel flag. The idea was probably brought to Sweden

in 1837 by the Swedish Seamen's Society; Sal. Olofsson, Lerberget, Sweden, to Malcolm Rosholt, February 17, 1969.

9. K. F. F. Stohlmann (1810–1868) was born at Kleinbremen, Germany. He accepted a call in 1838 to St. Matthew's German Lutheran church in New York City; J. C. Jensson, *American Lutheran Biographies*, 766 (Milwaukee, 1890).

10. A typographical error or inaccurate use of Latin. *Vosa* should be *vasa*, plural of *vas*, for vessel, presumably the sacred vessels used in the communion service.

11. Oscar I (1799–1859), king of Sweden and Norway from 1844 to 1859.

12. Not to be confused with the American Lutheran Church (1930) or The American Lutheran Church (1960). The reference is to the Evangelical Lutheran Ministerium (Synod) of New York.

13. Footnote by Dietrichson: "Lest there be any misunderstanding, I should point out that what I say in the following about the Methodists is by no means a judgment of the entire Methodist church body. I refer only to what I have experienced in regard to Methodism in America."

14. Dietrichson's quote is in English.

15. No doubt F. J. Brohm, a Missouri Synod pastor who served a German Lutheran church in New York City, 1843–1858. See H. E. Jacobs and J. A. W. Haas, eds., *The Lutheran Cyclopedia*, 64 (New York, 1889).

16. Footnote by Dietrichson: "In the census of 1840 there were 2,487,213 slaves in America."

CHAPTER III

17. Footnote by Dietrichson: "I have consistently stated distances in English miles. There are four of these in a geographic and six in a Norwegian mile."

18. Johannes A. A. Grabau (1804–1879); Jensson, *American Lutheran Biographies*, 271. A summary of Grabau's work and the migration of "Old Lutherans" to America in 1839 appears in Clarence A. Clausen and Andreas Elviken, eds., *A Chronicle of Old Muskego: The Diary of Søren Bache*, 88–89, n. 1 (Northfield, Minnesota, 1951).

19. No doubt Heinrich von Rohr, formerly an officer in the Prussian army, who came to Buffalo in 1839 to investigate conditions for the settlement of "Old Lutherans." Led by Grabau, they arrived in October the same year.

20. Footnote by Dietrichson: "When these emigrants compared what they had suffered on this short trip with how well they had

fared on the Atlantic crossing, they realized how much gratitude they owed our good skipper, Lt. Smith. He had arranged everything for their comfort and welfare and had taken care of his passengers solicitously. At great sacrifice of time, he had shipped their baggage from New York to Wisconsin. The company broke the contract, although it was carefully written; still, that was no fault of his. In sum, Smith deserves the deepest gratitude, not only from me, whom he always treated with the kindest courtesy and attention, but also from the emigrants. Many of them have asked me to express this feeling to him."

CHAPTER IV

21. Footnote by Dietrichson: "By prairie is meant a natural meadow the topography of which is flat, wet, rolling or undulating; the latter type of prairie, alternating with forest, is characteristic of Wisconsin. From the standpoint of health it is to be greatly preferred to the flat, wet terrain where malaria and bilious fever are common, and to the swampy, thick forests where illness is also common. The forest land, which in Wisconsin consists mostly of three kinds of oak: thick timberland, thin 'openings-land,' which derives its name from the fact that in it grow different species of oak." [This sentence in Dietrichson is confusing. He fails to mention "three" kinds of oak, and his description of "openings-land" is obscure. It also appears that he was still unaware of the great stand of pine in the northern half of the state.]

22. The reference is probably to the Fox River which flows through Lake Winnebago into Green Bay, not the Fox in southeastern Wisconsin that runs into northern Illinois.

23. *Alen*, plural of *ell*, is the equivalent of two English feet.

24. Dietrichson's description of Lake Koshkonong as "small" was correct when he wrote. A dam was later built on Koshkonong Creek, making the lake one of the largest in Wisconsin.

25. It seems clear that Dietrichson here is referring to the Fox River running into Illinois, not the Fox flowing into Green Bay.

26. Sauk-Washington was an early name for the present city of Port Washington.

27. Rockport, a "paper town," never became county seat. See Henry F. James, "Early Reminiscences of Janesville," in *Collections of the State Historical Society of Wisconsin*, 6:426–35 (1872).

28. The Pecatonica flows south into Illinois and eastward to join the Rock River south of Beloit.

29. Referred to by Søren Bache as "A. Hansen." See *A Chronicle*, 92. The passenger list of the brig *Washington*, which reached New York on July 5, 1843, identifies Hansen as an "artist" and his son

Hans M. as a "physician." His daughter Caspara was married to James Denoon Reymert by Pastor C. L. Clausen. Gerhard B. Naeseth, Madison, Wisconsin, to Malcolm Rosholt, November 5, 1970.

30. Claus Lauritz Clausen (1820–1892). See Introduction, p. 13. See also H. Fred Swansen, *The Founder of St. Ansgar: The Life Story of Claus Lauritz Clausen* (Blair, Nebraska, 1949); Carlton C. Qualey, "Claus L. Clausen, Pioneer Pastor and Settlement Promoter," in *Norwegian-American Studies and Records*, 6:12–29 (Northfield, Minnesota, 1931).

31. See Bache, *A Chronicle*, 35–43. See also Theodore C. Blegen, *Norwegian Migration to America: The American Transition*, 38 (Northfield, Minnesota, 1940) and Johannes Johansen and Søren Bache, "An Immigrant Exploration of the Middle West in 1839," in *Studies and Records*, 14:44–53 (1944).

32. P. A. Fenger and F. E. Boisen were Lutheran pastors and followers of Grundtvig.

33. Elling Eielsen (1804–1883). See Introduction, p. 12.

34. There is little question that Eielsen should be reckoned the first ordained pastor among Norwegian-American Lutherans. The charges of his opponents have been effectively dissipated by the historical records. See especially C. J. Carlsen, "Elling Eielsen, Pioneer Lay Preacher and First Norwegian Lutheran Pastor in America," an unpublished master's thesis, University of Minnesota, 1932. The ordaining clergyman was probably Francis Arnold Hoffmann (1822–1903) from Westphalia, Germany, who came to Chicago in 1840, worked as a bootblack in a hotel, later served as a teacher of a pastorless church at Dunkley's Grove (now Addison), Illinois; *Dictionary of American Biography*, 5:118.

35. Ole Munch Ræder, accompanied by Dietrichson, once met Eielsen and his wife on a public highway. Ræder reports that the conversation between Dietrichson and Eielsen was "friendly," and what impressed him was "Eielsen's confidence in his own position" and his "free and at the same time modest bearing." See Gunnar J. Malmin, ed., *America in the Forties: The Letters of Ole Munch Ræder*, 52 (Northfield, Minnesota, 1929). During part of his tour in Wisconsin, Ræder accompanied Adam Løvenskjold, the Norwegian consular official who was making a study of Scandinavian settlements. Since Ræder was in America in 1847–1848, it is clear that he was not present at the first meetings between Eielsen and Dietrichson in 1844, but his testimony does suggest that Dietrichson, after his return to Wisconsin in 1846, following a year's absence in Norway, had come to accept or at least tolerate Eielsen.

36. Listed as Christen Olsen Hole in the Koshkonong church reg-

ister, reproduced in George T. Flom, *History of Norwegian Immigration to the United States,* 315 (Iowa City, Iowa, 1909), but as Christian Olsen in the subscription lists of *Nordlyset* and *Democraten.* Dietrichson's question mark after the name Hole might suggest that he was uncertain whether the man went under the name of Hole or Olsen.

37. "Hauge's Friends." refers to the followers of Hans Nielsen Hauge. The name was sometimes applied in America to the followers of Elling Eielsen.

38. The Norwegian expression *Ellinganerne* was commonly used by Norwegian Synod people in references to the followers of Elling Eielsen. The term conveyed a certain disdain.

39. It appears fairly certain that a typographical error was made in this sentence. See the original edition printed in Norway, 40 (1846); no effort was made to correct it in the American edition published by R. B. Anderson, 38 (1896).

40. Tollef Olsen Bache (1770–1848). Søren Bache refers to his father several times in his diary; Søren's return to Norway was prompted mainly by the illness of his father.

41. Footnote by Dietrichson: "About this sect more later."

CHAPTER V

42. Dietrichson spoke in the hay barn of Amund Anderson Hornefjeld's farm in East Koshkonong on September 1. On the 50th anniversary of the founding of the East Koshkonong congregation, October 10, 1844, a large granite stone marker was unveiled at the site of the one-time barn. It stands in the farmyard of Sanford Anderson, a fourth-generation farmer. The marker calls attention to the first service and to the founding of East Koshkonong, but it fails to mention Dietrichson. A photograph of two oak trees, purported to be at the spot where Dietrichson preached in West Koshkonong on September 2, 1844, appears in *Minde fra jubelfesterne paa Koshkonong,* 13 (Decorah, Iowa, 1894).

43. In a letter to *Nordlyset* (January 6, 1848), Smith signed his name "Johan Gustaf Schmidt," a pastor of St. John's Church in Chicago. His letter begins with the quotation: "Forgive us our sins as we forgive others," and discusses the "pure church" and its doctrines, ending by wishing the editors of the paper "a merry Christmas, good luck, and salvation in eternity." A contributor to the paper replied to this letter in the next issue with the opening words: "But lead us not into temptation." Eventually Smith created so much dissension that he was forced to leave.

44. See *The Parish Journal*, 155, n. 20.

45. Erich Pontoppidan, *Collegium Pastorale Practicum* (Copenhagen, 1757).

46. The term *degn* is an old designation, generally synonymous with *forsanger* (precentor).

47. *Sit venia verbo* (to be spoken with permission), apparently an indication of the zeal with which Dietrichson guarded the pulpit as the symbol of the preaching office.

48. These were the original East Koshkonong and West Koshkonong congregations. On January 4, 1845, Dietrichson paid sixty-three cents to Mr. and Mrs. Gustein Rolfsen for a tract of land to be used for the East Koshkonong church. It is described in the warranty deed as "one-half acre from SE corner of NW-SW, Sec. 26, T. 6, R. 12E." See *Koshkonong Centennial 1844–1944*, 17. A piece of land purchased from Thone Aslaksdatter for the West Koshkonong church was described as half an acre, "being a part of the NW-NE, Sec. 14, T. 6, 11E;" *Koshkonong Centennial*, 17–18. The East Koshkonong congregation replaced the original log church in 1858 with a stone edifice built in rectangular style, on or near the site of the log church or about the center of the south line of the present cemetery. In 1852, the West Koshkonong congregation built an octagonal structure of stone and brick, also on or near the site of the original log church. After the split in both congregations in the late 1880s, over the question of pre-destination, these second buildings were demolished and new churches were erected in both East and West Koshkonong. Those breaking away from the old Norwegian Synod—later to join the United Norwegian Lutheran Church of America—in each case appropriated the "second" buildings. The eastern group built on or near the site of the stone church; in fact, some of the footings for the new church were taken from it. The western group, which joined the United Church, erected a new building on or near the site of the former octagonal building. Meanwhile, members of the congregations of East and West Koshkonong who remained loyal to the old Norwegian Synod also built new churches, the one in the east standing directly west of the cemetery or about a hundred yards northwest of the "United" church. Those in West Koshkonong remaining loyal to the old Synod built a rectangular structure about two hundred yards to the north of the United church higher up on the hillside.

49. These chests, made of hard wood, were often decorated with *rosemaling* (rose painting) and dates. They were used to store food as well as clothing for the long trip at sea.

50. See *The Parish Journal*, 156. The title "nobleman" is apparently a misnomer. There is no evidence to date that representatives

of the Swedish nobility ever settled around Koshkonong, but it is interesting that Dietrichson was under the impression that they had.

51. *Barselkvinders indledning*, the ceremony of readmitting a woman recently in childbirth into the church. Such a member was known as an *indgangskone* or "churched woman."

52. In the text of the Anderson or American edition, these numbered requirements jump from 2 to 4, omitting 3.

53. The expression used by Dietrichson is *"præst og sjelesørger."* Etymologically, *præst* is the English word priest but among American Lutherans it is translated pastor or minister. But *sjelesørger*, also pastor, more correctly understood is the term for the clergyman in private, personal ministry as distinct from preaching and administering the sacraments. The English word shepherd, which is poetic, is often used for *sjelesørger*.

CHAPTER VI

54. For the "affair Funkelien," see Nelson and Fevold, *The Lutheran Church*, 1:109.

55. *Bindenøgle*, literally the "binding key," an expression from Matthew 16:19: "I will give you the keys of the kingdom of heaven, and whatever you bind on earth shall be bound in heaven." The so-called "power of the keys" forms a part of the doctrinal content of the Lutheran confessions.

56. I Timothy 5:22.

57. Philipp Jakob Spener (1635–1705) was a German Lutheran churchman, the father of Pietism, and author of the famous *Pia Desideria*. See *Encyclopedia of the Lutheran Church*, 3:2245–46.

58. This was Whitsunday, the seventh Sunday after Easter, a church festival day commemorating Pentecost, which in 1845 fell on May 11.

59. Footnote by Dietrichson: "In every township, elections are held for the office of justice of the peace. These officers, elected for two years, enforce the laws that concern public safety and act as judges in cases involving $50 or less. They also make out land deeds, but they have no legal training whatsoever."

60. Footnote by Dietrichson: "A panel of 18 men is drawn who give their oath to uphold the law. From these 18, prosecution and defense counsel can each strike six. The remaining six constitute a jury and assist in making the decision."

61. Isaac Brown was an attorney in Cambridge, Wisconsin. See Einar Haugen, "Pastor Dietrichson of Old Koshkonong," in *Wisconsin Magazine of History*, 29:310 (March, 1946).

62. *Lige børn lege bedst* ("like children play best"), or, in English parlance, "birds of a feather flock together."

63. Dietrichson could easily have misspelled the name, making it Parmer for Palmer, although the possibility that he spelled it correctly need not be ruled out. The 1850 census lists a Samil (Samuel?) Palmer, a young farmer, in the township of Dunkirk. The township of Christiana, where Dietrichson lived, touches Dunkirk in the southwest corner.

64. Footnote by Dietrichson: "By Seventh Day Baptists is meant a religious group which agrees with the Baptists in rejecting infant baptism and also in other matters. They are different in that they observe Saturday, the Jewish Sabbath, as their day of worship. They keep this Sabbath with pharisaic strictness. It is the only proper day of rest. They are generally very hostile to people who observe Sunday. Many of them who came to our church and likewise a few [Norwegian?] Methodists declared their displeasure with our ritual, our black wooden cross on the altar, the pastor's robes, etc. To them this was open papistry. Also, and to many of the Methodists living nearby, it was a thorn in the flesh that the Koskonong congregation paid a fixed salary to its pastor who, according to their idea, should live by the work of his hands in spite of the apostle's word, 'those who preach the gospel shall live by the gospel.' "

65. Dietrichson is in error. He left before the appeal came up. The case did not wait until November. The records of the district court for Dane County show that it was brought in on June 2 and dismissed by Judge David Irvin on June 3, 1845. See Haugen, "Pastor Dietrichson of Old Koshkonong," 310, n. 20.

CHAPTER VII

66. The Pine Lake referred to here lies in Waukesha County, which was set off from Milwaukee County in 1846.

67. Gustaf Elias Marius Unonius (1810–1902), Swedish pioneer in Wisconsin, Episcopal clergyman and author, arrived in New York on September 11, 1841.

68. Hans Jacob Gasmann (1787–1857) purchased a quarter section from the United States on August 19, 1843, in Section 1, northeast corner of Oconomowoc Township, Waukesha County. See C. A. Clausen, tr. and ed., "The Gasmann Brothers Write Home," in *Norwegian-American Studies*, 23:71–107 (1967).

69. A reference to the Milwaukee and Rock River Canal Company charter in 1838. See Theron W. Haight, ed., *Memoirs of Waukesha County*, 104–105 (Wisconsin State Historical Society, 1907).

70. Lawrence (or Laurits) Jacob Fribert, Danish-born publisher and editor, came to America in 1843. In 1847 he published a "Handbook for Emigrants to the American West—With Directions for the Voy-

age, and Description of the Life and Agricultural Methods, Especially in Wisconsin" (*Haandbog for emigranter til Amerikas vest*). See Blegen, *Norwegian Migration, 1825–1860*, 256. He is also referred to as the founder of the Norwegian settlement at Port Washington in 1845. See Qualey, *Norwegian Settlement*, 63, and Bache, *A Chronicle*, 127. In English *Cameralvidenskaberne* (also spelled with an initial K) is called "cameralistics," which is defined by the *Oxford Universal Dictionary* (1955) as "relating to the management of the state property (in Germany)."

71. Dietrichson fails to explain how he came to see the archbishop's letter. Unonius must have shown it to him. The original dispute between Dietrichson and Unonius was settled without rancor. Unonius has this to say: "He [Dietrichson] went to extremes in certain matters, but in spite of the small misunderstandings which arose between us, these were soon set right, and under the existing conditions, could hardly have been avoided." See N. W. Olsson, ed., and J. O. Backlund, tr., *A Pioneer in Northwest America, 1841–1858: The Memoirs of Gustaf Unonius*, 2:100 (Minneapolis, 1960).

72. Peter Böckmann "whose stay in America was short and unfruitful," as adjudged by Adolph B. Benson and Naboth Hedin, eds., in *Swedes in America, 1638–1938*, 129 (New Haven, 1938). For more on the amazing but brief career of Böckmann in Wisconsin, see Olsson and Backlund, ed. and tr., *A Pioneer in Northwest America*, 2:59–64.

73. St. Luke's Lutheran Church, probably organized in 1844, became the center of the Rock River colony of Norwegians west of Pine Lake but across the range line in Jefferson County. The first church building was probably erected in 1850. See O. M. Norlie, ed., *Norsk lutherske menigheter i Amerika, 1843–1916*, 1:116 (Minneapolis, 1918).

74. Aamodt and Uhlen (Ulen) came to the United States on the *Johanna* in 1843. See passenger manifest in Bache, *A Chronicle*, 227–32.

75. This probably refers to what came to be called St. Olaf's Lutheran Church. One of its members, Christopher Olson Saeter (Sether), went to Dietrichson and asked him to visit his colony. See T. Helgeson, *Fra "Indianernes lande,"* 1:149 (Iola, Wisconsin, 1915 [?]).

76. No doubt a reference to the Watertown Plank Road begun in 1847 and completed four years later.

77. Astherland was Dietrichson's spelling for Aztalan, a prehistoric Indian village site east of Lake Mills, in Jefferson County.

78. Dietrichson errs slightly. The Chippewa Indians claimed the north and northwest of Wisconsin Territory in 1844. A map dated 1835 shows that the Menominees held the area between Lake Pepin on the west and Green Bay on the east, north of Fort Winnebago.

See S. C. Mazzuchelli, *Memoirs, Historical and Edifying, of a Missionary Apostolic of the Order of St. Dominic among the Catholics and Protestants in the United States of America*, 154 (Chicago, 1915).

CHAPTER VIII

79. Hamilton Diggings, now Wiota, was named for William Stephen Hamilton, a son of Alexander Hamilton.

80. For Knud Knudsen (1810–1889) see Beulah Folkedahl, "Knud Knudsen and His America Book," in *Norwegian-American Studies*, 23:108–25 (1967).

81. Harald Ommelstad, no doubt the Harald Pedersen Omstad whose name appears in the passenger manifest of *Johanna*, which entered New York harbor July 22, 1843. He was listed as a farmer and his age was given as 49. See Bache, *A Chronicle*, 228.

82. See Halvor L. Skavlem, *The Skavlem and Odegaarden Families* (Madison, Wisconsin, 1915).

83. Ole Nastad, more commonly known as Nattestad, was probably the first Norwegian to settle in Wisconsin Territory, in 1838. See Nattestad's "Description of a Journey to North America Begun in 1837," by R. B. Anderson, in *Wisconsin Magazine of History*, 1:178 (December, 1917).

84. Aslak Olsen Gjerrejord, written Gjergjord in the Koshkonong church register. Hvidsøe, the modern Kviteseid, is in central Telemark.

85. Dietrichson errs when he says it is west of Koshkonong. It would have to be east to lie "half way between Koskonong and Muskego."

86. James Denoon Reymert emigrated in 1842. In 1847 he was one of the founders of the first Norwegian newspaper in Wisconsin, *Nordlyset*, and its first editor. He also became the first Norwegian (his mother was a Scot) to enter the state legislature. See Johs. B. Wist, ed., *Norsk-amerikanernes festskrift*, 10 (Decorah, Iowa, 1914).

CHAPTER IX

87. The Fox and Illinois rivers join below Ottawa and flow into the Mississippi. Dietrichson neglected to mention the Rock River.

88. The Rand McNally *Road Atlas* today lists 102 counties in Illinois.

89. See Tosten Kittelsen Stabæk, "An Account of a Journey to California in 1852," tr. by Einar J. Haugen, in *Norwegian-American Studies and Records*, 4:99–124 (1929).

90. Christian Haraldson (Haralsen) ran a notice in *Democraten* on November 3, 1850, asking if any immigrant who had arrived that year had a letter for him from Lensmand Hansen in Slidre Parish, Valdres. He said he would be grateful if the letter were enclosed in an envelope

and addressed to him as "Mr. Christian Haraldson Ommelstad, Beloit P. O., Rock Co., Wis." A *lensmand* is a bailiff or sheriff of a district.

91. Dietrichson refers to a German congregation with roots in the Prussian Union (1817). It was dissatisfaction with the Union that had led Grabau and the Old Lutherans to emigrate. Dietrichson (or the typesetter) misspells the German word *unierte* in his *Reise*.

92. Dietrichson's question mark after the year 1825 would have been unnecessary if he had taken the time to check his sources. The year was 1825 and it was also in 1825, not 1824, that the "Sloopers" left Stavanger.

93. Kleng Pedersen Hesthammer (1783–1865), whose name is spelled Cleng Peerson in a letter written to the *Prairie Herald*, Chicago, August 3, 1850, and reprinted in *Democraten*, September 7, 1850. His reports on a tour of America in 1821–1824 influenced the first movement of emigrants to the United States on the sloop *Restauration*. He later founded the Fox River colony in La Salle County, Illinois, and other settlements in Iowa and Missouri, but in his last years he preferred Texas to the northern states. His letter to the *Prairie Herald* extolls the good life in Texas. He died in Bosque County, Texas.

94. This incident was mentioned in a report from which Dietrichson may have borrowed the anecdote. See Theodore C. Blegen, tr. and ed., *Ole Rynning's True Account of America*, 72 (Northfield, 1926).

95. This became the most celebrated incident in the early records of Norwegian-American maritime history. The ship's captain and its owners were eventually freed under a special pardon issued by President John Quincy Adams. See Blegen, *Norwegian Migration to America: The American Transition*, 599–628.

96. Probably a reference to Lars Larsen, leader of the Sloop party; Blegen, *The American Transition*, 695.

97. Ole Rynning founded the ill-fated Beaver Creek colony in Iroquois County, Illinois (about 60 miles south of Chicago), in 1837.

98. Hans Barlien (1772–1842) is mentioned by Johan Reiersen as the founder of Sugar Creek colony in Lee County, Iowa. See *Norwegian-American Studies and Records*, 1:117 (1926). He emigrated to the United States in 1837, when he made the statement: "Now for the first time I am able to breathe freely." See "Hans Barlien," in *Norsk biografisk leksikon*, 1:378–80, and D. G. Ristad, "A Doctrinaire Idealist: Hans Barlien," in *Norwegian-American Studies and Records*, 3:13–22 (1928).

99. Madam Lauman, probably the widow of Johan Joseph Laumann, a glassblower who emigrated from Faaberg in 1839, aged 47, and died near Keokuk, Iowa.

CHAPTER X

100. Joseph Smith (1805–1844) was the founder of the Mormon religion.

101. Sidney Rigdon (1793–1876), born at Piny Fork, Pennsylvania. "Some writers maintain that Rigdon rewrote and expanded a novel written by Solomon Spaulding and that Joseph Smith, with Rigdon's connivance, palmed it off as the Book of Mormon." After the murder of Smith, Rigdon remained in Nauvoo for several weeks until excommunicated on September 8, 1844, by a new group under Brigham Young. See *Dictionary of American Biography*, 8:600.

102. "And it came to pass that the Lord commanded me; wherefore I did make plates of ore, that I might engrave upon them the record of my people." See *Book of Mormon*, First Book of Nephi, chapter 5, authorized version from Reorganized Church of Jesus Christ of Latter Day Saints, 63 (Independence, Missouri, 1951).

103. "He [Smith] cannot be shown to have met Rigdon, the most likely source of its doctrinal matter, until after [*The Book of Mormon's*] publication;" Bernard De Voto, in *Dictionary of American Biography*, 9:311.

104. Footnote by Dietrichson: "This book is called 'the Book of Mormon.' I have heard that it takes its name from the prophet who wrote the inscriptions on the plates. His name is believed to be Mormoni and from that came the name Mormons." See De Voto: "The burden of the visions, conveyed to him [Smith] by the angel Nephi (later corrected to Moroni) was that no existing sect represented God's will." *Dictionary of American Biography*, 9:310.

105. Footnote by Dietrichson: "Upon my asking High Priest Gudmund Haugaas what desert wilderness the church of Christ had disappeared in, whether in the American or in some other desert, he replied, after some thought, 'to the people's wilderness.' When this answer did not satisfy me, I said that as the church of Christ must be a visible fellowship in the world, could he show me the exact place where Christ's church had been all the time until Joseph Smith was called by the Lord to reestablish it, or would he acknowledge that this directly contradicted the Lord's promise 'that the gates of hell shall not prevail against it.' The high priest could not answer my first question, nor could he reply to the second, so I got no further."

106. Solomon Spaulding (1761–1816), author of *The Manuscript Found*, became successively a clergyman, a businessman, and a novelist. See Max J. Herzog, ed., *The Reader's Encyclopedia of American Literature*, 1066 (New York, 1962).

107. The First Book of Nephi, according to Mormon chronology,

is dated about 600–570 B.C.; the Second Book of Nephi, 588–545 B.C. Lehi, according to the First Book of Nephi, was the father of Nephi and his three brothers.

108. Footnote by Dietrichson: "In the thinly settled area of the West there are only a very few places where a real inn can be found, so the settlers often take in travelers overnight for a fee."

109. Footnote by Dietrichson: "The Mormon church in Nauvoo carries on an extensive trade, for which this town on the Mississippi River is ideally located."

110. Ole Olson Heier was one of the first two emigrants to leave Tinn, Telemark; he was an "exceedingly eloquent man with a very winning disposition which made him a big power among the Mormons." H. R. Holand, *De norske settlementers historie: En oversigt over den norske indvandring til og bebyggelse av Amerikas nordvesten fra Amerikas opdagelse til Indianerkrigen i nordvesten, med bygde- og navneregister*, 89 (Ephraim, Wisconsin, 1908). Heier later broke with the Mormons and joined, or at least preached to, a Baptist group.

111. Gudmund Danielsen Haugaas was one of the "Sloopers" who arrived in New York in 1825 on board the *Restauration*. He first settled near Kendall, New York, but removed to La Salle County, Illinois, in 1834. As a subscriber to *Nordlyset*, he gave his address as Norway, Illinois. See Langeland, *Nordmændene*, 105. Haugaas died of cholera on his farm in 1849.

112. Knud Pedersen was "the most important man among Norwegians in the Mormon church." Holand, *De norske settlementers historie*, 90. He was from Eidsfjord in Hardanger and went to Fox River in 1837. He was later sent to Denmark and Norway as a Mormon missionary and returned to the United States in 1856 with 600 converts, many of whom settled in Utah. Pedersen eventually became a bishop.

113. Footnote by Dietrichson: "The Mormons frequently read these two Bible passages to disbelieving assemblies. They wish to show that the Mormon sect is the true apostolic church because it alone has, as it claims, the order of the ministry found in the first church and as the Lord has appointed some to be apostles, others to be prophets, evangelists, pastors, and teachers. See Ephesians 4:11 and I Corinthians 12:28; likewise, 'But the manifestation of the Spirit is given to every man to profit withal.' See I Corinthians 12:8–12." [The latter quotation, however, is from I Corinthians 12:7].

114. Footnote by Dietrichson falls after the word *tvende* (two) in the text. He says: "Missionaries sent out by the Mormon church always travel in pairs."

115. The question mark after the name Danielsen in the text is

Dietrichson's, probably because he was uncertain of the name or its spelling. Søren Bache says that he had heard that Danielsen, after conversion to Mormonism, had "been very cruel to his wife [and] curses her for not having joined the new faith also." Bache, *A Chronicle*, 140.

116. Footnote by Dietrichson: "Next to *The Book of Mormon*, the Book of Revelation and the Prophet Daniel are their favorite reading material."

117. Dietrichson "had visited Haugaas at his home the day before and had had a talk with him. There he saw, hanging above his sofa, a facsimile of the golden tablets. The writing, he says, was a strange mixture of Greek, Hebrew, Syriac and other letters and of strange figures like Chinese writing, so that it was impossible to make out a single word." R. B. Anderson, *The First Chapter of Norwegian Immigration*, 429.

CHAPTER XI

118. The canal cost $7,143,789; see *Nelson's Encyclopaedia*, 8:533A (1915).

119. Dietrichson had been a prison chaplain's assistant in Norway before coming to America. See Introduction, p. 21.

120. Dr. Charles Rudolph Demme (1795–1863), born in Thüringen, Germany, wounded at Waterloo, and later called to St. Michael's and Zion churches in Philadelphia as assistant to Frederick David Schaeffer in 1822; see Jensson, *American Lutheran Biographies*, 159.

CHAPTER XII

121. Footnote by Dietrichson: "It might appear from this that there is no hope that any theologian or clergyman in the homeland feels called to go to America, let alone four who would be willing to go as I propose. For my part, I believe that one of the main reasons why no one has come forward, even though some may have felt the call, is that they do not have the necessary means for making this long and expensive journey. With two empty hands it is impossible to undertake the trip, no matter how willing the spirit. Actually, I think that it would be easier to get four to go than one; working together in such a field of battle is both easier and more pleasant. Besides, if this cause is the cause of our gracious and almighty God's own church, then he will also manage to call able workers for this harvest when his time comes."

122. Footnote by Dietrichson: "It has surely not escaped the attentive reader that, in the various settlements, congregations have been established which are still entirely isolated and have no formal union

with other churches. It is plain to see that union is an absolute necessity for both inner and outer vigor if the church order already established is to become permanent. Lack of it will only be remedied if more clergymen emigrate and, together with the representatives of the several congregations, organize a synod and conduct synodical meetings."

123. Dietrichson seems to forget that he was earlier talking about four pastors in addition to the evangelist-traveler.

124. The Norwegian original reads: *"mange bække smaae gjør en stor Aa,"* the words *smaae* and *aa* giving it rhyme—something like our "great oaks from little acorns grow." The *ort* equaled 24 Norwegian shillings.

125. Footnote by Dietrichson: "This sum [500 specie dollars] was what Sørensen, the dyer in Christiania, gave me for my travel expenses and my stay in America. I naturally considered it a paramount duty to save all I could of this money, given as a Christian sacrifice. All told, I used, on my trip over and back and during my stay in America, 332 specie dollars. On my return to Christiania, I gave a detailed account of each shilling spent and returned 168 specie dollars to Sørensen. I write this to show that, with economy, it does not require so much even to go to America. I owe it to truth and to the cause for which I worked to state publicly that I was not motivated by 'material interests' as Herr Reiersen has been pleased to allege. I dare say I returned home poorer than when I left."

CHAPTER XIII

126. Provost Hans Gynther Magelssen (1806–1886) was parish pastor in Aafjorden, Nord-Trøndelag, in 1837 and dean at Foss from 1838. In 1847 he went to Østre Moland, and in 1874 to Østre Aker. Christian Johannes Brodtkorb (1804–1887) was a candidate in theology in 1830 and parish pastor at Hitra in 1831. He resigned from the ministry in 1866. Bishop Emeritus Johannes Smemo, Oslo, to Malcolm Rosholt, January 12, 1968.

The Koshkonong Parish Journal

1. The spelling of persons and places is that given in the Parish Journal. Dietrichson always spelled Koshkonong without the "h."

2. His catalog of "sects" included Presbyterians, Methodists, Baptists, Quakers, Mormons, and, of course, the followers of Elling Eielsen.

3. The reader will note Dietrichson's frequent use of the words "true saving doctrine" and "edifying church order." Both of these phrases could be a sign of Lutheran scholastic orthodoxy, but from the pen of Dietrichson they are perhaps better interpreted in a Grundtvigian sense with emphasis on the creed and baptism as "the Living Word" or "true saving doctrine" within the framework of the constitutional structure ("edifying church order") of the Church of Norway.

4. Neither the Andersen barn nor the two oaks on the Juve farm are standing today, but both are commemorated by monuments. The two farms are still in the possession of the original families. Local tradition has it that deep niches were cut in the oaks to provide support for a communion table, and that this action killed them.

5. An old spelling for "Oslo." The Opsloe Church was originally a Franciscan foundation located at the foot of Ekeberg (hill) near the present residence of Oslo's bishop. The church, called *Gamlebyens Kirke* (the church in the old town) is presently used as a hospital chapel.

6. Hans Riddervold (1795–1876) was parish pastor and school headmaster in Fredrikstad from 1819 to 1832. He was elected bishop of Trondhjem (modern Trondheim) in 1843.

7. This examination, a prerequisite to entrance to the university, corresponds chronologically with graduation from junior college in America, but it is academically more advanced. Dietrichson was privately tutored in preparation for this examination, as there was no *gymnasium* (junior college) in Fredrikstad. See P. Botten-Hansen, *Norske studenter*, 30 (Christiania and Copenhagen, 1893).

8. This was the third of four possible passing marks in the Norwegian grading system.

9. Before the study of theology was permitted, the university student was required to pass the so-called "second" examination. It covered such pretheological subjects as Hebrew, Greek, Latin, history, and philosophy.

10. The foreign missions movement in Norway was blossoming at

this time (the Norwegian Missionary Society was formed in 1842), and Dietrichson's interest in it was "both positive and active." See A. S. Burgess, "Burning Zeal: Missionary Endeavor," in J. C. K. Preus, ed., *Norsemen Found a Church*, 337 (Minneapolis, 1953).

11. Whether Dietrichson could properly refer to this appeal by Sørensen as a "call" is a debatable question. It is clear from the records that the Norwegian officials were aware of this fact (see n. 12). However, the authorities seem to have waived the formality in the face of evident spiritual need among the emigrants. See *Departements-Tidende*, 15:717 (Christiania, 1843). Lutheran theology has generally maintained that a proper "call" must originate with a congregation or the church at large through one of its agencies or arms. Dietrichson's view that ordination conferred "authority" also generally has been rejected by Lutheran theologians, who relate authority to the call of God mediated through the church. The church, in turn, sets apart the "regularly called" person for the office of the holy ministry by the rite of ordination.

12. The Royal Resolution granting permission for Dietrichson's ordination is found in *Departements-Tidende*, 15:715 (1843): "Under the date of 12th instant it has pleased His Majesty graciously to approve the recommendation made by the Norwegian government on September 20th this year, to wit: That gracious permission be given for Candidate of Theology Johannes Wilhelm Christian Dietrichson, who during his stay in the Free States of North America proposes to minister in the clerical office to the Norwegian emigrants there, to be ordained by the Bishop of Christiania in the usual manner, but with the modifications the Bishop thinks necessary in view of the extraordinary nature of the situation, and without granting the ordinand the right to perform ministerial acts in Norway before he shall have been appointed to a pastorate here in this country. Christiania, October 16, 1843."

13. A slip of memory or of proofreading in the *Reise* (p. 4) makes the ordination date February 26, 1844. See *The Travel Narrative*, 46.

14. "L. S." is the abbreviation for the Latin words *loco sigilli* (in the place of the [bishop's] seal). These letters were commonly used on copies made from original documents which bore the official seal. Bishop Christian Sørenssen (originally the name was spelled with a double "s") was the last Norwegian bishop consecrated in Copenhagen. He enjoyed the favor of the Swedish-Norwegian king Karl Johan. A good "pastoral" bishop, he was considered neither an able administrator nor a competent theologian. He was a rationalist and a high-ranking member of the order of Freemasons. See J. O. Andersen et al., eds., *Kirke-leksikon for Norden*, 4:482 (Copenhagen, 1929).

15. *Ritualet* (the *Ritual*), as it was commonly known, included regulations governing occasional services as well as the main liturgy. See *Dannemarkes og Norges kirke-ritual* (Copenhagen, 1762).

16. It is quite clear that Dietrichson had already adopted the American or free-church principle of a "gathered church." The adherents of this theology in Norway would be found among small groups of Moravians and Quakers. The Haugeans never formally separated from the Church of Norway, but considered themselves a movement of renewal within the church. On occasion Dietrichson later admitted new arrivals without interrogation as if to imply that the individuals in question were merely transferring from the Church of Norway to the Church of Norway in America.

17. For details on Smith, see Bache, *A Chronicle*, 214, n. 4.

18. This dedication antedated that of the Muskego Church, although work was begun earlier there.

19. Literally, "bell-ringer" or "precentor." The *klokker's* duties included leading the congregation in singing and reading the opening and closing prayers in the liturgy.

20. Trovatten is referred to by Dietrichson hereinafter simply as Ole Knudsen. For an account of Trovatten's life before coming to Koshkonong, see Clarence A. Clausen, ed., "The Trials of an Immigrant: The Journal of Ole K. Trovatten," *Norwegian-American Studies and Records*, 19:142–59 (Northfield, Minnesota, 1956).

21. *Medhjælpere*, literally, "assistants."

22. The reference is to Bishop Erich Pontoppidan's manual of practical theology: *Collegium Pastorale Practicum* (Copenhagen, 1757). Two copies of this edition, as well as two copies of the 1850 edition, are to be found in the library of Luther Theological Seminary, St. Paul. Dietrichson's reference is to the 1757 edition.

23. This sentence reflects Dietrichson's own determination to protect the congregations from such persons as Elling Eielsen.

24. See Appendix A, "Agreement for Sale of Original Property, 1844." See also Appendix C.

25. It should be noted that, at this time, the "material" duties were assigned to the deacons. Somewhat later, Dietrichson placed "spiritual" matters in the hands of deacons, and financial matters in the hands of trustees. Cf. n. 55 below.

26. The first letter of call to a Norwegian Lutheran clergyman in America was drafted by Pastor Clausen for the congregation at Rock Prairie (Luther Valley), Wisconsin, in February, 1844. See J. A. Bergh, *Den norsk lutherske kirkes historie i Amerika*, 34 (Minneapolis, 1914). A comparison of that letter of call with the one presented to Dietrichson shows striking similarities; in fact, whole sentences are identical.

27. One of the "matters to attend to" was no doubt his interest in remarriage. As noted in his *vita*, his first wife died not long after giving birth to a child. It was apparently known among the Norwegian immigrants that Dietrichson had romantic interests back in Norway. Bache, *A Chronicle*, 121.

28. The original salutation is "S. T. Hr. Pastor Clausen." The letters "S. T.," often used in letter writing during the eighteenth and early nineteenth century, were an abbreviation for *salvo titulo*, which, freely translated, means "No titles mentioned, no titles forgotten" or "I know you have titles. I am not using them, but I have not forgotten them either."

29. *Loco sigilli*; see p. 253, n. 14.

30. For a more extended account of the Funkelien affair based on additional sources, see Nelson and Fevold, *The Lutheran Church Among Norwegian-Americans*, 1:109 (Minneapolis, 1960).

31. The decision is reported later in *The Journal*; see p. 168.

32. An interesting commentary on Dietrichson's sojourn in Muskego can be found in Bache, *A Chronicle*, 159–63.

33. Note that this entry in the Parish Journal was dated May 19, 1845, and written at Muskego, not Koshkonong. See Bache, *A Chronicle*, 159.

CHAPTER II

34. It should be noted that this and subsequent page references (chiefly parenthetical) are to volume I of the original manuscript of the Parish Journal.

35. Clausen had been ordained in German by Pastor L. F. E. Krause. Cf. the chronicle of Pastor L. F. E. Krause in Carl S. Meyer, ed., *Moving Frontiers* (St. Louis, Mo.: Concordia Publishing House, 1964), pp. 130–31.

36. Dietrichson had already begun to separate financial matters from the "spiritual" duties of the deacons.

37. The reference is to the 1757 edition.

38. See n. 34.

39. Rock Prairie, later named Luther Valley, was a short distance northwest of Beloit, Wisconsin.

40. Midsummer Day, June 24.

CHAPTER III

41. Dietrichson's use of the word "permanent" should be interpreted, if not translated, as "regular." Dietrichson always made it clear that he did not intend to remain permanently in America. His use of "permanent" was no doubt directed against itinerant preachers such as Elling Eielsen.

42. The original of this letter has been preserved. See Appendix B for a translation of its text.

43. In the summer of 1956, the editor found the long-forgotten chalice behind the altar of the West Church. A second examination in April, 1958, showed it to be in good condition, the Latin inscription being quite legible.

44. "Matthias Sigvardt, bishop of Christiansand Diocese, very respectfully presents this cup to the bishop of Akershus Diocese, the most venerable Christian Sørensen, as a pledge of deepest friendship and reverence."

45. "A Journey among the Norwegian Immigrants in the United North American Free States." The reference is to the first edition, Stavanger, 1846.

46. The specie daler was worth nearly $1.50 at that time, although opinions vary.

47. The original is *kirkeverge* (verger).

CHAPTER IV

48. Dietrichson kept his records according to the church year, beginning in Advent, not the calendar year.

49. Catfish was a creek running from Stoughton, Wisconsin, through Dunkirk to the Rock River at Indian Ford, about eight or nine miles north of Janesville, Wisconsin. The road referred to by Dietrichson extended diagonally southwest from Cambridge, Wisconsin, across Christiana Township and the southeast corner of Pleasant Springs Township to Dunkirk on the Catfish. See *Roads in 1847. Map of Wisconsin* (Philadelphia, 1847), found in the manuscript and map room, Wisconsin State Historical Society, Madison.

50. Dietrichson is wrong at this point. He seems unconsciously to have transferred the Norwegian state-church relationship to America.

51. Dietrichson misunderstood the situation. The decisive point was not that it was necessary for Wisconsin Territory to become a state but rather that the territorial legislature had not yet enacted the appropriate law. As noted below, this was soon done.

52. See Appendix C. This deed was to rise up and haunt the congregation during the election (predestination) controversy of the 1880s, when Pastor J. A. Ottesen sought to retain possession of the property despite the fact that the congregation had forced him to resign. See Gerald Anderson, *The West Koshkonong Story: 1844–1969*, 14–17 (Rockford, Illinois, 1969).

53. The date is illegible in the original.

54. This is the first time the title "trustees" appears in The Parish Journal, and it is believed to be the first time it makes its appearance in the Norwegian Lutheran church in America.

55. Dietrichson's faulty interpretation of this law of 1847 was un-doubtedly the source of the dichotomy between deacons and trustees, and "spiritual" and "temporal" service. The law as enacted by the Territory of Wisconsin used Protestant Episcopal terminology, but was quite clear in indicating that the members of the church council (Episcopal, vestrymen; Norwegian Lutheran, *medhjelpere* or deacons) "shall be trustees of such church or congregation." *Laws of the Territory of Wisconsin . . . in 1847*, 86 (Madison, 1847). Dietrichson was wrong in asserting, "They are not to involve themselves in the spiritual and purely churchly matters of the congregation." Actually the deacons (vestrymen or council) were authorized to act as trustees over against the requirements of the civil law. The Dietrichson dichotomy persisted in the congregational and synodical structure of Norwegian Lutheranism for over one hundred years and influenced the polity of The American Lutheran Church (1960). The constitution of The American Lutheran Church assigned "spiritual" duties to its church council (the deacons writ large) and "business affairs" to its board of trustees. *Handbook of The American Lutheran Church*, Edition of 1960, 37, 39.

56. The quotations from the text of the law are given in English by Dietrichson.

57. See p. 176.

58. See Introduction, p. 36.

59. "The Northern Light." For an account of this newspaper, see Bache, *A Chronicle*, 217, n. 7. The paper carried news from Norway, items about American politics and other affairs, and articles about and by the immigrants themselves.

60. Colonel Alexander Botkin (1801–57) was twice a member of the Wisconsin Territorial legislature and later served one term in the state senate and another in the assembly. He was an unsuccessful candidate for United States senator. Dietrichson's opinion of Botkin apparently was shared by his colleagues in the legal profession. His necrology attempts to describe him as "public spirited," but these words are crossed out and he is then judged "active in public affairs." The writer of the biographical sketch assesses Botkin as "a remarkably 'strong-minded' man, of wonderful self-reliance and self-assurance, but it was his misfortune that his education had been very greatly neglected [no mention is made of any formal education whatever, let alone law training], of which, however, he appeared all unconscious. . . . In a speech in the Senate denouncing the action of a secret caucus, he said 'We want a fair fight. We don't want to go crawling around in the brush about this measure. We want action on it to be SUB ROSA and ABOVE BOARD.'" *Report of the Proceedings of the Meetings of the State Bar Association of Wisconsin*.

For the Years 1878, 1881 and 1895, 182 (Madison, 1905). The necrology referred to is a handwritten document, "Necrology, Wisconsin, 1846–1881," in volume 1, p. 227, in the library of the Wisconsin State Historical Society, Madison.

61. Quoted by Dietrichson in English.

62. According to the election results in Christiana and Pleasant Spring townships, the Koshkonong settlers, at least at this stage, were Democrats. They voted overwhelmingly in favor of Cass over Zachary Taylor in the presidential election of 1848. They gave Botkin's opponent a tremendous majority in both 1848 and 1850, and in the latter year the vote was almost identical in the respective races for state senator and for United States congressman. Madison was the center of Whig strength in Dane County. See Bayrd Still, "Norwegian-Americans and Wisconsin Politics in the Forties," in *Norwegian-American Studies and Records*, 8:58–64 (Northfield, 1934).

63. Here Dietrichson signs himself *sogneprest* (parish pastor), whereas ordinarily he used the title *prest* (pastor). This indicates that he is now the "permanent" (read "regular") pastor of this specific parish.

CHAPTER VI

64. Dietrichson entitles this section "Fifth Year from the Founding of the Congregation"; that is to say, at the end of the year he would have fulfilled his promise to remain five years.

65. Norwegian, *blodsot*. Translation here is a conjecture, based on the theory that the settlers did not know what tuberculosis was, and that the afflicted often coughed up blood.

66. When the Lord's Supper was not celebrated, the pastor used the extra time (perhaps an hour or more) to check the "homework" of the children; that is, he questioned them to determine if they had memorized the assigned portions of Luther's Small Catechism and the commonly used "explanation" in question-answer form.

67. Dietrichson gives an extended account of his role in the discussions to form a synod of congregations in "Den norsk-evang. lutherske kirke i Amerika," in *Theologisk Tidsskrift for den Norske Kirke*, 3:510–27 (Christiania, 1851). It should be noted that when Dietrichson lays down the conditions for unity, he goes beyond the Lutheran confessions to which he subscribed. "Order" (by which Dietrichson meant organization, ritual, discipline) is not a condition of unity in the Augsburg Confession, which says it is "enough to agree in the doctrine of the gospel and the sacraments" (Article VII).

68. H. A. Stub (1822–1907) succeeded Clausen as pastor of the Muskego congregation in 1848. He was the father of H. G. Stub, the

first president of the Norwegian Lutheran Church of America (1917) and of the National Lutheran Council (1918).

69. Though the letter is no longer appended to the original parish register, it has been preserved in J. A. Bergh, *Den norsk lutherske kirkes historie i Amerika*, 63–65 (Minneapolis, 1914).

70. See Nelson and Fevold, *The Lutheran Church*, 1:117–18.

71. Dietrichson organized and served "annex congregations" from the main congregation (*hovedmenighed*) at Koshkonong. He lists them in the document quoted a few lines below.

72. The original is no longer appended to the Parish Journal.

73. That is, special delivery.

74. The editor has been unable to locate the source or sources of Dietrichson's views on ecclesiastical polity. An examination of the three most likely sources (Pontoppidan, *Collegium Pastorale Practicum* [1757], *Dannemarkes og Norges kirke-ritual* [1762], *and Forordnet alterbog udi Danmark og Norge* [1688]) reveal nothing. The reference in Article IV to synodical-presbyterian government leads one to assume American influences. But Dietrichson mentions no American sources as being at hand.

75. The word *kirkemøde* (church meeting) is translated by either "synod" or "convention."

76. The duties of the superintendent, as hereinafter described, are definitely episcopal, but without, of course, the implication of the "historic episcopacy" as taught in Roman, Anglican, and Orthodox churches.

77. Dietrichson's "Regulations" are the first and perhaps only codification of "canon law" among Lutherans in America, i.e., regulations which are unabashedly called canons.

78. The question mark is Dietrichson's.

79. Does the expression "ecclesiastically invalid" mean that a baptism performed by a pastor under discipline is no real baptism? If so, Dietrichson's regulation is perilously close to Donatism. If the expression had no theological or religious implications for Dietrichson, but was purely "ecclesiastical," it would still pose a problem in interpretation.

80. The manuscript has Friday, August 21, 1849. Because September 6, 1849, was a Thursday and November 19, 1849, was a Monday, then August 21, 1849, had to be a Tuesday. See *infra*, pp. 211 and 213.

81. Near Skien in the province of Telemark.

82. The Norwegian word is *medhjelperne* (the assistants).

83. They are no longer appended to the Parish Journal.

84. A. C. Preus was to bring an anti-Grundtvigian emphasis to Koshkonong. When he returned to Norway (1872), he became pastor

of the Holt Parish near Østre Moland, where Dietrichson was in difficulty. It will be remembered that Preus denied Dietrichson permission to receive Holy Communion on the grounds that he was "heterodox." Preus's "orthodoxy" was no doubt strengthened by the influence of E. W. Hengstenberg (1802–1869), Lutheran "repristinationist" at the University of Berlin. See Einar Boysen, *J. W. Cappelen 1805–1878: Noen blad av norsk bokhandels og norsk kulturkamps historie*, 307 (Oslo, 1953).

85. Guldberg's Hymnal was compiled by two Danes, Bishop Ludvig Harboe (1709–1783) and Ove Høegh-Guldberg (1731–1808), and published in Copenhagen in 1778. It is sometimes known as the Harboe-Guldberg Hymnal.

86. The reference is to Bishop Erich Pontoppidan's Explanation of Luther's Small Catechism.

87. Luther's Small Catechism.

88. Wilhelm Andreas Wexels (1797–1866) was assistant pastor of the Cathedral Church of Our Saviour in Oslo. He was Norway's leading exponent of Gundtvigianism.

CHAPTER VII

89. Dietrichson leaves a blank at this point in the Parish Journal. He probably intended to insert a listing of the books, but there is no such list in the original Journal. Perhaps it was Dietrichson's intention to provide a list and to insert the page number later.

Index